YOU
CAN'T
SAY
THAT!

YOU CAN'T SAY THAT!

THE GROWING THREAT TO CIVIL LIBERTIES FROM ANTIDISCRIMINATION LAWS

DAVID E. BERNSTEIN

INSTITUTE

Washington, D.C.

Library of Congress Cataloging-in-Publication Data

Bernstein, David E.
   You can't say that! : the growing threat to civil liberties from
     antidiscrimination laws / David E. Bernstein.
     p. cm.
   Includes bibliographical references and index.
   ISBN 1-930865-53-8 (cloth : alk. paper)
    1. Civil rights--United States.   2. Discrimination--Law and
legislation--United States. I. Cato Institute. II. Title.

KF4749.B47 2003
342.7308'53--dc22

                                         2003055808

Cover design by Amanda Elliott.
Printed in the United States of America.

CATO INSTITUTE
1000 Massachusetts Ave., N.W.
Washington, D.C. 20001

To the memory of my grandparents and great-grandparents, the Bernsteins, Jozefsons, Kaplans, and Steins, who fled Europe for their lives and their freedom and found a haven of liberty for themselves and their progeny in America.

Contents

vii

Acknowledgments

I have been intrigued by conflicts between antidiscrimination laws and freedom of expression since 1990, when writer Sheldon Richman told me that his brother had gotten into trouble for placing a real estate advertisement in the *Philadelphia Jewish Exponent* stating that a house he was selling was "walking distance to the synagogue." This was pertinent information for an ad in a Jewish newspaper because Orthodox Jews are forbidden to drive to synagogue on the Sabbath and on many holidays. Nevertheless, local fair housing officials thought the ad was discriminatory. They claimed that, by noting proximity to a synagogue, the ad illegally expressed an implicit preference for Jewish buyers, thereby violating laws banning housing discrimination on the basis of religion. Appalled and intrigued, I did some further research, from which I discovered that the Fair Housing Act was consistently being enforced in ways that seemed to violate the First Amendment. I also began to notice news reports suggesting that other antidiscrimination laws were increasingly impinging on civil liberties. I resolved that someday I would write a book on the subject.

An opportunity to start work on such a book came in 1998, when a fellowship grant from the John M. Olin foundation relieved me of my teaching and committee responsibilities at the George Mason University School of Law for a year. My primary project for the year was to complete *Only One Place of Redress: African Americans, Labor Regulations, and the Courts from Reconstruction to the New Deal* (Duke University Press, 2001), but I made substantial progress on this book as well.

One problem I confronted in starting this book was that I understood that outside of the academic press market, the market for serious nonfiction is limited, and that authors who take politically incorrect positions, as I knew I would, face a particularly difficult time finding publishers among leading trade presses. David Boaz and the Cato Institute came to the rescue. As further incentive to get going, I was invited to publish initial versions of bits and pieces of what ultimately became the book as symposium articles: "The Right of Expressive Association and Private Universities' Racial Preferences and Speech Codes," *William and Mary Bill of Rights Journal*

9 (2001); "Antidiscrimination Laws and the First Amendment," *Missouri Law Review* 66 (2001); and "Sex Discrimination Laws Versus Civil Liberties," *University of Chicago Legal Forum* 1999. Michael Abramowicz, Neal Devins, Richard Epstein, Eugene Volokh, and Todd Zywicki commented on one of more of these articles. An earlier version of Chapter 12 appeared in *Liberty* magazine.

As the book progressed, I received assistance from a variety of sources. The Law and Economics Center at the George Mason University School of Law provided generous summer research funding. Daniel Polsby, Associate Dean for Academic Affairs at George Mason Law, arranged a reduced teaching schedule in exchange for a promise to complete a book manuscript. Walter Olson gave me helpful early advice. Lillian Bernstein read part of the book manuscript and insisted that I eliminate legal jargon. Michael Abramowicz, Stanley Bernstein, Gene Healy, Robert Levy, and Sara Pikofsky each read and commented on at least one complete draft of the book. Conversations with Eugene Volokh, both in person and via e-mail, helped clarify several important constitutional issues for me. I bounced many of the ideas in this book off my law professor colleagues on the ConLawProf listserv.

Nate Oman and James Winn provided outstanding research assistance. Nate's services were provided by the Institute for Humane Studies at George Mason University, which has been helpful to me in many ways since I was a senior in college. Olson's Overlawyered.com and Volokh's "Freedom of Speech vs. Workplace Harassment Law" (www.1.law.ucla.edy/~volokh/harass/) were extremely useful in providing leads on cases and other ammunition for this book. Readers who enjoy this book should be sure to visit both of those sites. John Showalter and Marni Soupcoff provided excellent editorial assistance. Micah Thorner went above and beyond the call of duty in providing amazingly prompt and efficient secretarial help while I was completing the final draft of the manuscript as a visiting professor at the Georgetown University Law Center in Spring of 2003. Finally, I would like to thank David Boaz for reading and commenting on several drafts of the book manuscript, and for otherwise shepherding this book through the publication process.

Introduction

Intolerant activists are determined to impose their moralistic views on all Americans, regardless of the consequences for civil liberties. These zealots are politically well organized and are a dominant force in one of the two major political parties. They have already achieved many legislative victories, especially at the local level, where they often wield disproportionate power. Courts have often acquiesced to their agenda, even when it conflicts directly with constitutional provisions protecting civil liberties. Until the power of these militants is checked, the First Amendment's protection of freedom of speech and freedom of religion will be in constant danger.

To many civil libertarians, the preceding paragraph reads like a description of the Christian right. But it also describes left-wing egalitarian activists, many of whom are associated with the "civil rights" establishment. Their agenda of elevating antidiscrimination concerns above all others poses an acute threat to civil liberties. The First Amendment prohibits the government from interfering with freedom of expression, which includes free exercise of religion, freedom of speech, freedom of the press, and the right to petition the government for a redress of grievances. All of these civil libertarian restrictions on government power are at risk from antidiscrimination laws. For example:

- In Berkeley, the federal Department of Housing and Urban Development threatened to sanction three neighborhood activists for organizing community opposition to a plan to turn a rundown hotel into a homeless center. HUD alleged that the activists had violated the Fair Housing Act by interfering with a project that would serve a group of people who would be disproportionately mentally ill or recovering substance abusers, protected groups under the Act. HUD spokesperson John Phillips, trying to parry free speech concerns raised by the media, instead stoked them. "To ask questions is one thing," Phillips

1

told reporters. "To write brochures and articles and go out and actively organize people to say, 'We don't want those people in those structures,' is another."[1]

- In San Francisco, Krissy Keefer is using an antidiscrimination law to challenge the artistic autonomy of the San Francisco Ballet. She is suing the ballet for height and weight discrimination for refusing to accept her daughter Fredrika into its preprofessional program. Fredrika is of average height and weight, while modern ballet's aesthetic standards require that dancers be tall and lithe.[2]

- In Denver, the city government refused to issue a Columbus Day parade permit unless the organizers signed an agreement stating that "there will be no references, depictions, or acknowledgment of Christopher Columbus during the parade; and no speeches or wreath laying for Christopher Columbus will be conducted." The city was responding to pressure from American Indian activists, who alleged that a parade celebrating Columbus would create an illegal "hostile public environment."[3]

- In New York City, Michelle Ganzy sued the Allen Christian School for firing her after she became pregnant out of wedlock. Ganzy, like all of the school's teachers, had agreed to serve as a role model for her students, in part by behaving in accordance with the school's conservative moral beliefs. Nevertheless, Ganzy sued for sex discrimination. A federal court, seemingly oblivious to the threat this lawsuit posed to the autonomy of religious institutions, ruled in her favor, holding that "[r]estrictions on pregnancy are not permitted because they are gender discriminatory by definition."[4]

- In Minneapolis, a group of librarians complained of sexual harassment because patrons using the library computers viewed images the librarians saw and found offensive. The Equal Employment Opportunity Commission found that the librarians had "probable cause" to pursue their claim. Because of this and similar cases, public and private libraries throughout the United States are under pressure to install filtering software on their computers, lest a librarian inadvertently view offensive material and file a sexual harassment lawsuit. Defining the issue precisely backwards, a representative of the National Organization for Women told the *New York Times* that she wondered "how far First Amendment rights may go before they infringe on sexual harassment laws."[5]

- In Eugene, Oregon, the state Newspaper Publishers Association published a list of 80 words and phrases that its members should ban from real estate advertisements to avoid liability under federal, state, or local fair housing laws. The forbidden words and phrases include language that signifies an obvious intent to violate fair housing laws (e.g., "no Mexicans"), but also language that is merely descriptive, such as "near church" or "walking distance to synagogue." Fair housing officials over-zealously interpret such phrases as expressing an illicit preference for Christians and Jews, respectively. The list also includes phrases that some fair housing officials believe are used as codes to discourage minorities ("exclusive neighborhood," "board approval required") or families with children ("quiet tenants," "bachelor pad").[6] There are a number of other phrases that did not make the Oregon list, but that some realtors avoid nonetheless for fear of liability, including the following: master bedroom (either sexist or purportedly evocative of slavery and therefore insulting to African Americans), great view (allegedly expresses preference for the nonblind), and walk-up (supposedly discourages the disabled).[7]

- Religious conservatives have also jumped on the antidiscrimination bandwagon. In Wellsville, Ohio, Dolores Stanley celebrated her new job as manager of the local Dairy Mart by removing *Playboy* and *Penthouse* from the store's shelves. "It goes against everything I believe in as a Christian," Stanley said. "There's no way I could participate in that." Stanley's superiors at corporate headquarters, attempting to exercise Dairy Mart's First Amendment right to sell legal magazines, told Stanley to replace the periodicals. She refused and was fired. The American Family Association, a conservative antipornography organization, represented Stanley in a lawsuit against Dairy Mart for sex and religious discrimination and for subjecting her to a "hostile workplace environment."[8] The case settled before trial for a sum "well into the six figures."[9]

These anecdotes are just a few examples of the growing threat antidiscrimination laws pose to civil liberties. Some civil libertarians

3

have attempted to finesse the issue by redefining civil liberties to include protection from the discriminatory behavior of private parties. Under this view, conflicts between freedom of expression and antidiscrimination laws could be construed as clashes between competing civil liberties. For purposes of this book, however, civil liberties retains its traditional definition, referring to constitutional rights protected by the First Amendment and related constitutional provisions.

The clash of civil liberties and antidiscrimination laws has emerged due to the gradual expansion of such laws to the point at which they regulate just about all aspects of American life. This expansion of antidiscrimination laws, in turn, reflects a shift in the primary justification for such laws from the practical, relatively limited goal of redressing harms visited upon previously oppressed groups, especially African Americans, to a moralistic agenda aimed at eliminating all forms of invidious discrimination. Such an extraordinarily ambitious goal cannot possibly be achieved—or even vigorously pursued—without grave consequences for civil liberties.

* * *

The civil rights movement initially focused on integrating African Americans into the nation's economic life. Civil rights activists persuasively argued that since the end of slavery, whites in the United States had used a combination of social pressure, violence, and law to exclude African Americans (and, to a lesser extent, other minorities) from certain jobs, leisure activities, and neighborhoods. In the South, especially, a web of law and custom had relegated African Americans to something akin to a lower caste than whites. Righting matters, activists argued, required federal laws banning discrimination not only by state and local governments, but also by large private employers and business proprietors.[10] Other groups received protection from the 1964 Civil Rights Act by piggybacking on the moral authority of the African American freedom struggle.

The provisions of the 1964 Civil Rights Act banning racial discrimination by state and local governments were uncontroversial outside of the often overlapping racist and "states' rights" circles. The provisions banning discrimination by private parties, however, ran against a strong libertarian streak in American society that values freedom of association. Civil libertarians had traditionally been wary of antidiscrimination laws that applied to the private sector. In 1945, for example, a group of civil libertarians, including *Nation* publisher and NAACP cofounder Oswald Garrison Villard, publicly opposed a proposed New York fair employment law. They urged civil rights supporters to respect freedom of association and to "rely on the force of slow but steadily growing public opinion," not legal compulsion, to combat employment discrimination.[11] In 1959, liberal philosopher Hannah Arendt published an essay in which she denounced discrimination by government, especially bans on interracial marriage—a taboo subject in those days—but also made clear her opposition to antidiscrimination laws that applied to the private "social sphere."[12] "Discrimination," she wrote, "is as indispensable a social right as equality is a political right."

By the 1960s, however, civil rights advocates had persuaded most civil libertarians that it was impossible to defeat the quasi-caste system faced by African Americans without some interference with the private sector. In particular, civil libertarians agreed that freedom of association, which had already been effectively quashed for generations by both government and private violence in the Jim Crow South and elsewhere, could not suddenly become the governing principle of American race relations. A hands-off policy was especially unattractive in the South, where state and local government remained firmly in the hands of segregationists who could pressure businesses to retain Jim Crow. Federal antidiscrimination law instead provided business owners—of whom many had found Jim Crow to be a costly nuisance—with the wherewithal to integrate, by freeing them from the threat of retaliation by local officials. [13]

Civil libertarians' concerns were also assuaged because the 1964 Civil Rights Act did not drastically infringe on civil liberties. The Act did impinge on freedom of association, but it only applied to relatively large businesses—those with 15 or more employees—and to places of public accommodation. Large businesses were already subject to myriad government regulations, and public accommodations had a centuries-old common law legal duty to serve all comers.[14] The Act covered educational institutions, but applied only to institutions that wished to receive federal funds, a relatively minor source of revenue for most universities at the time. Religious organizations received exemptions from some aspects of the law.

Civil rights advocates' respect for the First Amendment helped ensure that the early laws created little conflict with civil liberties.

The source of this respect was that the constitutional protections afforded speech, assembly, and religion had been crucial to the success of the civil rights movement. Supreme Court decisions enforcing civil rights activists' First Amendment rights consistently checked attempts by southern states to stifle the movement. Meanwhile, the movement established a base in black churches because even racist southern governments felt compelled to provide them a large measure of autonomy. Civil rights supporters, including government officials charged with enforcing the new laws, therefore thought it both shortsighted and wrong to eviscerate civil liberties in the name of civil rights. Major civil rights groups, including the NAACP and the American Jewish Congress, even opposed hate speech laws, which enjoyed a brief wave of popularity in the late 1940s and early 1950s.[15] For many years following passage of the 1964 Civil Rights Act, few if any cases brought under antidiscrimination laws impinged on freedom of expression or free exercise of religion.

Destroying the quasi-caste system that had excluded African Americans from many employment opportunities and public accommodations seemed a daunting task in 1964, but the system was dismantled surprisingly quickly and easily. Within a few years of the passage of the 1964 Civil Rights Act, racial exclusion and segregation by hotels, restaurants, theaters, and other commercial spaces virtually disappeared. Within a decade, major corporate employers not only stopped barring African Americans (and women) from many positions, but began to aggressively recruit and promote them—at times in preference to white males with better paper credentials. Universities, once notorious for exclusionary practices, engaged in particularly aggressive affirmative action policies, as did many government agencies.

Support among whites for equal opportunity continued its long-term dramatic rise. The proportion of the public telling pollsters that African Americans should have the same job opportunities as whites rose from 42 percent in 1944 to 87 percent in 1966.[16] Employment discrimination persisted, especially in blue-collar redoubts such as the construction industry, and integration remained elusive in both education and housing. Nevertheless, many barriers that had seemed almost insurmountable in 1964 had ceased to exist less than a decade later.

Once the racial caste system was largely dismantled, and newly organized groups—such as older Americans, gays, and the disabled—began to use civil rights terminology in expressing their demands for government intervention on their behalf, antidiscrimination activists shifted their rhetorical emphasis. They no longer focused on historical and economic arguments regarding the need to end racial discrimination in employment and places of public accommodation. Rather, they argued that discrimination—as expansively defined by organized interest groups—should be banned as a moral evil. Once private-sector discrimination was portrayed primarily as a secular sin, rather than as an economic issue, the rhetorical goal of civil rights advocates became the *elimination* of invidious discrimination.

Ironically, conservatives were partly responsible for this shift in emphasis. Conservatives had generally opposed the 1964 Civil Rights Act on states' rights grounds. Eventually, they became supporters of the Act and adopted the argument that antidiscrimination law's basic purpose was to eliminate the moral evil of discrimination. For example, the first President Bush, who had voted against the 1964 Civil Rights Act as a congressman from Texas, in 1990 called discrimination "a fundamental evil that tears at the fabric of our society."[17] In part, this shift was a result of a genuine change of heart among conservatives who were embarrassed by their previous tolerance of Jim Crow. But the emphasis on the moral component of antidiscrimination law also served a tactical goal: some conservatives believed that this emphasis would advance their argument that affirmative action preferences for minorities, whether voluntary or demanded by the government, should be banned as discrimination against whites.[18]

As the primary justification for antidiscrimination laws shifted from aiding previously oppressed groups to an austere moralism, the laws broadly expanded at the local, state, and federal levels. Antidiscrimination laws came to protect more and more groups against more and more types of discrimination. Enforcement of the laws gradually took on authoritarian traits, encouraged by the establishment of bureaucracies at all levels of government charged solely with the enforcement of antidiscrimination laws. Indeed, many jurisdictions came to call their civil rights enforcement bureaucracies "human rights" agencies—the term suggesting that enforcing antidiscrimination laws against private parties is analogous to enforcing bans on other activities widely regarded as violations of human rights, such as slavery, torture, and genocide.

As the intense moralism of modern antidiscrimination ideology became entrenched in American politics and society, antidiscrimination advocates, especially those who worked for the enforcement bureaucracies, increasingly viewed civil liberties as, at best, competing rights to be balanced against efforts to wipe out bigotry. At worst, they saw civil liberties as inconvenient and unnecessary obstacles to a discrimination-free world. This had grave practical implications for the First Amendment. HUD, for example, consistently interpreted ambiguous provisions of the Fair Housing Act in ways that threatened freedom of expression. Meanwhile, many courts interpreted antidiscrimination laws broadly, at times absurdly so. For example, courts consistently broadened the definition of "places of public accommodation" subject to antidiscrimination law to encompass entities like membership organizations that are neither "places" nor "public" nor "accommodations" according to the dictionary definitions and common usages of those words.

By the mid-1980s, antidiscrimination laws had emerged as a serious threat to civil liberties. Courts found that these laws punished everything from refusing to cast a pregnant woman as a bimbo in a soap opera, to giving speeches extolling the virtues of stay-at-home mothers, to expressing politically incorrect opinions at work, to refusing to share one's house with a gay roommate, to refusing to fund heretical student organizations at a Catholic university. Defendants protested that their First Amendment rights were being trampled on, but to no avail. Through the early 1990s, courts consistently refused to enforce First Amendment rights and other constitutionally protected civil liberties when their enforcement would have limited the reach of antidiscrimination laws. The trend of recent court decisions seems more friendly to civil liberties, largely because the courts have been populated with conservatives less committed to the antidiscrimination agenda. However, the final outcome of the conflict between civil liberties and antidiscrimination laws remains unresolved. Meanwhile, the fear of litigation—fear not only of actually losing a lawsuit, but also fear of being vindicated only after a protracted, expensive legal battle—is having a profound chilling effect on the exercise of civil liberties in workplaces, universities, membership organizations, and churches throughout the United States.

* * *

This book is a broad critical overview of the growing conflict between antidiscrimination laws and civil liberties. Chapter 1, by necessity the densest and most academic chapter of the book, discusses the normative and constitutional reasons why the clash between civil liberties and antidiscrimination laws should be resolved firmly in favor of civil liberties. The next four chapters discuss the growing regulation by antidiscrimination laws of speech, including workplace speech, artistic expression, political speech, and campus speech. The sixth chapter explores the government's use of antidiscrimination laws to force individuals and businesses to engage in speech. Chapters 7 and 8 recount how the growing scope of laws banning discrimination in public accommodations threatens the autonomy of private institutions and threatens to squelch the formation of organizations established for expressive purposes. In the next two chapters, the book discusses conflicts between antidiscrimination laws and religious freedom, focusing on religious schools and religious landlords, two groups that risk discrimination lawsuits when they act in accordance with their beliefs about sexual morality. Chapter 11 raises the issue of whether there are any organizations or activities too intimate to come constitutionally within the scope of antidiscrimination laws. The final chapter discusses the American Civil Liberties Union's unwillingness to consistently defend civil liberties against antidiscrimination laws.

Given the moral authority of antidiscrimination law in a society still recovering from a viciously racist past, writing a book critical of many of antidiscrimination law's applications is necessarily perilous, the law professor's equivalent of a politician disparaging mom and apple pie. The laudable goal of the ever-broadening antidiscrimination edifice is to achieve a fairer, more just society. Yet even—or perhaps especially—well-meaning attempts to achieve a praiseworthy goal must be criticized when the means used to achieve that goal become a threat to civil liberties.

The student who callously utters a racial epithet, the business executive who excludes Jews from his club, the coworker who tells obnoxious sexist jokes, the neighbor who lobbies against housing for the mentally ill—the actions of these individuals can be infuriating, especially to those who, like the author of this book,[19] have been personally victimized by bigots. But the alternative to protecting the constitutional rights of such scoundrels is much worse: the gradual evisceration of the pluralism, autonomy, and check on government power that civil liberties provide.

Students and others interested in delving into the issues discussed in *You Can't Say That!* in more detail should visit this book's accompanying website, http://mason.gmu.edu/~dbernste/book/, which provides links to all sources cited in the footnotes that are available online and other links to topics discussed in each chapter. The site also provides frequently updated links to reviews of *You Can't Say That!*, opinion editorials by the author, and videos of the author discussing the book.

1. Why Civil Liberties Should Be Protected from Antidiscrimination Laws

Almost all of the conflicts described in this book between civil liberties and antidiscrimination laws involve laws that impinge on some form of freedom of expression protected by the First Amendment and related constitutional provisions. In the normal course of things, constitutionally protected civil liberties trump conflicting statutory rules. Yet various courts, including at times the Supreme Court, have held that the government has a "compelling interest" in eradicating discrimination sufficient to warrant overriding civil liberties. The courts have not, however, coherently explained why they have granted antidiscrimination laws this extraordinary immunity.

Most Americans consider limiting invidious discrimination against historically disadvantaged groups to be an important governmental interest, an interest that the average citizen might find "compelling" in lay terms. But for an interest to be constitutionally compelling, and therefore capable of trumping civil liberties, the interest should not simply be important. Rather, that interest should be so vital that it would be virtually suicidal for society *not* to limit civil liberties in order to pursue it.[1] Indeed, many important governmental interests, such as the government's interest in reducing violent crime, are routinely subordinated to the First Amendment because they are not, constitutionally speaking, compelling interests. For example, incendiary speech currently protected by the First Amendment can encourage violent behavior by glorifying violence against women, as much "gangsta rap" does. Yet courts have shown no inclination to uphold bans on such speech.

By contrast, from the late 1970s until the early 1990s courts abandoned civil liberties in favor of antidiscrimination principles with stunning blitheness. State courts went even further, expanding the

11

compelling interest paradigm to antidiscrimination interests that don't even seem objectively important, much less constitutionally compelling. For example, the Alaska Supreme Court found that the state's interest in protecting unmarried heterosexual couples from housing discrimination is sufficiently compelling to override First Amendment rights.[2]

If judges routinely announced that the government's compelling interest in eradicating violent crime trumped the enforcement of constitutional rights, civil libertarians—in common with other thoughtful Americans—would strongly protest. Yet few civil libertarians protested when courts allowed the government to eviscerate civil liberties to pursue its interest in eradicating discrimination.[3] Indeed, many liberal law professors with otherwise impeccable civil liberties credentials went out of their way to justify the courts' malfeasance. The professors argued that the Thirteenth, Fourteenth, and Fifteenth Amendments, passed largely to aid African Americans after the Civil War, create a governmental obligation to enforce equality among groups.[4] This obligation, they contend, can in turn supersede explicit protections provided by the Bill of Rights, including the First Amendment.

This argument is wrong, both textually and historically. The Civil War amendments do not purport to guarantee substantive equality, much less to override the First Amendment. The Thirteenth Amendment abolished slavery, the Fourteenth Amendment required states to provide all persons with equal protection of the laws (not equality *per se*), and the Fifteenth Amendment guaranteed African Americans the right to vote. None of the Civil War amendments established a right to be free from private-sector discrimination.

Some scholars argue, however, that First Amendment rights should be subordinated to antidiscrimination claims because the "constitutional value" of equality as reflected in the Fourteenth Amendment is in tension with the First Amendment "value" of freedom of expression.[5] The Constitution, however, is first and foremost a legal document, not a mere expression of abstract values. The First Amendment's prohibition on government regulation of freedom of expression does not conflict with the Fourteenth Amendment's requirement that states may not deny equal protection of the laws. For example, an individual who engages in racist speech is protected by the First Amendment and is not violating the Four-teenth Amendment because he is neither an agent of the state nor denying anyone equal protection of the laws.

Arguments that courts should abstract egalitarian values from the Civil War amendments and find that those values trump the First Amendment are not only specious but also extremely dangerous. If courts were to accept such arguments, the slippery slope to broad censorship of speech would be short indeed. For example, public safety, like equality, is an important societal and constitutional value. Under a paradigm that important values override constitutional protections, the government could ban *any* incendiary speech that implicitly or explicitly encourages violence or criminal activity because such speech could be considered a threat to public safety.[6] Any movie, book, or play with an outlaw hero would lose constitu-tional protection; say goodbye to *Robin Hood, Antigone, Bonnie and Clyde,* and virtually every Martin Scorsese movie. Moreover, if the constitutional values paradigm were adopted by the courts, the criminal procedure protections of the Fourth, Fifth, and Sixth amend-ments, such as the right to remain silent and the right to a jury trial, could ultimately be eviscerated. After all, these rights conflict with the "constitutional value" of public safety.

The lack of a sound constitutional justification for sacrificing civil liberties to antidiscrimination laws, combined with the increased encroachment of antidiscrimination laws on previously untouched elements of civil society, has led the Supreme Court to become increasingly protective of civil liberties. In 1992, the Court unani-mously invalidated a hate speech law as unconstitutional govern-ment interference with free speech.[7] Several years later, the Court unanimously held that Massachusetts had violated the First Amend-ment when it tried to force a privately sponsored St. Patrick's Day parade to allow a gay rights group to march under its own banner.[8] Most recently, the Court, in a five-to-four decision, upheld the right of the Boy Scouts of America to exclude a gay scoutmaster whose sexual identity, according to the BSA, undermined the BSA's promo-tion of traditional sexual morality.[9] In all these cases, the Court rejected the argument that the government's purported compelling interest in eradicating discrimination trumped the First Amendment.

* * *

In theory, the Constitution's protection of civil liberties is inviolate and therefore not subject to changing intellectual fashion. In practice, however, history teaches that when constitutional provisions lose the support of the public, and especially the support of the legal elite from which federal judges are drawn, those provisions are enervated. Judges will continue to pay lip service to such provisions, but they will fail to properly enforce them until eventually they lose all force.

Given this dynamic, the prospect for continued judicial protection of civil liberties when they impinge upon antidiscrimination concerns is uncertain. Many academics are already disparaging constitutional protection of freedom of expression. Over the last two decades, radical scholars, including many feminists and "critical race" theorists, have vociferously attacked the First Amendment as a barrier to the government's ability to pursue sexual and racial equality. Anti–free speech feminists have stated that they would ban what they call "expressive means of practicing inequality," such as publishing "academic books purporting to document women's biological inferiority to men ... or [claiming] that reports of rape are routinely fabricated."[10] Critical race theorists, meanwhile, suggest that racist expression is "so dangerous, and so tied to perpetuation of violence and degradation of the very classes of human beings who are least equipped to respond, that it is properly treated as outside of the realm of protected discourse."[11] From their ivory towers at Harvard, Yale, Chicago, and other elite universities, influential liberal law professors increasingly echo the feminists' and critical race theorists' views.[12] The First Amendment is therefore in dire need of a powerful, consistent, defense.

The primary civil libertarian defense of freedom of expression from government suppression is that such freedom is necessary to ensure the existence of a robust marketplace of ideas. Advocates of this position suggest that freedom of expression helps ensure the triumph of reason over prejudice, of enlightened public opinion over entrenched political and economic power. This argument has some force, given the notable successes of the marketplace of ideas in recent American history. In the 1940s, Catholics and Jews were excluded from many universities, private clubs, and corporations; African Americans were segregated by law in the South and subjected to routine discrimination almost everywhere else; Japanese

14

Americans were incarcerated in internment camps; American Indian children were frequently removed from their parents and forcibly assimilated in boarding schools; and male homosexuals were thought to be pedophiles and perverts, and with few exceptions felt obliged to live closeted lives. Sixty years later, the status of all of these groups has improved dramatically. The remarkable social and political transformation in the status of American minority groups was possible only because the Constitution's guarantee of freedom of expression prevented defenders of the discriminatory status quo from using government power to stifle challenges to orthodox attitudes.

Nevertheless, critics of freedom of expression argue that the marketplace of ideas paradigm is an inadequate justification for inhibiting government regulation of speech. They point out that the unregulated marketplace of ideas is highly imperfect, and indeed far less effective than an unregulated economic market when it comes to protecting minorities. Economists point out that a free economic market protects minorities from discrimination to some degree because businesspeople have an economic incentive to hire the most productive workers and to obtain the most customers. Concern for the financial bottom line mitigates the temptation of business owners to indulge their prejudices.

However, minorities get comparatively little innate protection in the political marketplace of ideas because individual citizens have no corresponding incentive (economic or otherwise) to overlook or overcome personal prejudices or opinions about minorities. The average citizen seeking an ideology to guide his voting and other political activity has virtually no incentive to seek and find truth, especially because his opinion is highly unlikely to be decisive on any given matter. Even voters who genuinely seek the truth regarding particular issues will have difficulty finding it. The human mind is cognitively limited and much more suited for certain tasks, such as pursuing economic self-interest, than for others, such as adopting sensible ideological positions. As Nobel economics laureate Ronald Coase points out, "It's easier for people to discover that they have a bad can of peaches than it is for them to discover that they have a bad idea."[13] Moreover, while in competitive economic markets minorities can generally find safe havens in the private sector even if most organizations discriminate, there is no safe haven for minorities if racist ideas dominate politics and find their way into law.

If anything, then, restrictions on speech that denigrates vulnerable groups are more likely to protect minorities and women over time than are laws banning discrimination in employment. Free speech critics exploit the power of this point by criticizing liberal civil libertarians who vigorously oppose laissez faire economics, especially when it comes to protecting minorities from discrimination, but support an unregulated marketplace of ideas.[14] If the government can make the economic marketplace fairer and more efficient by regulating it, they ask, why can the government not do the same for the less-efficient speech marketplace?

One answer, provided by law and economics luminaries such as Ronald Coase and Richard Epstein, is that government regulation of the economic marketplace is at least as wrongheaded as government regulation of the marketplace of ideas. Epstein therefore argues in favor of both the robust protection of First Amendment liberties and the repeal of antidiscrimination laws that apply to private parties.[15] Indeed, Epstein suggests that these two policies are synergistic, because he doubts that the freedoms of speech and religion can ultimately be defended from antidiscrimination laws once it is conceded that an antidiscrimination norm is an appropriate legal limit on freedom of contract.

But even civil libertarians who strongly support basic employment and housing discrimination laws can offer a compelling rejoinder to those who advocate allowing such laws to run roughshod over the First Amendment. In contrast to the Panglossian straw men that censorship advocates build and demolish, realistic civil libertarians recognize that the free marketplace of ideas is imperfect, perhaps highly so. However, civil libertarians also recognize that they must still ask the most important question in political economy: compared with what? Although much private speech is wrongheaded or even dangerous, it is even more dangerous to put the government in charge of policing it.[16]

The alternative to allowing an unregulated speech marketplace is permitting government censorship, leaving "the government in control of all the institutions of culture, the great censor and director of which thoughts are good for us."[17] For good reason, civil libertarians believe that the government cannot be trusted with the power to establish an official orthodoxy on any issue, cultural or political, or to ensure the "fairness" of political debate. As one scholar puts it, "freedom of speech is based in large part on a distrust of the ability of government to make the necessary distinctions, a distrust of government determinations of truth and falsity, an appreciation of the fallibility of political leaders, and a somewhat deeper distrust of governmental power in a more general sense."[18]

Freedom of expression is necessary to prevent government from entrenching itself and expanding its power at the expense of the public. As federal court of appeals judge Frank Easterbrook wrote in an opinion striking down an antipornography statute inspired by academic feminists, "free speech has been on balance an ally of those seeking change. Governments that want stasis start by restricting speech. . . . Without a strong guarantee of freedom of speech, there is no effective right to challenge what is."[19] First Amendment scholar John McGinnis likewise notes that government officials have a natural tendency to suppress speech antithetical to their interests. As McGinnis notes, the free flow of information related to politics and culture threatens "government hierarchies both by rearranging coalitions and revealing facts that will prompt political action."[20]

The framers of the American Constitution also recognized that government is in constant danger of capture by factions that desire to use the government for their own private ends, a phenomenon known in modern academic literature as "rent-seeking." The Constitution and Bill of Rights were intended to establish a system of government that limits such rent-seeking. The First Amendment's protection of freedom of expression is particularly important in this regard. The founders believed that once in power, factions would exploit any government authority to regulate speech in self-serving ways. The founders' insights have been confirmed by experience around the world and by modern research into human political behavior by economists and evolutionary psychologists. Permitting government regulation of information relating to politics or culture would come at a very high price to society.[21]

Contrary to the insinuations of some critics,[22] then, all but the most starry-eyed civil libertarians recognize that freedom of expression can have many negative side effects, or, as economists put it, negative externalities. But civil libertarians are also familiar with the voracious lust for power and pursuit of self-interest endemic in politicians and their rent-seeking allies. Civil libertarians apply the cold calculus that the negative externalities caused by government regulation are likely to outweigh any negative externalities that arise from freedom of expression. Or, more simply put, civil libertarians believe that allowing politicians to decide the scope of freedom of speech is simply more dangerous than any damage the speech itself may cause. This is especially true in the United States. In contrast to more statist social systems, the United States has largely maintained a Tocquevillian nature, in which political and cultural innovations arise from the grass roots, not from the government. Freedom of expression is therefore necessary for economic and cultural progress.[23]

Some scholars recognize the dangers of government regulation of speech but still call for limited censorship to achieve what they consider particularly important antidiscrimination ends. Professor Andrew Koppelman of Northwestern University, for example, argues that there should be a presumption in favor of freedom of expression because "[r]acist speech may be substantively worthless, but outlawing it would give the state the power to decide *which* political views are worthless because racist." However, although Koppelman acknowledges that government power to censor speech can be "easily abused," he adds that censorship can be justified if the speech in question is "exceedingly harmful."[24] Koppelman believes that in such cases "a significant, but limited, infringement on free speech" is appropriate. He says he would discard any speech restrictions once they had served their purpose of achieving "workplace equality" for previously excluded minorities and women.

Koppelman's proposal demonstrates the dangers of divorcing political philosophy from practical political economy. He never clarifies how the government could objectively determine which speech is sufficiently harmful to merit censorship. With the First Amendment effectively nullified under Koppelman's preferred regime, censorship decisions would ultimately be made through ordinary politics, in which voter ignorance, rent-seeking, and similar problems would arise. In the long run, speech restrictions would likely serve the interests of dominant political factions, with no guarantee that those factions would represent the progressive political forces Koppelman supports.

Moreover, even assuming speech restrictions could be limited to the goals set for them by Koppelman, he provides no guidance on how such restrictions would ultimately be abolished once they are in place. He fails to explain how Congress or state legislatures would reach a consensus that the speech restrictions' goals have been achieved, and how legislators would buck the lobbying power of the interest groups that would inevitably coalesce to defend the restrictions. For example, in the 80-plus years since the end of World War I, Congress has not been able to summon the will to permanently abolish the mohair subsidies that were enacted to ensure fabric availability for World War I military uniforms.[25] It hardly seems likely, then, that Congress would have the wherewithal to abolish entrenched censorship rules.

* * *

Some civil libertarians argue that the government should force large private institutions, such as universities and large corporations, to adhere to "First Amendment standards." In other words, the government should prohibit large private institutions from penalizing expression if the government itself could not lawfully punish that expression. For example, the California affiliate of the American Civil Liberties Union supported a state law that requires private high schools and universities to permit any speech that the First Amendment requires a public school to tolerate.[26] The national ACLU then backed a bill introduced in the U.S. House and Senate that would have extended that rule to universities nationwide.[27]

As we have seen, the underlying rationale for the First Amendment is to protect the private sector from government regulation of speech. Moreover, the First Amendment—"Congress [and, under modern doctrine, the states] shall make no law"—applies only to the government. The ACLU's argument that the government should impose "First Amendment standards" on the private sector is therefore paradoxical. A constitutionally based, normatively sound civil libertarian perspective dictates instead that private entities must be free to adopt idiosyncratic policies regarding expression, even if powerful lobbying groups such as the ACLU believe such policies are unwise. As Professor Randall Kennedy of Harvard Law School suggests, the proper response to private-sector experimentation with speech rules is to "let a thousand flowers bloom."[28] Indeed, Supreme Court precedent suggests that the First Amendment prohibits the government from interfering with private institutions as they promote and defend particular ideological orthodoxies.[29]

An exception to the principle that civil liberties concerns are not implicated when private institutions adopt speech rules arises when a private institution adopts a speech rule because the law requires it to do so. For example, a university speech code adopted to comply with sexual harassment laws is an indirect regulation of speech by the government, not a voluntary speech restriction by a private institution. From a First Amendment perspective, such indirect government censorship is just as problematic as direct government control over speech.

* * *

Some scholars, most prominently law professor and literary critic Stanley Fish of the University of Illinois at Chicago, argue that neutral protection of freedom of expression is impossible. In our society, the task of interpreting the First Amendment falls mainly to the judiciary, and Fish argues that judicial invocation of freedom of expression merely masks politically motivated actions. Therefore, according to Fish, the only question worth discussing is who will get the power to censor whom.[30]

Fish is correct that judges are not Platonic guardians immune from political motivation. However, that does not mean that judges are motivated solely, or even primarily, by politics. Fish's left-wing academic allies have faulted "law and economics" scholars for relying on too narrow a view of human nature. In particular, economists tend to treat individuals as rational utility-maximizers, while ignoring the powerful roles played by psychology and social norms in shaping behavior. Fish likewise ignores the role played by psychology and social norms in shaping judicial behavior. Judges who are trained from their law school days that the role of the judiciary is to fairly enforce constitutional rights will find their self-image bound up in their ability to eschew personal prejudices and act fairly. This has practical consequences. For example, federal judges in the late 19th and mid-20th century protected the rights of Chinese immigrants and African Americans, respectively, even though the judges often had little personal sympathy for these minority groups' aspirations, and even though local political culture was strongly hostile to those groups.[31] Political temptations will always exist for judges, but they will remain tempered by the norm of judicial objectivity—

unless Fish and his colleagues succeed in destroying that norm by persuading judges that law and politics are indistinguishable.

Another irony is that Fish and his allies attack claims of neutrality by "employ[ing] an epistemology that denies all eternal verities." Simultaneously, however, "they establish current notions of racial and gender equality as an unquestionable, transcendent truth."[32] For example, Fish writes that "'[f]ree speech' is just the name we give to verbal behavior that serves the substantive agendas we wish to advance; and we give our preferred verbal behaviors *that* name when we can, when we have the power to do so, because in the rhetoric of American life, the label 'free speech' is the one you want your favorites to wear."[33] Because the concept of freedom of expression is merely a political device to promote particular agendas, according to Fish, there is no reason to suffer racist and sexist expression in its name, given the dangers such speech poses to the dignity and equality of its targets.[34] Yet if we accept Fish's view that there is "no such thing as free speech" because everything comes down to politics, then surely there can be no such thing as "dignity" or "equality" either. Those who argue that purportedly illusory notions of freedom of speech should be sacrificed to equalitarian commitments that are based on notions at least as delusive cannot possibly explain why.

* * *

Protecting freedom of expression from government regulation will ultimately benefit left-wing scholars who support censorship, such as radical feminists and critical race theorists, as much as anyone. These scholars advocate speech regulations while living primarily in the very left-wing academic world, where their views are only marginally out of the mainstream. Yet, if the First Amendment is weakened sufficiently by antidiscrimination law and the government gains the power to suppress speech more broadly, radical feminists and critical race theorists, as holders of views wildly at variance with those of the public at large, are likely to be among the new censorship's first victims. That leftists writing in a society that has long been, and continues to be, hostile to their ideologies would want to weaken the principle that government may not suppress unpopular expression seems counterintuitive and shortsighted, to say the least.[35]

Indeed, many critical race scholars and radical feminists argue that the United States is innately and irredeemably racist and sexist. One need not accept this vision to realize that the Critical-Race-and-Radical-Feminist-Party, if such a thing existed, would not exactly take the American electorate by storm, at least not anytime soon. Because many critical race theorists and feminists claim to believe that American society is so hostile to their values, they should find constitutional protections against the majority especially important.

Of course, left-wing censors imagine a world in which the government silences only their ideological enemies, and they advocate censorship as an integral part of a much broader scheme for reconstructing society along egalitarian lines. Yet, it should be a cardinal principle of political advocacy that one should not support a regime with regulatory powers that one would not want applied to oneself. Acceptance of this principle would not only reduce hypocrisy, it would also remind political activists that politics is unpredictable and driven by power rather than morality. Power granted to government is often ultimately used against those who advocated that the power be exercised against others. As Yale political science professor William Graham Sumner remarked many years ago, "The advocate of [government] interference takes it for granted that he and his associates will have the administration of their legislative device in their own hands. . . . They never appear to remember that the device, when once set up, will itself be the prize of a struggle; that it will serve one set of purposes as well as another, so that after all the only serious question is: who will get it?"[36]

2. The Threat to Freedom of Expression in the Workplace

Jerold Mackenzie worked at Miller Brewing Company for 19 years, eventually achieving executive status and a $95,000 salary. One day, he made the career-ending mistake of recounting the previous night's episode of the sitcom *Seinfeld* to his coworker Patricia Best. In the episode, Jerry Seinfeld cannot remember the name of the woman he is dating, but he does recall that she said kids teased her as a child because her name rhymes with a part of the female anatomy. Jerry and his friend George brainstorm, but the best guesses they can come up with are the unlikely "Mulva" and "Gipple." Jerry's girlfriend breaks up with him when she realizes he doesn't know her name. As she leaves him forever, Jerry finally remembers the elusive rhyming name and calls after her, "Delores!"

Mackenzie related the details of this episode to Best, but she told Mackenzie she did not get the joke. To clarify the somewhat off-color punch line, Mackenzie gave her a copy of a dictionary page on which the word "clitoris" was highlighted. Best—who was apparently known to use salty language at work herself—complained to Miller Brewing officials of sexual harassment, and Miller Brewing fired Mackenzie for "unacceptable managerial performance." Mackenzie responded with a lawsuit alleging wrongful termination and other wrongs. At trial, Miller Brewing officials acknowledged that the direct cause of Mackenzie's termination was the *Seinfeld* incident and the ensuing fear of a sexual harassment lawsuit. The jury awarded Mackenzie $26.6 million, including $1.5 million in punitive damages against Best for interfering with Mackenzie's employment relationship with Miller Brewing. The verdict was later overturned on appeal because Wisconsin law does not have a law banning wrongful termination.[1]

Miller Brewing's firing of Mackenzie may seem like an absurd overreaction, but it was very much consistent with the counsel of employment law experts. They advise employers to enforce a zero

23

tolerance policy for any type of sex-related remarks by employees, especially those made by supervisors or executives like Mackenzie. Consultant Beau Crivello suggests, "A rule of thumb is that if you can't say it or do it in a house of worship or in front of children, then don't say it or do it at work."[2] The rather startling message from the experts is that speech generally protected from government sanction loses that protection the moment it enters the workplace. Frank Carillo, president of Executive Communications Group, warns that just because you hear something in the media "doesn't mean you can say it [at work]. The media has a certain license to say things that the average person can't."[3] Consultant Monica Ballard concurs: "People think that if they hear something on TV or the radio, they can say it at work. But that, of course, is not the case."[4] Jerold Mackenzie, among others, would agree.

The roots of all of this censorship lie in the "hostile environment" component of antidiscrimination law. Beginning in the late 1970s, feminist legal scholars argued that the ban on employment discrimination against women should include a ban on sexual harassment.[5] Sexual harassment, they argued, includes the act of subjecting women to a "hostile work environment" by exposing them to offensive speech. The speech need not be directed at any individual woman to constitute harassment. For it to qualify as harassment of a woman coworker, it is enough that the speech could reasonably be construed as hostile to women generally. Further, the determination of whether a hostile environment existed does not depend on whether anyone *intended* to make any or all of their female coworkers feel unwelcome. An innocently offered comment can as easily be charged with creating a hostile environment as a deliberate slur or threat.

The feminists achieved a great victory when the Supreme Court held in 1986 that an illegal hostile work environment exists when "the workplace is permeated with discriminatory intimidation, ridicule, and insult, . . . that is sufficiently severe or pervasive to alter the conditions of the victim's employment."[6] Thousands of lawsuits of varying degrees of legal merit followed. Legal filings grew exponentially after the attention given to the issue of sexual harassment during the Clarence Thomas–Anita Hill hearings. Government agencies quickly produced pamphlets that urged victims of sexual harassment to file complaints and that often defined "hostile environment" far more broadly than the law justified.

Many employers responded to the growth of hostile environment law by attempting to regulate the potentially offensive speech of their employees.[7] The result was an implicit, but nonetheless chilling, nationwide workplace speech code that banned any speech that could offend women. The Supreme Court, perhaps realizing that it had opened a veritable Pandora's box of litigation, has recently emphasized that sporadic abusive language, gender-related jokes, and occasional teasing are not enough to meet the legal test for a hostile environment.[8] Prudent employers still feel compelled, however, to enforce speech guidelines that go well beyond what the letter of Supreme Court precedent requires.

There are several reasons for this caution. First, as four Supreme Court justices have noted in a related context,[9] the fuzzy guidance provided by hostile environment precedents simply does not give employers a clear indication of what they must do to remain within the confines of the law. For example, while a single offensive joke will not create liability, some courts have held that a pattern of jokes by different employees can create a hostile environment.[10] The safest route for employers is to ban *any* banter with sexual connotations, lest the aggregation of speech by different employees constitute a hostile environment. Better to be safe (if silent) than sorry.

Second, and relatedly, the severe and pervasive liability standard is sufficiently vague, good counsel sufficiently expensive, and trial judges and juries sufficiently unpredictable that employers feel compelled to settle even highly dubious claims to avoid the risks and costs of litigation. After all, juries have awarded tens of thousands of dollars to plaintiffs in cases appellate courts later dismissed.[11] Although clearly meritless claims rarely survive federal appellate review, no sensible attorney would advise his clients to depend on appellate courts—which can only overturn "clearly erroneous" jury verdicts—to save them from unjustified claims. This is especially true because fighting a claim to the appellate level can cost hundreds of thousands of dollars, with the costs disproportionately borne by the defendant. Victory may be sweet, but saving one's company six-digit sums by avoiding litigation entirely is even sweeter. Risk-averse employers will settle pending cases, and prevent future lawsuits by cracking down on potentially offensive speech.

Third, disgruntled employees or former employees can impose large costs on employers without going to the effort and expense of filing a lawsuit, simply by complaining of harassment to the Equal Employment Opportunity Commission. The EEOC is legally required to investigate every complaint of sex discrimination, no matter how weak or unconvincing a complaint seems. Even a trivial complaint can lead to a broad investigation of the underlying claim, costing the employer thousands of dollars in legal fees and lost time. And petty complaints are actually encouraged by official government pronouncements that propagate inaccurate, overbroad definitions of what constitutes illegal sexual harassment. For example, an official U.S. Department of Labor pamphlet states that harassment includes cases in which a coworker "made sexual jokes or said sexual things that you didn't like, so long as the jokes made it hard to work."[12] A very sensitive or very religious person may find that *any* sex-oriented remarks make it hard to work. Such a person is encouraged by government publications to complain of sexual harassment the first time a coworker tells a dirty joke. The offended worker will likely lose, but not before her employer wastes resources on its defense.

Fourth, many states and localities have their own antidiscrimination laws with standards for hostile environment liability that are sometimes significantly broader than the federal laws' requirement of severe and pervasive harassment. For example, a New Jersey court held that under state law employees who forwarded one list of crude jokes to their colleagues via e-mail had created an illegal "offensive work environment," even though this act would be unlikely to create liability under federal law.[13] Even if state and local law are no broader than federal law, employers are often at a special disadvantage when a hostile environment complaint is filed under state or local law because, unlike in the federal system, in states administrative tribunals often make the initial ruling on hostile environment claims. Because these administrative bodies are part of executive branch agencies charged specifically with enforcing the relevant antidiscrimination laws, they naturally tend to be more sympathetic to discrimination claims and less sensitive to free speech concerns than are federal courts, which have broader responsibilities and are part of the judicial branch of government.

* * *

Hostile environment law has spread well beyond the sex discrimination context, with claims successfully prosecuted for race, religion, and national origin harassment. One court, for example, found that publishing religious articles in a company newsletter and printing Christian-themed verses on company paychecks constituted "harassment" of a Jewish employee.[14] Another court found that an employee who hung in her cubicle pictures of the Ayatollah Khomeini and of Iranian protestors burning an American flag was guilty of national origin harassment against an Iranian-American employee who happened to see the display.[15] Court rulings and EEOC guidelines suggest that religious harassment includes both a religious employee proselytizing a coworker and a secular employee ridiculing a religious coworker for the latter's beliefs.[16]

As in the sex discrimination context, a hostile environment claim for race discrimination and other types of workplace discrimination can arise even when the speech in question was not directed at the plaintiff. For example, the EEOC charged a company with national origin harassment after a Japanese-American employee filed a complaint about the firm's advertising campaign. Some of the company's ads featured images of samurai, kabuki, and sumo wrestling to represent the firm's Japanese competitors. The employee also charged that officials of the company called Japanese competitors "Japs" and "slant-eyes." The case was eventually settled for an undisclosed amount.[17]

Standards for racial and ethnic harassment are at least as vague as they are in the sexual harassment context, which leads to unpredictable jury verdicts. Even highly questionable claims can result in large verdicts, giving employers strong incentives to heavily regulate workplace speech as a preventive measure.

One especially meritless claim that led to a six-figure verdict involved Allen Fruge, a white Department of Energy employee based in Texas. Fruge unwittingly spawned a harassment suit when he followed up a southeast Texas training session with a bit of self-deprecating humor. He sent several of his colleagues who had attended the session with him gag certificates anointing each of them as an honorary "Coon Ass"[18]—usually spelled "coonass"—a mildly derogatory slang term for a Cajun. The certificate stated that "[y]ou are to sing, dance, and tell jokes and eat boudin, cracklins, gumbo, crawfish etouffe and just about anything else." The joke stemmed from the fact that southeast Texas, the training session location, has a large Cajun population, including Fruge himself.

An African American recipient of the certificate, Sherry Reid, chief of the Nuclear and Fossil Branch of the DOE in Washington, D.C., apparently missed the joke and complained to her supervisors that Fruge had called her a "coon." Fruge sent Reid a formal (and humble) letter of apology for the inadvertent offense, and explained what "Coon Ass" actually meant. Reid nevertheless remained convinced that "Coon Ass" was a racial pejorative, and demanded that Fruge be fired. DOE supervisors declined to fire Fruge, but they did send him to "diversity training." They also reminded Reid that the certificate had been meant as a joke, that Fruge had meant no offense, that "Coon Ass" was slang for Cajun, and that Fruge sent the certificates to people of various races and ethnicities, so he clearly was not targeting African Americans. Reid nevertheless sued the DOE, claiming that she had been subjected to a racial epithet that had created a hostile environment, a situation made worse by the DOE's failure to fire Fruge.

Reid's case was seemingly frivolous. The linguistics expert her attorney hired was unable to present evidence that "Coon Ass" meant anything but "Cajun," or that the phrase had racist origins, and Reid presented no evidence that Fruge had any discriminatory intent when he sent the certificate to her. Moreover, even if "Coon Ass" had been a racial epithet, a single instance of being given a joke certificate, even one containing a racial epithet, by a nonsupervisory colleague who works 1,200 miles away does not seem to remotely satisfy the legal requirement that harassment must be "severe and pervasive" for it to create hostile environment liability. Nevertheless, a federal district court allowed the case to go to trial,[19] and the jury awarded Reid $120,000, plus another $100,000 in attorneys' fees.[20] The DOE settled the case before its appeal could be heard for a sum very close to the jury award.

Even if a disgruntled worker decides not to take a case all the way to a jury, he can still impose costs on his boss or ex-boss by alleging that he was subjected to a hostile environment, even if he has scant supporting evidence. For example, a gay man named John Dill put his former employer, CPA Referral, in a pickle when he filed a complaint of employment discrimination with the Seattle Human Rights Department. Dill claimed that his ex-boss Bryan Griggs had created a "hostile work environment" for homosexuals in violation of a local antidiscrimination ordinance. According to

Dill, Griggs's offensive behavior consisted of playing conservative and Christian radio shows that Dill felt conveyed an antigay message, posting a letter from a congresswoman in which she endorsed the military's policy of excluding gays, and having a note on his desk reminding himself to lobby against allowing gays to adopt children. Dill acknowledged that Griggs did not know he was gay, and Dill never told Griggs that any of Griggs's actions offended or upset him.

Dill had been employed by CPA Referral the previous fall, but Griggs had laid him off when business slowed. Griggs had allowed Dill to come back to work as a volunteer, promising him the first available paid job. Much to Griggs's surprise, Dill suddenly tendered his resignation in a letter stating that "I feel I must 'come out' and stop playing 'don't ask, don't tell.' " In his letter, Dill explained that he was leaving CPA Referral for "a supportive environment." He then filed his complaint, and the SHRD launched a full investigation of CPA Referral.

The befuddled Griggs told the SHRD that he listened to the conservative talk shows to make sure they played the advertising he had paid for, and that he posted many letters from politicians to encourage political participation among his employees. Another gay employee signed an affidavit swearing that he had never perceived any antigay animus in the workplace. There seems to have been no evidence that Dill suffered antigay discrimination, and a cynic might surmise that Dill filed the complaint mainly to get revenge on Griggs for having fired him. Dill eventually withdrew his complaint, but only after Griggs had spent thousands of dollars on legal fees defending himself and his company.[21] If Dill's goal was to punish Griggs, he managed to achieve it even without being formally vindicated by a court.

* * *

Most hostile environment employment cases have focused on whether the behavior at issue crossed the line from merely annoying or offensive conduct into conduct sufficiently severe and pervasive to meet the law's definition of creating a hostile environment. A few private employers, however, have unsuccessfully tried to claim First Amendment immunity from speech-based hostile environment claims.

The first reported hostile environment lawsuit in which the defendant invoked a free speech defense involved Lois Robinson, a welder at a Florida shipyard, who brought a case in federal court alleging that her employer, Jacksonville Shipyards, countenanced a hostile environment by permitting photos of nude and partially nude women to be displayed in various areas of her workplace.[22] She also complained about sexual and derogatory remarks made in her presence about her and other women, and about indecent and obscene graffiti directed at her.[23] Jacksonville Shipyards responded that the First Amendment protected at least some of this speech and asked the court to prohibit Robinson from relying on constitutionally protected speech to support her hostile environment claim.

The court ruled that the First Amendment does not protect workplace speech from employment discrimination law.[24] The court then issued an incredibly broad injunction that banned from the Jacksonville Shipyards' workplace not only pornography but also any "sexually suggestive" material. Employees on lunch break could no longer read *Cosmopolitan* magazine or Danielle Steel novels, or listen to Eminem or Britney Spears on a Walkman.

The court found that the First Amendment did not protect the workplace speech at issue for several reasons, none of which is persuasive. First, the court asserted that the company was not expressing itself through the offensive expression of its employees. What the court failed to discern was that because the company was being held liable for the speech of its employees, the relevant question was whether the *employees'* speech was constitutionally protected. There is no doubt that the Constitution protects such speech from government regulation, even when the speech conflicts with a broader regulatory scheme like hostile environment law.[25] The court failed to recognize that employers may assert a First Amendment defense on behalf of their employees, and may have their own First Amendment right to refuse to prohibit workplace speech.[26]

Next, the court opined that the nude pinups and expressions of hostility toward women in the shipyard were not protected speech, but were discriminatory conduct in the form of creation of a hostile work environment. Here, the court was correct insofar as it pointed out that speech can sometimes be considered conduct—for example, threats, intimidation, libel, and other forms of misconduct engaged in through speech do not receive First Amendment protection. Similarly, quid pro quo harassment (e.g., "Sleep with me or else!") is not protected by the First Amendment. Arguably, the government may even regulate as an action harassing speech targeted at a particular person for discriminatory reasons. But merely labeling speech "discrimination," as the *Robinson* court did, does not make it so. Posting a nonobscene pinup or expressing a politically incorrect opinion is protected outside of the workplace, and a mere change in venue from the sidewalk to the office cannot convert such protected speech into unprotected discriminatory action. Given that most adults spend much of their time in the workplace and that almost any speech beyond the most banal is likely to offend *someone*, allowing the government to regulate any offensive speech that occurs in the workplace would invite an incredibly broad assault on freedom of speech.

The *Robinson* court next determined that regulation of offensive workplace speech was a permissible regulation of the time, place, and manner of speech. Government can regulate these aspects of speech, restricting parades and protests to certain times of the day or limiting the volume of a megaphone in a residential area. But time, place, and manner restrictions can only be valid if they do not regulate speech on the basis of the speaker's viewpoint. Thus, a rule disallowing the use of megaphones during protests in residential neighborhoods may be valid, but a rule forbidding megaphones only when they are used to criticize affirmative action would be illicit viewpoint discrimination. Hostile environment law clearly discriminates based on viewpoint.[27] For example, hostile environment law potentially penalizes expression of the viewpoint that "women are stupid and incapable of being physicists," but not that "women are brilliant and make excellent physicists." Therefore, hostile environment law cannot be considered an appropriate time, place, and manner regulation.

Finally, the court insisted that plaintiff Robinson was a "captive audience" in the shipyard and therefore the First Amendment did not protect speech that offended her. Yet we are all at times captive to expression we find offensive, in the sense that we must take action to avoid seeing or hearing it. Nevertheless, that speech is still constitutionally protected. Of course, avoiding some types of offensive speech is relatively easy, while avoiding offensive workplace speech by finding new employment can be difficult and costly. But if courts accepted *Robinson*'s view that the First Amendment does not protect offensive speech that is very difficult or costly to avoid, much of modern First Amendment law would need to be discarded. For example, contrary to Supreme Court precedent, strikers would not have the right to picket outside their workplace, and antiabortion protestors would not have the right to assemble outside abortion clinics.[28] The Supreme Court has even protected the right of an individual to wear a jacket displaying the phrase "Fuck the Draft" inside a courthouse where many people who will see the profanity are truly a captive audience, in that they are legally required to be there.[29] If offensive speech is thus protected when avoiding it would require committing a crime by refusing to show up in court when required, surely it must also be protected when avoiding it would only involve switching jobs. Even if the captive audience rationale *could* be used to justify speech restrictions in the workplace, any such restrictions would have to be viewpoint-neutral, which, as noted previously, hostile environment law is not.

Despite the seemingly fatal weaknesses in *Robinson*'s First Amendment analysis, many other courts have relied on it in rejecting First Amendment defenses in hostile environment cases.[30] Most commonly in cases favorably citing *Robinson*, the plaintiff had been subjected to a pattern of severe individualized harassment, and the First Amendment defense applied only to a fraction of the behavior that allegedly created a hostile environment. However, nothing in *Robinson* limits its application to cases in which constitutionally protected expression is only a minor element. One court, in fact, cited *Robinson* favorably in a case in which the plaintiff's sole allegation was that her opponents for a union position had cirulated a satirical flyer during an election campaign.[31] The satire featured a picture of the plaintiff's head superimposed over an anonymous woman's naked body. This was tasteless, to be sure, but it was also political speech clearly protected by the First Amendment, as indicated by a landmark Supreme Court opinion protecting an even more offensive satire of Jerry Falwell that appeared in *Hustler* magazine.[32]

* * *

Just as the injunction granted in *Robinson* created an unprecedented prior restraint (proactively censoring speech before it is spoken) on sexist speech, the California Supreme Court recently upheld an unprecedented prior restraint on racist speech. A jury had found that an Avis Rent A Car outlet had engaged in employment discrimination, in part by allowing an employee to repeatedly utter racial epithets targeted at the Latino plaintiffs. Besides awarding damages, the trial court issued an injunction prohibiting Avis employees "from using any derogatory racial or ethnic epithets directed at, or descriptive of, Hispanic/Latino employees of [Avis]."[33] An appellate court limited the injunction to the workplace and attempted to narrow the scope of the injunction via a proposed list of specific words that the district court could ban. Not satisfied that these modifications made the injunction comport with the First Amendment, Avis appealed to the California Supreme Court.

A four-to-three majority of the state supreme court upheld the appellate court's decision. The three dissenters argued that the injunction amounted to a prior restraint on constitutionally protected speech. They pointed out that U.S. Supreme Court precedent shows that prior restraints are not allowed for speech that might, but won't necessarily, be illegal. The reason for this rule is that such restraints have a chilling effect on what could have been legal, protected speech. For example, a single future pejorative use of a racial epithet, although banned by the injunction, cannot be the severe and pervasive harassment required to create an illegal hostile work environment; in some contexts it might be severe, but a single comment cannot be "pervasive." For that matter, racial epithets can be uttered in contexts that do not evince hostility. For example, epithets could be mentioned during "diversity education" or could be used ironically, yet these uses of the epithets would be equally banned by the injunction's prior restraint. Justice Clarence Thomas urged his colleagues to hear Avis's appeal to the U. S. Supreme Court because of the "troubling free speech issues" raised by the case,[34] but he was not successful, and the injunction stood.

The ultimate outcome of the battle between the First Amendment and the speech-regulating aspects of hostile environment law thus remains unresolved and will remain that way until the Supreme Court chooses to resolve the issue. No court has yet held directly that the First Amendment prohibits workplace speech from being the basis of Title VII liability if that speech would be protected in other contexts. However, four Supreme Court justices have suggested that hostile environment law sometimes violates the First Amendment,[35] and other federal courts have expressed alarm at hostile environment law's growing conflict with freedom of speech.[36]

Federal courts have also been sympathetic to First Amendment objections to prophylactic measures ordered by state and local governments to avoid creating a hostile environment in the public sector workplace. For example, courts have held that prohibiting prisoners and on-duty firefighters from reading *Playboy* unconstitutionally restricts expression, despite claims that allowing pornographic magazines to be read creates a hostile work environment for female prison guards and firefighters.[37]

In the absence of definitive Supreme Court guidance, however, hostile environment law marches on. In February 2002, for example, Anchorage, Alaska, fearing lawsuits by female firefighters, banned from its firehouse not only *Playboy* and other pornographic magazines, but also the slightly racy men's magazine *Maxim*.[38] And the law continues to grow. The latest trend in this expansion is employees suing employers for not preventing hostile environments allegedly created by patrons. For example, the Equal Employment Opportunity Commission has declared that 12 Minneapolis librarians were subjected to a sexually hostile work environment when they were exposed to pornography accessed on the Internet by library patrons. If courts agree with the EEOC, all libraries, public and private, will need to ban Internet access to "offensive" sites or face hostile environment liability.[39]

* * *

There are signs that the public is growing impatient with the corrosive effect of hostile environment law on freedom of expression. One of the more amusing manifestations of this disquiet is an episode of the animated series *South Park*. After a visit from the "Sexual Harassment Panda," the children of South Park begin to sue each other for harassment over minor insults. Eventually, the children pursue deeper pockets, the school at which these insults take place. The school is bankrupted, while Kyle's attorney father, who represents all of the plaintiffs, becomes wealthy. This leads to the following exchange:

> Father: You see, son, we live in a liberal democratic society. The Democrats [sic—it was a mostly Republican EEOC and Supreme Court] created sexual harassment law, which tells us what we can and cannot say in the workplace, and what we can and cannot do in the workplace.
> Kyle: But isn't that fascism?
> Father: No, because we don't call it fascism.

3. The Threat to Artistic Freedom

In 1999, a San Francisco gym put up a billboard with an illustration of space aliens and a warning: "When They Come, They'll Eat the Fat Ones First." Outraged activists for the overweight protested outside of the gym, holding signs that said "Eat Me." The gym took the billboard down, but the activists used momentum from the protests to successfully lobby for a city ordinance banning discrimination based on height and weight.

Krissy Keefer, director of Dance Brigade, a company that produces political dance such as "Dance of the Endangered Species," soon became the first San Franciscan to take advantage the new ordinance.[1] The standards of modern ballet require dancers to be lithe and thin, because body fat obscures the separations between parts and, it is thought, unduly accentuates the trunk. Being thin also helps a dancer perform ballet moves quickly and artfully and makes it easier for a male dancer to lift his partner. Keefer, however, regards ballet's body-type criteria as a feminist issue, because, she says, they require a dancer to "have an unhealthy relationship" with her body, leaving ballerinas on diets so strict that they are vulnerable to eating disorders.

Keefer had a particularly keen interest in ballet's body-style requirements because of her medium-sized daughter, Fredrika. The elder Keefer had brought nine-year-old Fredrika to an audition for the San Francisco Ballet's preprofessional school. The school's Web site states that "the ideal candidate is a healthy child with a well-proportioned body, a straight and supple spine, legs turned out from the hip joint, flexibility, slender legs and torso and correctly arched feet, who has an ear for music and an instinct for movement." The school promptly rejected Fredrika for not having the right body type to succeed as a professional ballet dancer.

The Ballet instead offered Fredrika a full scholarship to its Dance in Schools Program. School admissions officers said that if she could prove the school's initial impression wrong or if her body style changed, Fredrika could enter the preprofessional regimen later. But Krissy Keefer was not mollified. Like many stage moms, she was convinced that her daughter was destined for great things. Keefer persuaded herself that the narrow-mindedness of the ballet school was interfering with nine-year-old Fredrika's "career." The elder Keefer told ABC's *Good Morning America* that "I need a program for my daughter that actually could satisfy her professional aspirations."

Keefer filed a complaint with the San Francisco Human Rights Commission, claiming height and weight discrimination and, because ballet schools enforce height and weight requirements less stringently for boys—largely because the pool of boys willing to pursue ballet is much smaller than the pool of girls—sex discrimination. Keefer told the media, "I am mad at them for not seeing how talented she is, for having such a narrow, myopic view of what makes a dancer." The San Francisco Ballet, Keefer wrote in a press release, "should have a program that reflects the real needs of San Francisco's citizens, and the SFB school should foster a program of physical, emotional and mental well-being of its female participants as it pursues artistic excellence."

Keefer's complaint charged that Fredrika's rejection had caused her "confusion" and "humiliation." Fredrika, however, actually seemed reasonably content. She told the *San Francisco Chronicle* that "I'm sad I didn't get in, but I'm happy because I like the Pacific Dance Theater [the school she had been attending] a lot and I didn't want to lose that." In fact, any confusion and humiliation suffered by Fredrika may have been the result of her mother dragging her into a media circus. Krissy subjected Fredrika to press conferences and television interviews, forcing Fredrika to relive her "rejection" countless times and to have her body repeatedly held up to public scrutiny.

Keefer's legal action drew howls of protest from dancers and dance critics. Paul Ben-Itzak, editor of *Dance Insider* magazine, wrote that "what we have here is a ballet mother whose vanity is vicariously wounded, and who is shamelessly, in the guise of public-spirited concern, trying to hurt the San Francisco Ballet because it, in her view, hurt her daughter Fredrika." Dance critic Octavio Roca added: "We are in a world where artistic canons are devalued, and every opinion, no matter how biased or uninformed, is worth the same as every other. . . . In the name of democracy, with the laudable goal of nondiscrimination, we end up bypassing excellence while propping up the mediocre and the bland." Even Lawrence Gold-huber, a six-foot-one, 350-pound modern dancer, mocked Keefer's complaint, and admitted that he preferred watching thin dancers, particularly in ballet. "Short people don't get hired by the NBA," he noted, "Should fat people be in the ballet?"

Critics also pointed out that little Fredrika was hardly being deprived of a potential career in dance. Many other dance styles, including musical theater, disco, modern dance, and most ethnic dance types, do not have stringent body type requirements. None of this swayed Keefer, however, who told a reporter that people act as if "there's something sacred about ballet, so that it can't be legislated at all outside of the artistic view. It's not untouchable by the rest of the standards for society." Eva Patterson, an attorney for the Lawyers' Committee for Civil Rights, gushed that Keefer's case was "really groundbreaking. I'm sure many people will pooh-pooh it but it sounds important because it could force us to reexamine our attitudes toward body image and culture."

Unfortunately, in their intense zealousness to right the wrongs attributed to ballet's slim-centric aesthetic, Keefer and Patterson overlooked one small but important detail: the First Amendment. Properly interpreted, the Constitution's protection of free expression from government interference bars the City of San Francisco from legislating ballet standards. Larry Brinkin, a member of the San Francisco Human Rights Commission, recognized as much. He told the *San Francisco Chronicle* that the San Francisco Ballet school has a First Amendment right to choose to train only performers who meet the school's subjective criteria.

As of this writing, however, the case against the Ballet is still pending. Fredrika's dance career is going strong despite her rejection by the San Francisco Ballet; she won rave reviews for her lead role in a 2003 production of "Einstein's Daughter." Meanwhile, another claimant under San Francisco's weight discrimination law, a five-foot-eight and 240-pound woman, forced Jazzercise, the nation's leading aerobic exercise company, to drop its requirement that instructors have a fit appearance.

* * *

The Keefer case is an extreme illustration of an emerging trend of activists and government agencies trying to use antidiscrimination law to make artistic expression more politically correct. For example, in March 1998 a group of women artists calling itself the Title IX Task Force filed a complaint with the National Endowment for the Arts against three of New York's leading museums—the Museum of Modern Art, the Guggenheim Museum, and the Whitney Museum of American Art. The complaint alleged that these museums do not display enough paintings or sculptures created by women.

Title IX, an amendment to the 1964 Civil Rights Act, bans sex discrimination by institutions that receive federal funds, a definition that encompasses the three art museums named in the Task Force's complaint. Title IX is famously credited with substantially increasing the funding universities give to women's athletics. Activists for women's athletics "so unequivocally succeeded in what they had set out to do, it inspired us," Task Force member Mary Beth Edelson remarked.[2]

Edelson claims that the paucity of art by women exhibited in the big three art museums is devastating to women's career prospects. "Collectors will go to the museums and see work and think, 'This is the *Good Housekeeping* seal of approval' . . . and they go to a dealer and they buy that work," Edelson explained, "If the museums don't include women . . . then the dealers have a very difficult time selling [art by] women." The museums' spokespeople respond that major exhibitions focus on the work of artists established over many years; therefore, if works by male artists are presently overrepresented at exhibitions, this reflects biases that shaped the art world years ago, not any biases currently informing the museums' choices.[3] Regardless of who is correct, it hardly seems consistent with artistic freedom to have the government dictate whose work art museums should display.

* * *

Antidiscrimination laws' threat to artistic freedom goes well beyond arts organizations such as the San Francisco Ballet and New York's leading art museums. Employers and university officials are increasingly facing the Hobson's choice of either removing "offensive" art from the workplace or facing antidiscrimination lawsuits. The ban on certain kinds of art is explicit in some jurisdictions. For example, Madison, Wisconsin, has a law specifically defining illegal "sexual harassment" to include "repeated display of sexually graphic materials which is not necessary for business purposes."[4] The Montana Human Rights Commission's guide for employers similarly states that "prohibited sexual harassment includes: [d]isplays of magazines, books, or pictures with a sexual connotation."[5]

At the end of the day, however, it is litigation or fear of litigation pursued under *federal* antidiscrimination law that lies at the root of most art censorship undertaken to satisfy antidiscrimination law. Title VII of the 1964 Civil Rights Act bans the creation of a "hostile workplace environment" for women as part of its judicially constructed prohibition on sexual harassment. For example, Penn State University took down a print of Goya's *Naked Maja* that had been hanging in a classroom when Nancy Stumhofer, an English professor, complained about its depicting a naked woman. Professor Stumhofer explained, "Whether it was a *Playboy* centerfold or a Goya, what I am discussing is that it's a nude picture of a woman which encourages males to make remarks about body parts."[6]

The Murfreesboro, Tennessee, city government removed from city hall an impressionistic painting by Maxine Henderson that depicts a nude woman with her breasts partially in view. The city was responding to a complaint by Laurie Crowder, an assistant school superintendent who did not work in city hall but passed the painting one day on the way to a meeting there. She threatened a hostile environment lawsuit, a move that led the city to take the painting off display.[7] Crowder said, "I personally find art in any form whether it be a painting, a Greek statue or a picture out of *Playboy* which displays genitals, buttocks, and/or nipples of the human body, to be pornographic and, in this instance, very offensive and degrading to me as a woman."

After the city removed the painting, City Attorney Tom Reed remarked, "I feel more comfortable siding with protecting the rights under the Title VII sexual harassment statutes than I do under the First Amendment."[8] Reed added, "You really can't be too cautious. A sexual harassment judgment usually has six zeros behind it."[9] Ironically, Reed's caution did not save Murfreesboro from a lawsuit. Henderson, the artist, successfully sued the city for removing the painting in violation of Henderson's First Amendment rights.[10] However, in stark contrast to the huge sum that Reed had worried about losing in a sexual harassment suit, Henderson recovered only one dollar along with her costs.[11]

Arguably, public schools like Penn State, local governments like Murfreesboro, and other government entities should, out of respect to prudish employees and citizens, avoid displaying nude art in public spaces. Despite the dubious First Amendment ruling in favor of Ms. Henderson, the objectionable aspect of the incidents described earlier is not that the art was removed—Penn State and Murfreesboro had no obligation to display the art in the first place—but rather that its removal was undertaken in response to threats of legal action. Stumhofer and Henderson turned issues of taste into issues of alleged illegal sexual harassment—developments that will give inevitable pause to any employer, public or private, who wishes to display potentially controversial art in the workplace.

* * *

Although many of the early sexual harassment complaints based on artistic displays involved feminist plaintiffs, individuals with conservative social views have also used sexual harassment law to promote censorship. For example, some Christian groups have argued that convenience stores should not be permitted to sell pornographic magazines, because the presence of such magazines creates a hostile environment for female and Christian employees.

For others, it is the combination of race and sex that proves especially provocative and objectionable. For example, University of South Florida freshman Nicole Ferry was offended by a photograph displayed in her art class. The photograph, titled "Nigger Lover," showed a black man and a white woman locked in a simulated sexual embrace.[12] It was the work of African American artist and class teaching assistant Derek Washington, who intended to use the arresting image to force viewers to examine their reactions to a depiction of interracial sex.

Washington, who also happened to be the black man in the photo, displayed the image in class as part of a lecture on controversial art. Although the explicit nature of Washington's photo may have surprised or bothered some students, it should not have come as a complete shock. Instructor Diane Elmeer had earlier warned students that they might find some images shown during this lecture offensive, and told them they were free to skip the presentation entirely or to leave at any time without being penalized.

Ferry apparently was not so sensitive as to skip the presentation, but Washington's photo made a strong negative impression on her. When she mentioned the photo to her father, he responded by sending an angry letter to the university, calling the photo "pornographic" and "smut." The university was unresponsive to this complaint, which seemed little more than the prudish concerns of a conservative parent. In a later meeting with university officials, however, Mr. Ferry hit school officials where it hurt. He claimed "sexual harassment" had been perpetrated on his daughter—by "an African American male," no less. The elder Ferry had clearly learned the proper buzzword ("sexual harassment") to get university censorship gears in motion, and move the censors did. The university general counsel ordered Washington reassigned to another class, because it would "penalize a victim of an alleged sexual harassment" if Washington were to continue to have "a position of power" in the original class. Fine Arts Dean Ronald Jones told students that "no sexual harassment claim or allegation made in my office or within my hearing will go unacted upon. I cannot tolerate an environment when something like that happens."

Washington's reassignment prompted a sit-in protest of the university president's office by most of the other 250 students in the class. Sophomore Alexia Bridges expressed concern that Washington's reassignment would cause other instructors to avoid controversial subjects. "Everybody is going to watch their step," she said, "dot their I's and cross their T's." Students contended that other art displayed in the class was far more sexually explicit than Washington's piece, and that Ferry had singled out Washington's photo because of its depiction of interracial sex. Elmeer reportedly told her class that the incident "reeks of racism." Following the protest, the university withdrew Washington's reassignment. All of this further upset Ferry, who alleged that she was being vilified for standing up to sexual harassment. Her father sent another letter to the university, this one accusing college officials of "evoking [sic] the protest," and the younger Ferry filed a sexual harassment lawsuit against the school. The complaint lent support to those who thought Ferry's agitation had a racial subtext when it gratuitously volunteered that she was white and Washington was black. The university caved again, settling with the Ferrys for $25,000.

Not surprisingly, Washington was upset by the university's cravenness. "This came down to a business issue," he said, "and I just don't think money should supersede ethics." An explicit university policy prohibiting instructors from displaying sexually explicit materials in their classes would probably be within a state university's constitutional authority to set academic policy (see Chapter 5). No such policy, however, existed at the University of South Florida. Given that the controverted art was directly related to the subject matter of the class, Washington had every reason and right to assume that, in the absence of an explicit policy to the contrary, his academic freedom in displaying this art was protected. As the Ferry debacle shows, vague sexual harassment policies have unfortunately become a means for enforcing ad hoc artistic censorship policies.

* * *

Inevitably, antidiscrimination laws threaten not only highbrow art, but lowbrow art and entertainment as well. The Supreme Court has declared that "the line between the transmission of ideas and mere entertainment is much too elusive for this Court to draw, if indeed such a line can be drawn at all."[13] Therefore, the First Amendment has been held to protect all forms of entertainment from government regulation, even those shows, books, and pictures that have no discernable value to society beyond entertainment. This principle, however, is being increasingly undermined by the enforcement of antidiscrimination laws.

In response to a "hostile environment" complaint on the basis of the prevalence of nude pinups at a shipyard, a federal court banned the display of any "sexually suggestive, sexually demeaning, or pornographic" material there.[14] Another court upheld a $125,000 sex discrimination award based in part on the plaintiff's coworker's playing "misogynistic rap music" and displaying music videos depicting an array of sexually provocative conduct.[15] The Americans with Disabilities Act has been held to require a comedy club to put a deaf interpreter on stage, even during a performance by an illusionist who must have the audience's full attention focused where he needs it to achieve his effects.[16]

Perhaps the most notorious case of antidiscrimination law impinging on lowbrow art involved actress Hunter Tylo. The producers of the steamy prime-time soap opera *Melrose Place* hired Tylo to play the show's latest promiscuous bimbo, "Taylor McBride." Predictably, given *Melrose Place*'s emphasis on form (and especially female form) over substance, Tylo's contract included a clause forbidding any "material change" in her appearance. When Tylo became pregnant before the new season started shooting, the producers fired her, explaining that they did not want their bed-hopping vixen character to be played by an obviously pregnant woman. To get an idea of where the producers were coming from, picture this: in one pivotal scene, Tylo, who gained 47 pounds during her pregnancy, was to be filmed cavorting pool-side in a thong bikini.

Tylo sued for employment discrimination based on sex and pregnancy. The producers of the show responded that Tylo's prepregnancy appearance was a bona fide occupational qualification (BFOQ) reasonably necessary to the proper casting of the show. Therefore, they argued, Tylo's claim failed under federal law.[17] The producers also claimed a First Amendment right to cast the part as they saw fit. The judge declined to dismiss the case on BFOQ or First Amendment grounds, and the jury found in Tylo's favor, awarding her $5 million. Tylo's attorney, Gloria Allred, enthused that Tylo "is absolutely a living Susan B. Anthony and a Rosa Parks all rolled into one."[18] After the verdict, the case was settled for an undisclosed sum.

But it's not only Hollywood's free, if sometimes raunchy, expression that is being compromised. Antidiscrimination laws even endanger something as quaint and apparently innocuous as the period theme of a restaurant, raising the question of whether ambience is an element of artistic freedom protected by the First Amendment. Cock of the Walk, a southern seafood chain, tried to provide an atmosphere in keeping with its 1800s riverboat theme. The waiters, dressed in period costume, were meant to represent the legendary fighters who brawled for the privilege of steering the riverboats, which netted them the best-of-the-best title: Cock of the Walk. Only males were hired as servers because, as Mike Fink Corporation, the owner of the chain, explained, women did not work on riverboat crews in the 1800s. It was a simple matter of historical accuracy.

Susan Mathis applied for a server job at one of the chain's restaurants, arriving equipped with a hidden recorder that taped a restaurant manager turning her down for a server position because she was a woman. At Mathis's behest, the Equal Employment Opportunity Commission sued Mike Fink for sex discrimination. The company responded that given the restaurants' historical theme, being male was a BFOQ. A jury disagreed and found the restaurant liable for discrimination. Following the verdict, the company agreed to pay a $70,000 settlement. The company also agreed to hire women for server positions and to allow the EEOC to monitor its hiring practices for the next five years.[19] Mathis's successful lawsuit led one frustrated commentator to ask, "What's the next logical target for discrimination cleanup?. . . How about a guy in the Dallas Cowboys cheerleaders? How about featuring a guy in the *Sports Illustrated* annual swimsuit issue?"[20]

Mike Fink failed to raise a First Amendment defense in the case, so the court did not address the restaurant chain's constitutional rights. However, one federal appellate court has held that the (late) Sambo's restaurant chain had a First Amendment right to use its name, despite claims that the name created a hostile environment for African American patrons.[21] A restaurant like Cock of the Walk may have a similar First Amendment right to create a particular historical ambience.

An opportunity for courts to decide whether a restaurant has the right to create a sexy ambience appealing to men was lost when the Hooters restaurant chain settled a sex discrimination complaint filed by the EEOC. The EEOC had sued Hooters, which relies on an image provided by voluptuous and tightly clothed waitresses, for refusing to hire male servers and for having a double-entendre name that suggested that only women could work there. Following a clever public relations campaign by Hooters, featuring a hairy, ugly "Hooters guy" —Hooters' comical take on being forced to abandon its female-only server policy—the EEOC backed off, but not before extorting $3.75 million from Hooters, and requiring Hooters to create three new gender-neutral categories of employees.[22]

In separate litigation, two women who worked at a New Orleans Hooters franchise won verdicts of $20,000 each after having their hours cut when they became pregnant. In response, the national chain expressed regret, and noted that corporate policy prohibits pregnancy discrimination and requires all of its restaurants to offer special maternity Hooters outfits to its staff. Not all patrons are pleased with this compromise, which is dictated by laws banning discrimination against pregnant women. "Who wants to look at a belly button looking at you?" asked Ryan Petty, a 22-year-old U.S. Air Force flight crew chief from Dallas with a talent for telling it like he sees it, "Under the law, it's discrimination, but I don't want to see a pregnant Hooters girl, cottage-cheese legs and everything."[23] A similarly blunt bachelor party participant added that if "the [Hooters] atmosphere was filled with 18 pregnant women in tights, we wouldn't be there."

Regardless of how antidiscrimination law affects waiters at Cock of the Walk and Hooters, though, the grand American tradition of dinner theater, in which actors double as waiters during intermissions, is apparently not at risk from sex discrimination law. For purposes of determining whether sex discrimination by eating places is permissible, the EEOC draws a distinction between "whether you're putting on a show or [just] serving food."[24] If servers at a restaurant actually perform gender-specific roles in a theatrical performance,[25] then sex discrimination in hiring is okay. Otherwise, the EEOC generally considers sex discrimination to be impermissible under federal antidiscrimination laws. The basis for this policy is the famous "Love Airlines" case from the late 1970s, in which Southwest Airlines asserted the right to hire only sexy young women as flight attendants in order to cultivate an image that would appeal to male business travelers. A federal court ruled that because the essence of the airline's business was transporting passengers, not sexual allurement, the airline's employment policy was illegal sex discrimination.[26] The implication, however, was that discrimination by a business that really was centered around sexual allurement *would* be licit. Ironically, then, Hooters' problem may be that its form of sexual entertainment is too subtle and tame. As an anonymous EEOC official noted, "Hooters claimed that . . . they [sic] were providing vicarious sexual recreation . . . but all along they were primarily a food business."[27] A bemused commentator concluded that "[i]f Hooters had wanted to avoid a civil rights lawsuit, and save $3.75 million, it should have dimmed the lights, bared the waitresses, and cut the menu down to nuts and nachos."[28]

* * *

After generations in which controversial art, especially art considered sexually indecent, was "banned in Boston" and across the United States, American artists have finally won First Amendment protection for their work over the past several decades. The result has been a flourishing and diverse arts and entertainment scene

unrivaled in the rest of the world. However, the growth of antidiscrimination law threatens this achievement. Feminists like Krissy
Keefer and the Title IX Task Force, prudes like Laurie Crowder,
prima donnas like Hunter Tylo, reactionaries like the Ferry family,
and government bureaucrats like the EEOC officials who went after
Hooters are all eager to use the force of antidiscrimination law to
compel the arts and entertainment world to conform to their vision
of a good society. Only the First Amendment's protection of artistic
freedom stands between such individuals and a return to widespread artistic censorship under the guise of combating discrimination.

4. Political Speech as Illegal Discrimination

One of the cornerstones of any healthy democracy is the citizenry's freedom to criticize and question government officials and policies. That is why the U.S. Constitution acknowledges a specific right to petition the government rather than relying on the general freedom of speech granted in the First Amendment to safeguard this essential liberty. Despite this crucial and clear protection, however, government officials are increasingly trying to punish the political speech they dislike as illegal discrimination.

Perhaps the most egregious example of this phenomenon involved an attempt to punish opponents of a proposed public housing project in Berkeley, California. Berkeley is divided between affluent neighborhoods in the coastal hills and the much poorer flatlands area. The liberal hills neighborhoods dominate local politics and elect representatives who vote to heavily invest city resources in public housing units, social services, and homeless shelters. Also in response to concerns of the affluent hills residents, the city places almost all these projects in the low-income neighborhoods of the flatlands, where the residents have traditionally been poorly organized and politically weak.

In May 1992, Resources for Community Development, a nonprofit housing developer, received a large grant from Berkeley to convert the run-down Bel Air Motel in the flatlands into a multifamily housing unit for the homeless.[1] Opposition to the Bel Air conversion became a unifying cause among the flatlanders. As one resident put it, "If the city wants to build low-income housing they should do so in an equitable fashion—everywhere within the city's districts—equally. It's time for other areas to participate in solving the 'affordable housing crisis.' "[2]

Alexandra White, her husband, Joseph Deringer, and their neighbor Richard Graham—a group the media later dubbed "the Berkeley three"—organized the opposition to the new housing units. Deringer and White's home abutted immediately against the Bel Air property, and Graham lived a few houses down the street. In newsletters and petitions, the Berkeley three asserted that the proposed location of the new center, near two liquor stores and a nightclub, was inappropriate because of the prevalence of alcoholism among the homeless population. They also noted the absence of local mental health and substance abuse treatment facilities, a factor seemingly neglectful of the needs of the many homeless who are mentally ill or addicted to drugs.

Despite this neighborhood opposition, led by the Berkeley three, and despite a lawsuit documenting irregularities in the process granting the needed zoning variance to the project, the Bel Air conversion ultimately went forward. However, bitter feelings remained, accompanied by a desire for revenge on the part of the housing activists who had supported the Bel Air project. Marianne Lawless, the director of Housing Rights, Inc., a federally funded housing advocacy group, decided to punish the Berkeley three for what she considered to be their politically incorrect community activism by filing a complaint with the San Francisco office of the federal Department of Housing and Urban Development claiming that the Berkeley three were guilty of discrimination against the disabled. Lawless's one-sentence complaint stated that the Berkeley three had tried to block the Bel Air project "because they perceive[d] the primary residents of the facility would be the mentally disabled or the disabled through substance abuse."[3]

Lawless's complaint relied on the 1988 amendments to the Fair Housing Act, which she contended banned political speech motivated by discriminatory animus that leads to the delay or cancellation of a project that would serve protected groups. HUD agreed, arguing that it could punish "individuals [who] have engaged in speech advocating illegal acts." HUD asserted that such speech includes asking the government to halt a publicly funded housing project because the facility will serve those "disabled" by drug addiction and mental illness.[4]

Therefore, HUD vigorously investigated Lawless's claim, issuing subpoenas for everything the Berkeley three had written about the controversy, for minutes of public meetings, for lists of members of their coalition, and for any other relevant documents. HUD warned the Berkeley three that failure to cease their activism immediately or to comply with the subpoenas could result in fines of up to $100,000 each and jail sentences of up to one year. The Berkeley three were further informed that if the investigation turned up evidence of discrimination, they would be subject to fines of up to $50,000 each and might be liable for compensatory and punitive damages.[5] Despite protests from the Berkeley three's attorney, HUD denied that its investigation impinged on their First Amendment rights. HUD soon announced the results of its preliminary investigation: the Berkeley three had violated the Fair Housing Act. HUD sent the case to the Justice Department for prosecution.

The Berkeley incident was just one of many during the early years of the Clinton administration in which HUD officials harassed and intimidated neighborhood activists.[6] One victim summed up the effects of HUD's investigation as follows:

> It financially ruined the neighborhood association and terrified residents. HUD investigators pressured neighbors to turn informer. Residents were afraid to join the association or to speak out at public meetings. The government even tried to deprive us of legal representation by threatening to call our attorney as a witness. We couldn't take minutes at meetings of our board because these could be seized and used as evidence against us. We tried to settle the case, but the terms of the consent decree drafted by the government were intolerable. They would have required residents to undergo an enforced course of political re-education and proposed unconstitutional restraints on our right to speak, write and association.[7]

After a media outcry over HUD's disregard of First Amendment rights in the Berkeley case and other cases,[8] the agency backed down, announcing that it would no longer investigate "any complaint . . . that involves public activities directed toward achieving action by a governmental entity or official; and do not involve force, physical harm, or a clear threat of force or physical harm to one or more individuals."[9] HUD also announced that it was dropping the investigation of the Berkeley incident because, it concluded, the Berkeley three had acted within their First Amendment rights.[10]

This all sounds very sensible, but the new policy was opposed by Assistant Attorney General Deval Patrick of the Justice Department, which prosecutes lawsuits under the Fair Housing Act. Patrick ignored HUD's new guidelines and ordered the Justice Department to bring new lawsuits against community activists.[11] He contended that "Congress intended the [Fair Housing Act] to proscribe any speech if it leads to discrimination prohibited by the FHA."[12] Two years after HUD acknowledged that prosecuting neighborhood activists for expressing their political viewpoints was unconstitutional and unwise, Patrick continued to defend the Justice Department's attempted squelching of free speech in a Fair Housing Act case in Fort Worth, Texas. In doing so, he analogized political leaflets to baseball bats, remarking that bats "are perfectly legal too. But if you wield one to keep people out of the neighborhood, we are going to use the bat as evidence of your intent to violate the civil rights laws."[13]

The problem with Patrick's analogy is that there are huge differences, both constitutionally and morally, between wielding a baseball bat as a physical threat and using speech to try to peacefully persuade others that a point of view is correct. The essence of the First Amendment is that peaceful persuasion is permissible, even when the potential consequences of that persuasion are unpalatable. Patrick assumed that speech, like wielding a baseball bat, can be restricted simply because it may result in harm to someone, but he was wrong. The First Amendment protects freedom of speech *even when the speech at issue could cause harm*. For example, a person has the right to propagate nasty and incendiary theories, such as the truth of racial superiority or the need to boycott stores owned by a particular ethnic group, even though speech may cause grievous harm. This outcome may be distasteful, but it beats the alternative, of trusting the government to use political criteria to decide which speech is too offensive or too dangerous to tolerate. And let's not kid ourselves; political criteria, rather than some highfalutin' academic or philosophical theory, is exactly what the government will use.

Luckily, the federal judge overseeing the Fort Worth case had a better grasp of the First Amendment than did Patrick and rejected the latter's theory. The judge held that "leafleting, petitioning, and soliciting" against the placement of a group home in one's neighborhood are actions protected by the First Amendment.[14] More generally, the federal courts have steadfastly protected First Amendment rights against legal assaults on neighborhood activists. For example, the Berkeley three successfully sued HUD in federal court for its violation of their constitutional rights.[15] In that case, the court even took the unusual step of holding individual HUD employees personally liable for this violation because their conduct was so clearly and outrageously unconstitutional. In the few other cases that have squarely addressed the First Amendment issue, courts have similarly decided in favor of citizen activists and against HUD.[16]

However, one judge did leave the door open for future government lawsuits after dismissing a Fair Housing Act case filed by a real estate developer against Travis Compton. Compton had been appointed by the mayor of Fresno, California, to serve on an advisory committee charged with making recommendations on proposed development plans. As part of his duties, Compton voted and spoke out against a public bond issue for a low-income housing project. The developer who had hoped to build the project sued Compton for violation of the Fair Housing Act.

Tens of thousands of dollars in legal fees later, the judge found that the plaintiff failed to provide sufficient evidence to support his claim. But the judge also opined gratuitously that "the First Amendment does not necessarily trump the Civil Rights Act or state and federal fair housing laws. . . . Unlawfully discriminatory conduct carried out by speech activities is not immunized by the First Amendment."[17] Cases in which developers sue citizens opposed to their plans are especially dangerous, because developers, unlike HUD officials, are not government officials and therefore cannot be sued for violating the First Amendment. Until the Supreme Court makes clear that citizen activists may not be punished under the Fair Housing Act for engaging in political speech, public housing developers will attempt to use the Fair Housing Act to intimidate their political opponents and bully their way past obstacles to their projects.

* * *

Neighborhood activists opposing housing projects are not the only lightning rods for attempts to suppress political speech. Anyone taking action to oppose the current orthodoxy on antidiscrimination principles is at risk of being silenced by the powers that be. Critics of affirmative action preferences in higher education seem especially likely to be threatened with censorship. For example, Professor James Bell of Chicago's Daley College mocked the school's affirmative action "diversity" policy in a sarcastic column for the teachers' union newspaper. He wrote the following:

> I think this is a marvelous idea, and because I also subscribe to the idea of diversity . . .
>
> . . . When I buy a dozen eggs I try to make sure that at least two or three of them are rotten.
>
> . . . I want a law passed that says one-fourth of all doctors must be incompetent.
>
> . . . now and then I make a point to date an ugly woman.
>
> . . . I believe we should encourage more Egyptians to come to the U.S. so that our country could also enjoy the advantages of female genital mutilation. . . . I think we should also welcome more Mauritanians and Sudanese to the United States, so we could also have human slavery in this country.
>
> . . . I think all colleges should be required to hire administrators and teachers with IQs below 80. (I was just told this law already exists; it's called "affirmative action.")
>
> . . . I think there should be a law forcing companies to hire employees even though they can't do the job. (Someone mentioned that there already was such a law; it's called "affirmative action.").
>
> . . . Finally, I think the President [of the College] should fire himself and the Vice-President in order to make room for more non-Hispanic administrators at Daley College.[18]

Not surprisingly, the column evoked some controversy. No doubt that was part of the author's intent, but those who disagreed with Bell did not seem willing to debate or share their views on the contentious issue. It was perhaps easier to muzzle the pesky messenger. The college's Board of Trustees filed a complaint against the union newspaper that had carried Bell's column with the Chicago Commission on Human Relations. The complaint relied on the Chicago Human Rights Ordinance, which bans discriminatory "harassment in places of public accommodation." The complaint alleged that Bell's antidiversity article "contribute[d] to deep-seated problems in attitude and behavior that makes students uncomfortable in an institution where comfort is essential for learning." According to the board, "The First Amendment is not blanket authorization for provocative hate speech at a public institution." The Commission eventually dismissed the action, but only because it found that the newspaper at issue was not a "place of public accommodation" under the law.[19]

Other professors have also found themselves under fire for expressing politically incorrect sentiments outside of the classroom. David Deming, professor of geology and geophysics at the University of Oklahoma, wrote to the campus newspaper, *The Oklahoma Daily*,[20] responding to a syndicated pro–gun control editorial by Yale student Joni Klotter. Klotter's piece had stated that "easy access to a handgun allows everyone in this country . . . to quickly and easily kill as many random people as they want."

It wouldn't take a gun nut to object to Klotter's hyperbole, but Deming, a zealous gun rights advocate with a history of making eccentric statements, had an especially cantankerous reaction.[21] His response letter stated that Klotter's "easy access" to a vagina enabled her to "quickly and easily" have sex with "as many random people" as she wanted. He added that her "possession of an unregistered vagina equipped her to work as a prostitute and spread venereal disease." Deming concluded his letter by stating that he hoped Klotter was as responsible with her dangerous "equipment" as most gun owners are with theirs.

It was a strange and aggressive way to express a pro–gun rights position, and it is hard to imagine that Deming's analogy won over many readers, but his letter clearly argued the merits of a political position. A few days after Deming's letter appeared, Becky Herbert, director of the University of Oklahoma's campus ministry center, filed a sexual harassment complaint against Deming with university administrators. Herbert found it "unacceptable" that Deming had "resort[ed] to using an individual's human sexuality as a means of entering into a debate." Herbert stated that "having my [sic] vagina equated with a handgun is degrading, and for this to go unaddressed by the university is demoralizing."[22] She told the media that she wanted the university to reprimand Deming and require him to undergo sensitivity training on women's issues.[23] Twenty more formal complaints from other members of the University of Oklahoma community followed.

Most observers would agree that Deming's letter was, at best, intemperate and vulgar, although Deming subsequently argued that he had simply tried to show that "my gun no more makes me a killer than her vagina makes her an immoral person."[24] Regardless, a letter to a school paper making a political argument hardly comes within the standard definition of sexual harassment. Moreover, the letter was clearly political speech protected by the First Amendment, and the University of Oklahoma, as a public university, was obligated to abide by First Amendment rules.

The university nevertheless allowed a sexual harassment investigation to proceed. The dean of the College of Geosciences, John T. Snow, criticized Deming for upsetting students, alumni, and the administration, and he warned Deming that the controversy might affect his career.[25] As proceedings against Deming progressed, university president and former U.S. senator David Boren declined to intercede on his behalf. Boren's primary concern, he told Deming, was not academic freedom but "restoring civility to public debate."[26] Eventually, two libertarian-leaning organizations, the Center for Individual Rights and the Foundation for Individual Rights in Education, threatened to sue the university for violating Deming's First Amendment rights. In an astounding coincidence, shortly after receiving these threats the university's administration suddenly discovered that Deming's letter was actually not covered by the university's sexual harassment guidelines, and the university dismissed the complaints against him.

* * *

We have examined some very blatant and overt attempts at censoring unpopular political ideas, but antidiscrimination laws threaten freedom of expression in more subtle and insidious ways. Corporate CEOs, university presidents, members of the clergy, and other prominent individuals often develop a high profile outside of their workplaces and are subsequently asked to speak about public issues. One would think that on these occasions the speaker could say what he liked, as he is speaking on his own private time and in his own personal capacity, but one would be wrong. As former Boston University president John Silber discovered the hard way, plaintiffs in employment discrimination lawsuits can use a prominent person's public statements against him.

Professor Julia Brown of BU's English Department sued the university when it denied her tenure.[27] During trial and in his closing argument, her attorney discussed a speech that had been delivered by then-university president Silber, a vocal social conservative. In his speech, delivered a few years earlier to a policy group in Washington, D.C., Silber had expressed concern about the growing number of working women who he felt did not spend sufficient time and energy on child-rearing. Brown's attorney cross-examined Silber about this speech, and the judge jumped in, gratuitously asking, "Some of those career women are in the universities, including your own? . . . And I suppose one way to get them back in the kitchen, is to get them out of the university; is that so?" In his closing argument, Brown's attorney stated that based on Silber's views, "at BU, women and not men carry the burden of being seen as wives and mothers and not just as scholars."

The jury awarded Brown $215,000 and tenure. An appellate court criticized the trial court for admitting the evidence regarding Silber's speech. The court observed that the evidence presented was marginally relevant at best and that allowing evidence of a university official's political and social views to support a discrimination claim had the potential to chill academic freedom. The court nevertheless let the verdict stand, finding that the admission of the speech was "harmless error" that had not affected the verdict—a curious finding given the attention Brown's attorney had lavished on the evidence in his closing. Indeed, posttrial interviews with jurors revealed that while they liked Brown,[28] they did not believe that BU had discriminated against her. They had nevertheless ruled in her favor because they felt that Silber was arrogant and sexist in believing that women should stay home and take care of their kids. Had the district court excluded the evidence of Silber's speech, BU would likely have won the case.

Courts have even used individuals' stated opposition to or distaste for antidiscrimination laws as evidence of discrimination. For example, one court began an opinion finding liability under the Equal Pay Act of 1963 by quoting a manager who had pronounced the law "foolish" when it was under congressional consideration.[29] In another case, an appellate court upheld a verdict for the plaintiff in a sex discrimination lawsuit against Keene State College in part because a Keene State official had, in an unrelated letter, written to the president of Smith College for information on how that school had responded to a charge of sex discrimination because he was "concerned that that form of anarchy may creep north into our virgin territory."[30] And when *Forbes* magazine was sued for age discrimination, the plaintiff relied on a column publisher Steve Forbes had written 15 years earlier opposing proposed laws that would end age-based mandatory retirement.[31]

This trend of admitting past remarks on legal or social policy law as evidence of current discrimination is disturbing. The fact that a defendant criticized an antidiscrimination law may be marginally relevant to the question of whether the defendant broke the law. However, most people obey even laws they disagree with, and allowing the plaintiff to present the defendant's critical remarks to the jury about popular law is grossly and unfairly prejudicial. Admission of such statements therefore violates standard rules of evidence.[32] Moreover, allowing discrimination plaintiffs to rely on a defendant's past political speech creates a severe risk of chilling the exercise of First Amendment rights, a risk that is not worth taking for introducing evidence of minimal value.

* * *

Even criticisms of perceived government racism can get a speaker in trouble with civil rights authorities when the form of the criticism is deemed offensive. St. Paul, Minnesota's Human Rights Director, Tyrone Terrill, sought to punish the St. Paul *Pioneer Press* for running a biting editorial cartoon critical of the school's failure to properly educate black athletes. The cartoon, entitled "The Plantation," depicted a basketball game with three anonymous African American University of Minnesota basketball players visible. Two middle-aged, well-dressed white males are watching the game from the stands, and one says, "Of course we don't let them learn to read or write."[33] Cartoonist Kirk Anderson was protesting the UM athletic program's perceived exploitation of African American athletes— only one in four UM basketball players graduates from the university.

Terrill's complaint nevertheless alleged that the cartoon created an illicit "hostile public environment," an allegation similar to the one leveled against the teachers' union newspaper in the Daley College case. Terrill claimed that by creating such an environment, the newspaper illegally "discriminated against African American student-athletes past, present and future in the area of public accommodations on the basis of race."[34] Terrill told the *Pioneer Press* that he believed the cartoon was not protected by the First Amendment, because it was analogous to an employee hanging nude centerfolds in the workplace or directing racial epithets at coworkers, behavior other courts had punished (see Chapter 2). After meeting with the newspaper's attorney, Terrill agreed to drop the complaint, but only because the attorney persuaded him that the newspaper's editorial column could not have violated St. Paul's antidiscrimination ordinance, because an editorial column is not a "place of public accommodation" under the law.[35]

* * *

One of the most cherished freedoms Americans enjoy is the right to lobby and criticize their government. It is both frightening and sad, then, that this liberty is undergoing such a serious and increasing threat from antidiscrimination laws. The only thing that now stands between a citizen with a contrarian political view to express and the Deval Patricks, Tyrone Terrills, and other eager censors of the world is the First Amendment. If we allow antidiscrimination laws to erode this protection, we will find ourselves at the mercy of a power elite able to muzzle any dissent from its vision of an egalitarian political orthodoxy.

5. Censoring Campus Speech

Public universities, like all government entities, must comply with the First Amendment. Nevertheless, many public universities have established speech codes to censor expression potentially offensive to women, African Americans, or other groups protected by civil rights laws. Universities commonly justify these rules as being necessary to prevent the creation of an illegal "hostile environment" on campus. University officials have not, however, been able to reconcile suppression of potentially offensive expression with the First Amendment.

The first wave of public university speech codes appeared in the late 1980s, with the rise of censorious political correctness. The University of Michigan's code, for example, banned speech "that stigmatizes or victimizes an individual on the basis of race" or that "has the purpose or reasonably foreseeable effect of interfering with an individual's academic efforts."[1] Another part of the code prohibited speech relating to sex or sexual orientation that "creates an intimidating, hostile or demeaning environment for educational pursuits."

In furtherance of its code, the university distributed a handbook with examples of illicit speech. For example, a student organization, the book stated, would violate the speech code if it "sponsors entertainment that includes a comedian who slurs Hispanics." The handbook also noted that expression of certain politically incorrect opinions, such as remarks by male students that "women just aren't as good in this field as men," were prohibited. Beyond these two examples, students could only guess at what speech was forbidden. A federal court concluded "that the University had no idea what the limits of the [p]olicy were and it was essentially making up the rules as it went along."

Ironically, complaints under the speech code overwhelmingly involved white students charging African Americans with hate speech. For example, the university punished an African American student for opining in class that homosexuality is a curable disease. Courts did not treat these early speech codes kindly: federal courts overturned on First Amendment grounds codes at Michigan,[2] the University of Wisconsin,[3] and Central Michigan University.[4] Through the early 1990s, advocates of speech codes argued that, despite these lower court decisions, the Supreme Court's "fighting words" doctrine allowed government regulation of "hate speech." Under the fighting words doctrine, the First Amendment does not protect speech likely to incite the listener to imminent violence.

In *R.A.V. v. City of St. Paul*,[5] however, the Supreme Court overturned a conviction under a hate speech law for cross burning. In its ruling, the Supreme Court held that the government may ban *all* fighting words but it may not ban only select fighting words on the basis of their content. The hate speech ordinance in question banned only racist fighting words and therefore violated the First Amendment.[6] The upshot of *R.A.V.* is that, first, public universities may not restrict student speech that allegedly creates a hostile environment when the speech does not rise to the level of fighting words.[7] Second, even when such speech does amount to fighting words, public universities may not enact speech restrictions that single out for punishment fighting words that offend only members of certain protected groups.[8] The only possible exception to the latter rule is if a university can show that the racist fighting words it banned are more likely to incite imminent violence than are other fighting words, and that this greater danger from racist fighting words, and not a desire to squelch racist speech as such, was the sole reason the university prohibited racist fighting words.

Given these constitutional barriers, public university speech codes were on the way out until the federal Department of Education revived them in 1994. Male students at Santa Rosa Community College had posted anatomically explicit and sexually derogatory remarks about two female students in a discussion group hosted by the college's computer network.[9] Several aggrieved students filed a complaint against the college with the DOE's Office for Civil Rights. The DOE found that the messages probably created a hostile educational environment on the basis of sex for one of the students. University toleration of such offensive speech, the government added, would violate Title IX, the law banning discrimination against women by educational institutions that receive federal funding.

Under this standard, to avoid losing federal funds, universities must proactively ban offensive speech by students and diligently punish any violations of that ban.

The DOE failed to explain how its rule was consistent with the First Amendment. Speech codes enacted by public universities clearly violate the First Amendment even if the codes are enacted in response to the demands of the DOE, so requiring public universities to enact speech codes or forfeit public funds would obviously be unconstitutional. Nevertheless, facing this choice, public university officials have ignored the First Amendment issue and complied with DOE guidelines. Although a few schools may truly be concerned about the potential loss of federal funding, the prevailing attitude among university officials seems to be that the DOE's Santa Rosa decision provides a ready excuse to indulge their preference for speech codes. University officials implicitly reason that if the DOE can get away with ignoring the First Amendment, then so can they. Unfortunately, they may be right.

In any case, many public universities retain speech codes despite the lurking First Amendment issues. Some codes are so broad that, when taken literally, they are absurd. The University of Maryland's sexual harassment policy, for example, bans "idle chatter of a sexual nature, sexual innuendoes, comments about a person's clothing, body, and/or sexual activities, comments of a sexual nature about weight, body shape, size, or figure, and comments or questions about the sensuality of a person."[10] So, at the University of Maryland, saying "I like your shirt, Brenda" is a punishable instance of sexual harassment. Further, because under Maryland's code the prohibited speech need not be specifically directed at an individual to constitute harassment, even saying "I really like men who wear bow ties" is out of bounds, at least if a man who wears bow ties hears about it.

Public university censorship to prevent a hostile environment extends well beyond the sex discrimination issues raised in the Santa Rosa case. Federal law also bans discrimination in education on the basis of race, religion, veteran status, and other criteria, and universities argue that they must censor speech to prevent a hostile environment for groups protected by those laws, as well. As a measure of just how far the law extends, consider the actions of the Office of Federal Contract Compliance Programs. That office charged illegal harassment based on Vietnam-era veteran status when an

61

exhibit at Ohio State University displayed pictures and postings criticizing the actions of American military personnel during the Vietnam War.[11] So much for academic freedom and the spirit of open debate in higher education.

A more typical case arose when a member of Phi Kappa Sigma at the University of California, Riverside, designed a T-shirt advertising a "South of the Border" party. The shirt featured a figure wearing a serape and sombrero sitting on a beach looking at the setting sun and holding a bottle of tequila, along with a picture of a set of steel drums and a wooden tiki head, in which was carved the word "Jamaica." The bottom of the shirt depicted a smiling Rastafarian carrying a six-pack of beer while standing in a Mexican cantina frequented by Riverside students, humming a lyric from an antiracist song by Bob Marley: "It doesn't matter where you come from long as you know where you are going."[12] Although not exactly a brilliant artistic gem, the shirt was nonetheless a little more creative and diverse than the average frat party ad.

Campus Latino activists, however, were not favorably impressed. They charged that the shirt "dehumanizes and promotes racist views of Mexican people" and they formally accused the fraternity of violating university rules by circulating "offensive racial stereotypes." The fraternity president, Rich Carrez, apologized to the activists and pointed out that he was part Native American, the vice president of the fraternity was Latino, the T-shirt creator was Latino, and the fraternity was the most racially diverse on campus, with 25 white and 22 nonwhite members. The activists were unmoved and stubbornly clung to their view that the innocuous T-shirt promoted offensive stereotypes.

Ultimately, the university required fraternity members to destroy all of the T-shirts, apologize in writing, engage in community service, and attend two seminars on multiculturalism—an ironic punishment given that almost half the fraternity members were themselves minorities. The university also stripped the fraternity of its charter and expelled it from campus for three years. The university eventually lifted all of the sanctions, but only after legal intervention by the Individual Rights Foundation, a national network of lawyers that responds to threats to the First Amendment by college administrators and government officials.

Lawsuits, or even the threat of lawsuits, certainly seem to get campus officials' attention. At some public universities, civil libertarians have used the threat of legal action to persuade school officials to abandon their speech codes. For example, in 1997, the Office of Social Justice at West Virginia University published a brochure defining illicit discriminatory behavior as, among other things, expression of politically incorrect sentiments. An example of such forbidden discrimination was provided: claiming that "women never do well" in a particular science class regardless, apparently, of whether the statement is true.[13] With such strict limits on what thoughts and feelings could be publicly shared, WVU students might well have had trouble finding anything neutral and sensitive enough to say to each other. But not to worry, the brochure provided helpful "advice" for encouraging a welcome environment, such as substituting "friend, lover, or partner" for the word boyfriend or girlfriend. The brochure further cheerfully suggested that failure to comply with its advice would be punishable.

Concerned faculty members wrote to the president of the university, David Hardesty Jr., seeking assurance that the brochure was not a speech and behavior code for students and faculty. Hardesty instead confirmed his correspondents' fears by writing that "[t]he right to free speech and the concept of academic freedom do not exist in isolation," and that freedom of speech does not include the right "to create a hostile environment on campus."[14] The university ultimately withdrew the brochure, but, as is no doubt becoming a familiar theme in these tales, only after the West Virginia Civil Liberties Union threatened to sue.[15]

* * *

Regardless of whether their universities have formal speech codes, public university officials frequently restrict "offensive" student speech on an ad hoc basis. For example, UCLA suspended an editor of the student newspaper for running an editorial cartoon ridiculing affirmative action preferences. In the cartoon, a student asks a rooster on campus how it got into UCLA. The rooster responds, "affirmative action." After the editor was sanctioned by UCLA, student editor James Taranto reproduced the cartoon in the California State University, Northridge, student newspaper and criticized UCLA officials for suspending the paper's editor for engaging in constitutionally protected expression. Northridge officials suspended Taranto from his editorial position for two weeks for publishing controversial material "without permission." However, when Taranto threatened a lawsuit, the school removed the suspension from his transcript.[16] Taranto continued to pursue a career in journalism and currently edits Opinionjournal.com.

In another incident, administrators at the University of Minnesota, Twin Cities, prohibited the College Republicans from distributing at the school's orientation fliers critical of then-president Bill Clinton. Several fliers contained R-rated humor, and one of them vulgarly satirized the president's views on gay rights. University officials argued that the fliers violated the university's nondiscrimination policy, violated orientation guidelines that require orientation to provide students with an "appreciation of diversity," and were not "consistent with the goals of the university."[17]

After severe criticism from the American Civil Liberties Union and the local media—especially the *Minneapolis Star Tribune*—the university relented and permitted the distribution of the fliers. However, university president Nils Hasselmo stubbornly insisted that the flyer incident had only had the "appearance of" suppressing speech.[18] He maintained that the orientation regulations that the fliers had violated were constitutional and had only been suspended, not repealed. Subsequently, an outraged Minnesota law student sued the university for violating its students' constitutional rights. The university capitulated, agreeing not only to stop censoring student materials but also, in a welcome twist on the usual forced sensitivity training ritual, to have its administration attend a lecture on the protection of freedom of speech afforded by the First Amendment.[19]

* * *

This chapter has so far dealt only with public universities, which, as government actors, are subject to the limits of the First Amendment. However, it is important to remember that private universities are not government actors and therefore are immune from the dictates of the First Amendment. The Constitution does not stop them from enacting speech codes. In fact, private universities probably have a First Amendment expressive association right to set speech guidelines on campus (see Chapter 8). Many private university speech restrictions would exist regardless of government antidis-crimination regulations. For example, one hardly expects universi-ties with a traditional religious mission to tolerate blasphemous comments from their students. Also, many elite private universities are controlled by politically correct administrators and professors who support stringent speech codes banning insensitive and intoler-ant comments regardless of legal requirements.

But although private universities have the right to enact and enforce voluntary speech codes, the First Amendment prohibits the government from *requiring* private universities to administer speech codes. Nevertheless, under the Santa Rosa case discussed previously, the government has threatened to strip private universities of federal funding if they don't enforce speech restrictions to ensure that their students are not exposed to a "hostile environment." Moreover, individual students may sue universities for tolerating a "hostile educational environment," in the same way that workers may sue their employers for tolerating a "hostile workplace environment" (see Chapter 2). There is no practical difference between the blatantly unconstitutional act of the government's directly censoring speech at private universities and what the government actually does, which is to enforce laws that create legal liability for private universities that fail to proactively censor speech. The latter course may be less obviously Orwellian than the former, but its effects, that is, govern-ment censorship, are the same.

Brad Kvederis, a student at Claremont McKenna College, a private school in Claremont, California, learned this lesson the hard way. He published for his dorm a gossip newsletter called the *Wohlford Free Press*. Like many college publications, the *Free Press* included sexually suggestive material. Depending on which account of the relevant events one reads, the newsletter was either a relatively sober, albeit profanity-laced, publication that occasionally men-tioned sex or a scandal sheet reporting on the drinking and sexual hijinks of dorm residents. In any event, three female students—only one of whom was mentioned in the newsletter—filed hostile environment complaints against Kvederis with the university. Fear-ing liability, the university suspended Kvederis for a semester and required him to undergo sexual harassment sensitivity training.

The ACLU sued on Kvederis's behalf under a unique California law that prohibits private universities from regulating student

65

speech (see Chapter 8). The court, however, dismissed the case on the grounds that Kvederis's publication had "the potential to create a hostile environment and could have become the basis of sexual harassment claims" if the college had not intervened.[20] Federal anti-discrimination law supersedes state free speech law, the court ruled. Before appeal, the college and Kvederis settled for undisclosed terms.[21]

* * *

For any university to function, its administration must engage in content-based regulation of its faculty's speech. That is to say, the administrators must, to a certain extent, dictate what professors will or will not talk about in class and the subjects they will or will not teach. For example, for a university to run smoothly, the administrators must determine what courses will and will not be taught, and on the basis of the applicants' academic writings, which professors will or will not be hired and granted tenure.[22] The inevitability of content-based regulation of academic expression on public university campuses suggests a strong civil libertarian case that government should not be in the business of running universities at all. After all, content-based speech restrictions are a clear no-no under the First Amendment. But once the government is allowed to control universities, university officials must be able to place reasonable restrictions on what their faculty members may say in the classroom.

Even the most hardcore proponent of academic freedom would have to concede that a professor assigned to teach 19th-century French literature can be penalized for using his class time to teach anthropology, in the same way that any other government employee can be punished for not doing his job. Similarly, a professor who uses his class as a forum to launch into irrelevant diatribes criticizing certain ethnic or religious groups may clearly be sanctioned for not doing his job. More problematic is the question of whether professors have the right to engage in classroom speech that is relevant to the topic at hand but that offends some students.

Academics, including the author of this book, generally believe that the danger to academic dialogue caused by restrictions on purportedly offensive speech outweighs the potential benefit of reducing offense to students. Indeed, sometimes the only way to get students to genuinely confront and engage in controversial issues is to risk offending them. The appropriate policy is one that fully protects professors' classroom speech, *as long as the speech has a reasonable relationship to the topic at hand* (there's no reason to tolerate a lecture on the glories of *Mein Kampf* from a woodworking professor), and as long as the offending speech does not constitute harassing behavior clearly directed *at particular students.*

Some federal court analyses of the constitutional issues involved in regulating professors' classroom speech adopt a similar analysis.[23] Other decisions, however, suggest that public universities have a broader latitude than this to set general guidelines on appropriate speech in class. In essence, under these decisions, universities are free to regulate any classroom speech as long as they can show that such regulations are reasonably related to legitimate pedagogical objectives.[24] For example, a university may bar the faculty from using obscene language during class, regardless of context, on the grounds that university officials have determined that any educational benefit that may be gained from using such language is outweighed by the fact that it will distract and upset many students, interfering with their ability to learn.[25] (A law professor at such a university would have a difficult time teaching many First Amendment cases, including the important "Fuck the Draft" case mentioned in Chapter 2.) Under this line of cases, arguably a university may even declare that certain controversial subjects, such as whether racial differences in IQ exist, are off-limits in the classroom because they are too distracting to students.

The caveat is that to comply with the First Amendment's guarantees of free expression and the Fourteenth Amendment's guarantee of due process, public universities must clearly spell out any restrictions on professors' classroom speech in advance.[26] However, because academic freedom is an extremely powerful and popular notion, few, if any, public universities promulgate detailed prospective speech regulations. Indeed, many universities spell out academic freedom guarantees in faculty contracts or in binding rules published in university handbooks. The threat of censorship remains, however, when universities adopt extremely vague guidelines banning "harassment" based on race, sex, and other attributes. The vagueness of these guidelines allows extremely sensitive or politically motivated students to launch harassment cases against unwary professors who offended them in class, which undermines the university's claimed commitment to academic freedom.

The case of Professor Donald Silva of the University of New Hampshire provides an instructive example. Silva's troubles started when, during his technical writing course, he used the concept of sexual intercourse to illustrate the process of focusing the thesis statement of a technical report. He told the class, "I will put focus in terms of sex, so you can better understand it. Focus is like sex. You seek a target. You zero in on your subject. You move from side to side. You close in on the subject. You bracket the subject and center on it. Focus connects experience and language. You and the subject become one." In a later class, he used a famous remark about belly dancing—"like jello on a plate with a vibrator under the plate"—as an example of a vivid metaphor.

Silva had used these similes in class for many years, and he argued that they were effective in getting the attention of his students. Six of his students did not agree, although judging by the poor grammar and the spelling errors that plagued the written sexual harassment claim they filed against Silva, they could have used all the writing help they could get.[27] One student wrote, somewhat incoherently, that "Silva started talking in a sexual manner which I thought was very inappropriated [sic] and also very affending [sic]." Another wrote, "During class we were discussion [sic] our technical reports when Don Silva . . . made [sic] a vulgar, inappropriate description of a 'bowl of jello and a vibrator,' to describe the belly dancer." A third added, "I had questions about our assignment on 26 Feb, but due to his use of sex as a 'focus,' I walked away rather than asked [sic] him to clarify again. I didn't want any more strange explainations [sic]." Yet another student was "very offended" by Silva's "sexual refferals [sic]."

Silva's comments were arguably in bad taste, but they hardly rose to the level of the severe and pervasive conduct normally required to support a sexual harassment claim. Moreover, the university's sexual harassment policy did not suggest that it regulated the comments at issue. The only examples the policy gave of remarks that could constitute sexual harassment were "unwelcome sexual propositions," "graphic comments about a person's body," "sexually degrading words to describe a person," "derogatory or sexually explicit statements about an actual or supposed sexual relationship," and "derogatory gender-based humor." None of these examples applied to Silva's statements. Nevertheless, after several hearings that could most charitably be described as almost comically unfair, university officials found that Silva's "focus" discussion had violated the university's sexual harassment policy. The university suspended Silva without pay for one year and required him to attend psychological counseling sessions at his own expense.[28]

Silva responded by suing the university in federal court. The court issued a favorable preliminary ruling after finding, among other things, that the university likely violated Silva's First Amendment rights. The court acknowledged that under appropriate circumstances the university's sexual harassment policy could be applied to classroom speech because it "seeks to address the legitimate pedagogical concern of providing a congenial academic environment." However, the policy was unconstitutional as applied to Silva's classroom speech because it "employed an impermissibly subjective standard that unreasonably limited academic freedom." The strong theme running through the court's opinion is that a public-university professor may not be sanctioned for classroom speech unless he has been given prior notice that such speech is prohibited. Before the case could proceed further, the parties settled, with the university agreeing to all of Silva's demands.[29]

* * *

Much of the threat to academic freedom from antidiscrimination laws comes from campus radical feminists who seek to use the hostile environment component of sexual harassment law to stifle discourse they dislike. A University of New Hampshire women's studies professor's diatribe, reacting to Silva's vindication, exemplifies the anti–free speech sentiment of many (though certainly not all) feminist academics:

> Academia ... has traditionally been dominated by white heterosexual men, and the First Amendment and Academic Freedom (FAF) traditionally have protected the rights of white heterosexual men. Most of us are silenced by existing social conditions before we get the power to speak out in any way where FAF might protect us. So forgive us if we don't get all teary-eyed about FAF. Perhaps to you it's as sacrosanct as the flag or national anthem; to us strict construction of the First Amendment is just another yoke around our necks.[30]

Ironically, preventing vague university antidiscrimination policies from becoming excuses to censor unpopular speech will ultimately benefit feminists and their anti–free speech allies in the multiculturalist and critical race theory movements as much as it benefits anyone else. One does not need much of an imagination to come up with examples of how antidiscrimination law could be used to silence left-wing academics like the New Hampshire women's studies professor. For example, men taking classes from extreme feminist professors sometimes claim that these professors create a hostile environment for them. These claims sometimes have a legitimate basis. After all, Professor Mary Daly of Boston College went so far as to ban men from her feminist ethics class over a 25-year period,[31] ensuring that male students had no access to her academic environment at all. More often, however, male students are simply uncomfortable with feminist professors' radical viewpoints.

Highly questionable claims of discrimination by male students have already been reported. For example, a male undergraduate in a human sexuality course accused Toni Blake, a female graduate student teacher, of sexual harassment. Blake used a banana to demonstrate condom application and joked that men, like basketball players, "dribble before they shoot." A male student complained that she "objectified the penis" and created a "hostile environment for him as a man."[32] In another incident, a married male Christian student filed a sexual harassment lawsuit after a lesbian psychology professor presented a lecture on female masturbation. The student claimed to have felt "raped and trapped" by the lecture.[33]

While it would be unfair to speculate about the motives of these students, one can easily imagine situations in which students would bring such charges because they disliked their professors for ideological or other reasons. Unfortunately, that is exactly the spiteful behavior that hostile environment law invites. Even the weakest discrimination complaints can lead, at a minimum, to a mandatory investigation by the Department of Education. Michael Krauss of George Mason University's law school, for example, spent months responding to one such investigation based on a frivolous student complaint, which he believes was motivated by a prior dispute he had with the student over grading. The complaint arose from Krauss's query to a torts class about whether burning a cross and shouting "kill the niggers" in front of someone's home constituted the tort of assault.[34] The student suggested that using the n-word in class was discriminatory per se. Such incidents make professors reluctant to discuss issues involving race relations, rape, and other extremely important issues for fear that an offended or vengeful student will file a complaint.

* * *

If left-wing professors wish to preserve their own academic freedom, they must learn to be more tolerant of those whose speech they currently seek to suppress. For the past several decades, the pressure to censor free speech on public university campuses has come primarily from the left. However, the current war against terrorism, and the frequent dissent within academe to that war, has shifted the censorship dynamic, putting many radical-left professors on the defensive. The First Amendment, and the values of academic freedom that have sprung up around it, will protect the vast majority of dissenters, but only because the radicals' war against the First Amendment has so far been largely unsuccessful. These academics would do well to consider what their plight might be should they ever succeed in doing away with constitutional protection of unpopular speech.

In Canada, left-wing academics are beginning to learn firsthand what it's like to have their own censorship vehicles used against them. For example, Professor Sunera Thobani of the University of British Columbia, a native of Tanzania, faced a hate crimes investigation after she launched into a vicious diatribe against American foreign policy. Thobani, a Marxist feminist and multiculturalist activist, had remarked that Americans are "bloodthirsty, vengeful and calling for blood."[35] The Canadian hate crimes law was created to protect minority groups from hate speech, but in this case it was invoked to protect Americans. The police revealed the investigation to the media, despite a general policy against doing so, because, a hate crimes investigator explained, "Here we have a complaint against someone who is obviously from a visible minority, whom the complainant feels is promoting hate. Normally, people think it's a white supremacist or Caucasians, promoting hate against visible minorities. . . . We want to get the message out that it's wrong, all around."[36]

The police eventually decided not to file charges for undisclosed reasons, perhaps because Thobani's speech was sufficiently rambling that her perceived attack on Americans could alternatively be construed as an attack on the "socially constructed" American nation invoked by President George W. Bush. Although still potentially insulting to Americans, this would not violate the hate crimes law. So, Thobani, who seethes with contempt for the Western world and the bourgeois liberties it protects, will stay out of jail—for now. Nevertheless, the incident reminds us that those who oppose freedom of speech would likely become the first victims of its demise. As Albert Jay Nock once wrote, "Whatever power you give the State to do things for you carries with it the equivalent power to do things to you."[37] With freedom of expression, as with much else in life, what goes around comes around.

6. Compelled Speech

Nothing is more repugnant to the First Amendment's protection of freedom of expression than the government's compelling individuals to express views contrary to their actual beliefs. As Justice Robert Jackson wrote for the Supreme Court almost 60 years ago, the nation cannot logically have a First Amendment that "guards the individual's right to speak his own mind, but left [sic] it open to public authorities to compel him to utter what is not on his mind."[1]

Despite these serious First Amendment considerations, an increasingly common method of punishing violators of antidiscrimination laws is to compel them to speak against their beliefs, as the case of Roy Frankhouser illustrates. Frankhouser, a Ku Klux Klan supporter with a long arrest record, harassed and intimidated Bonnie Jouhari, a fair-housing specialist for the Reading-Berks County Human Relations Council in Reading, Pennsylvania. Frankhouser sat on a public bench outside Jouhari's office and photographed her through the window. When Jouhari appeared on a television talk show, Frankhouser called in to warn her that "we're always keeping an eye on you." Even more ominous, Frankhouser displayed a picture of her obtained from a local neo-Nazi Web site on his "White Forum" public access cable television show. As on the Web site, the picture shown on television had a threatening caption: "Traitors like this should beware, for in our day, they will be hung from the neck from the nearest tree or lamppost." Jouhari decided to move to the West Coast—in part to get away from Frankhouser—but he continued to unnerve her until the last moment by appearing uninvited at the local bar that hosted her going-away party.[2]

The U.S. Justice Department and the local police declined to prosecute Frankhouser, because officials determined that his obnoxious behavior did not rise to the level of an actual threat, and he was therefore acting within his First Amendment rights. This decision was sound based on current First Amendment doctrine, which probably protects implicitly threatening speech more than it should. In

73

January 1999, an administrative law judge with the federal Department of Housing and Urban Development did charge the owner of the neo-Nazi Web site with violating the Fair Housing Act by threatening Jouhari. The judge, however, found no reasonable cause for charging Frankhouser, who had "reported" the threat by discussing it on his television show, but had never explicitly endorsed it.

A month later, however, the assistant secretary for fair housing and equal opportunity ordered that misdemeanor charges be brought against Frankhouser. Ultimately, the impecunious, unemployable Frankhouser agreed to a settlement. He promised to stay 100 feet away from Jouhari and her daughter and to pay Jouhari five percent of his annual salary for 10 years, in the unlikely event that it ever exceeded $25,000.[3] Frankhouser agreed to never mention Jouhari's name again and to attend HUD-sponsored sensitivity training. Frankhouser was also required to apologize to Jouhari on his "White Forum" television show and in letters to local newspapers, to broadcast HUD fair housing public service announcements as part of his television show, to read a government-scripted introduction to those announcements, and to display on the front of his house a poster produced by HUD, inveighing against discrimination in housing sales and rentals.

HUD Secretary Andrew Cuomo announced that "this settlement makes a very loud statement, not just to this particular case but to anyone who would think of engaging or involving themselves in this hideous type of behavior."[4] Columnist Michael Kelly, by contrast, interpreted the "statement" made by the settlement as, among other things, that the government may force an individual "to curtail his speech," to take reeducation classes, and to "make statements contrary to his beliefs."[5]

Not surprisingly, Frankhouser was not rehabilitated. "Clinton and Andrew Cuomo can kiss my rebel derriere," Frankhouser told columnist Dennis Roddy. "Yeah, I'm a sensitive guy. I'll end up liking gays, marry a [black] and maybe move to Mexico later on." Frankhouser said of his sensitivity training, "Hey, if the taxpayers want to foot the bill, God bless 'em. If they don't give me lunch, I won't go." Roddy opined that "[w]hen an irredeemable racist is sent to sensitivity training and made to say things he doesn't believe on a show that caters to an audience that won't listen, we are only left to remember how foolish a country gets to look when its secretary of housing becomes a closet attorney general."[6]

Indeed, during the Clinton administration, HUD was the federal agency that most consistently violated civil liberties on behalf of an antidiscrimination agenda. HUD's overzealousness went well beyond the Frankhouser case. As part of its war against neighborhood organizations that oppose local group housing initiatives (see Chapter 4), HUD tried to compel these organizations not only to give up their right to express their opinions but also to affirmatively support HUD's objectives. For example, a Seattle citizens' group, the Capitol Hill Association for Parity, opposed the proposed establishment by Pioneeer Housing Services of a complex of five buildings on one block to house the mentally ill and recovering addicts. HUD accused CHAP of violating the Fair Housing Act, and offered a conciliation agreement to avoid litigation.[7] Among other things, the agreement required the group to write to everyone on its mailing list in support of the PHS development, and to sponsor a block party "to which all residents, including residents of PHS housing, will be invited." The agreement specified that the group "shall solicit support for the block party from local businesses, and will ensure that free entertainment and inexpensive food are provided." HUD eventually dropped the case under public pressure.

Another case in which compelled speech was invoked as a remedy for discrimination involved Union Market, a store in Springfield, Massachusetts. After finding that a Union Market supervisor had discriminated against a Puerto Rican worker, the Massachusetts Commission Against Discrimination ordered standard remedies, including requiring back wages and emotional distress damages to be paid. However, the MCAD also required Union Market to "sponsor an event celebrating the Latino history and culture, drawing upon the resources of leaders and civic organizations servicing the Springfield Latino community."[8]

The MCAD justified this extraordinary remedy on the grounds that most of Union Market's employees and customers are Puerto Rican. "It not only provides an opportunity for the market to demonstrate its goodwill," the hearing officer wrote, "it sends a message to businesses . . . that they should honor the people they serve and show they appreciate their patronage." The MCAD did not attempt to explain how the commonwealth could require Union Market to "honor" customers of a certain ethnic group and to demonstrate that the store "appreciates their patronage" without violating the

First Amendment. The First Amendment issue is especially problematic in this case because it was an employee, not a customer, who complained of discrimination, so it is difficult to argue that the compelled speech honoring Latino customers was necessary to remediate a specific harm caused by a violation of the law.

The MCAD also dictated speech to a Boston bar owner charged with discrimination. In February 2000, the owner put up a display comprising vines, stuffed monkeys, a large stuffed gorilla wearing a crown, a wooden figure holding a spear, and coconuts painted with black faces and large red lips. A sign behind the stuffed animals proclaimed, "Hey, hey, we're the monkeys." The owner claimed he put up this display annually "because it's the dead of winter. People are sick of winter and want to go into a bar with a tropical flair."[9] He noted that the tropical display was part of a rotating series— frogs in the spring, fish in the summer, elephants and donkeys at election time. However, a bartender allegedly told patrons that the display mocked Black History Month and that the regal gorilla represented Martin Luther King Jr. When a report of the incident appeared in the *Boston Herald*, the chairman of the MCAD initiated proceedings against the bar for allegedly creating a hostile environment for African American patrons.[10] Rather than litigate, the bar owner agreed to the Commission's demands that he apologize and contribute money to events "addressing the topic of the history and contributions of Irish Americans and African Americans."[11] Surprisingly, the MCAD did not respond to the bar owner's annual display of frogs by requiring him to contribute money to events addressing the topic of the history and contributions of French Americans.

* * *

Government authorities have also sought to dictate to commercial entities the content of their advertisements. The Fair Housing Act, for example, has been construed to regulate the content of real estate advertisements. Federal regulations—currently suspended while HUD completes a review of possible conflicts between its regulations and the First Amendment—state that to prevent an inference that an advertiser prefers tenants from certain groups, if human models are used in display advertising campaigns, "the models should be clearly definable as reasonably representing majority and minority groups in the metropolitan area."[12] In other words, if you are a developer setting up a magazine ad to sell units in a new condominium complex, you had better be sure that some of those happy people cavorting in the pool and soaking up sun on their balconies are not white.

Liability for failure to use a suitably diverse group of human models extends not only to the party that places the ad but also to the newspaper publishing the ad and the ad agency that designed it. Several courts have agreed with HUD on this interpretation of the Fair Housing Act.[13] One court held that an ordinary reader, seeing ads that contained only white models, "would naturally infer from these ads . . . that white individuals were preferred as tenants."[14] Therefore, such ads violate the Fair Housing Act's ban on advertising that indicates a preference on the basis of race.

A federal appellate court rebuked the *New York Times* for suggesting that the only way to avoid a lawsuit—and potential liability for hundreds of thousands of dollars in damages[15]—under HUD's interpretation of the Fair Housing Act would be to institute quotas for African American models.[16] Yet the *Washington Post* was soon compelled to do exactly that. The *Post* avoided litigation only by agreeing with a local activist group that the newspaper would require a minimum of 25 percent African American models in all housing display ads.[17] One real estate company that faced claims for discriminatory advertising sought to avoid future liability by ending its use of human models entirely, only to be ordered by a federal court to first expiate its past sins by placing ads featuring racially diverse models.[18]

Fair housing laws protect many groups besides African Americans; in theory, advertisers who use human models and do not include Asians, Latinos, Hasidic Jews, disabled individuals, or families with children could be held liable for discrimination.[19] (The ad that did comply with such silly standards would be decidedly amusing to behold. The Afro-Asian Lubavitcher and his wheelchair-bound Latino daughter . . .) A federal judge has specifically argued that advertisements that did not feature all groups protected by the Fair Housing Act in proportion to their representation in the local metropolitan area could be found to be discriminatory.[20] Predictably, the result of all this has been that advertisers have given up on trying to meet such unreasonable standards; human models are now rarely used in real estate advertising. Ironically, the exception to this trend is on those occasions when HUD requires developers participating in certain federal housing programs to develop and implement "affirmative fair housing" marketing plans, which must include advertising specifically designed to appeal to groups that are not likely to apply for the housing.[21]

At one time, HUD's regulations clearly imposed liability for "discriminatory advertising" regardless of the intent of the advertiser. For example, the fact that it hadn't occurred to an apartment complex owner to include a couple of kids in the ad for downtown studios was no defense under the regulations to a charge of discrimination against families with children. HUD suspended those regulations as part of a general effort to get closer to the right side of the First Amendment, but the department stopped short of promulgating new regulations limiting liability to intentional discriminators. HUD currently takes no official position on whether discriminatory intent is necessary for advertising to violate the Fair Housing Act, instead leaving the issue up to the courts.[22] Some courts, meanwhile, do require plaintiffs to prove intent in human model cases.[23] One federal appellate court reasoned that forcing advertisers and newspapers that had no discriminatory intent to consider the race of advertising models would violate the First Amendment by chilling commercial speech.[24]

* * *

In contrast to HUD rules requiring real estate companies to have "inclusive" advertising if they advertise at all, the Equal Employment Opportunity Commission has prosecuted some employers for *not* advertising. The Chicago office of the EEOC has made something of a cottage industry out of suing small businesses that hire workers primarily through word of mouth, rather than through help-wanted ads placed in large-circulation newspapers. The department claims that the result of such hiring practices is a statistically determined "underrepresentation" of African Americans at the companies at issue.

For example, the agency went after Andrew Hwang, a Korean immigrant who owned Consolidated Service Systems, a small Chicago-based janitorial services company.[25] Hwang found his employees mostly by word of mouth in the local Korean community and through the Korean Association of Greater Chicago.[26] The EEOC decided that because 95 percent of the Chicago work force is composed of non-Asians, while Consolidated had mostly Korean employees, Consolidated was presumptively guilty of discrimination. The EEOC offered to settle if Consolidated agreed to pay $475,000 in "back pay" to non-Koreans who had applied to Consolidated and (like many Korean applicants) been rejected.[27] Consolidated's annual revenues were only about $400,000, so accepting a $475,000 settlement offer was well beyond Hwang's means. Not surprisingly, Hwang declined to settle.

The EEOC then sued Hwang and Consolidated in federal court, but the trial court dismissed the EEOC's case. On agency appeal, Judge Richard Posner wrote a rousing opinion affirming the lower court's ruling. Posner first stated that small businesses are not required to actively seek out workers from the broad community. He noted that if an employer "can obtain all the competent workers he wants, at wages no higher than the minimum that he expects to have to pay, without beating the bushes for workers—without in fact spending a cent on recruitment," he will do so to reduce his costs of doing business. Continuing, Posner stated that, notwithstanding the discriminatory impact it may have, word-of-mouth hiring cannot support an inference of intentional discrimination when it is clearly "the cheapest and most efficient method of recruitment." Posner concluded that "it is not discrimination, and it is certainly not active discrimination, for an employer to sit back and wait for people willing to work for low wages to apply to him. The fact that they are ethnically or racially uniform does not impose upon him a duty to spend money advertising in the help-wanted columns of the *Chicago Tribune*."

Posner also focused on the important role that small, ethnically based businesses play in the upward mobility of immigrants. Immigrants, Posner wrote, "tend to cluster in their own communities, united by ties of language, culture, and background." They often form small businesses, the "first rung on the ladder of American success," and employ "relatives, friends, and other members of their community, and they obtain new employees by word of mouth." Despite, or perhaps because of, "their ambition and hard work," recent immigrants "are frequent targets of discrimination, some of it violent." Posner suggested that "it would be a bitter irony if the federal agency dedicated to enforcing the antidiscrimination laws succeeded in using those laws to kick these people off the ladder by compelling them to institute costly systems of hiring."[28] Alas, Hwang's legal triumph turned out to be Pyrrhic. The huge legal fees he expended in successfully fighting off the EEOC forced Consolidated Service Systems out of business.[29]

The Chicago office of the EEOC also targeted Ted Grezeskiewicz, a Polish immigrant. After working for 16 years at a spring-making plant that employed mainly fellow Polish immigrants, Grezeskiewicz left in 1966 to form his own business, O & G Spring and Wire Forms Specialty Company. He took many of his former coworkers with him. By the 1980s, Grezeskiewicz employed around 50 workers, almost all of them Polish or Latino immigrants, hired primarily through word of mouth.[30]

In 1988, the EEOC sued O & G because, according to the agency's statistical models, O & G's work force should have been 22 percent African American. Although the EEOC had received no complaints of discrimination, the agency found that O & G's disproportionate percentage of Polish and Hispanic workers evidenced discrimination.[31] The district court sided with the EEOC and required O & G to place an ad in the *Chicago Tribune* inviting readers to submit claims against O & G.[32] More than 400 people eventually submitted claims. Amazingly, the EEOC made no attempt to screen applicants to determine whether or not they had actually sought work at O & G. Instead, the agency demanded that the company pay all of them, at a total cost of $378,754. Some of these purported victims had been in jail during the relevant time periods or had held better paying jobs.[33]

Grezeskiewicz appealed, but the court sided with the EEOC. Judge Daniel Manion wrote a dissent sharply criticizing the statistical evidence relied upon by the EEOC, the district court, and the appeals court. He quoted Judge Posner's opinion in the *Consolidated Services* case and suggested that "Judge Posner's prophecy has come to pass in this case."[34] As for O & G, besides the cost of the remedy, it had to endure 10 years of EEOC investigation and litigation, the company ultimately spending more than $400,000 defending itself.[35]

The EEOC's defenders observe that certain hiring policies can reinforce patterns of discrimination by allowing incumbent workers from dominant ethnic groups to choose their colleagues. The EEOC, for example, forced construction unions to adopt antinepotism policies. The unions in question not only had a history of excluding nonwhites but also restricted entry into their occupations through their unions' membership policies and through control of licensing boards.[36] However, the Chicago cases are very different. Polish and Korean immigrants are not established, incumbent workers trying to maintain their status at the expense of African Americans. Rather, they themselves are trying to establish a foothold in the American economy while competing with other Americans who have the advantages of better language skills, more familiarity with the labor market, and often better access to traditional credit.

The reason the Chicago companies sued by the EEOC failed to advertise widely in the media is that newspaper advertisements were obviously an inefficient use of the companies' limited resources. The Chicago EEOC tried to force small companies that employ mainly immigrants to have the same employment advertising policies as IBM or General Motors, with a public job search for each position and a premium placed on ensuring ethnic diversity. However, for the most part, the jobs offered by the Chicago small businesses in these cases involved low wages and hard work—the type of work generally scorned by native-born Americans of all races. Had these Chicago companies tried to advertise widely for unskilled workers, they would likely have found little interest from the general public, and therefore would have received little bang for their buck.

In contrast, word-of-mouth employment recruitment lowers costs for employers of immigrants. Not only does it save advertising costs, but, as Professor Richard Epstein notes, "It is easier and cheaper for everyone if Spanish-speaking workers work with Spanish-speaking workers and Polish-speaking workers with Polish-speaking workers, all other things held constant."[37] Moreover, employees hired through ethnic networks are likely to be reliable individuals, because current employees have vouched for them. Further, small immigrant manufacturing companies can compete with foreign competitors only because of their low labor costs relative to productivity. To the extent the EEOC forces higher employment costs on these businesses, it forces them closer to going out of business.

Finally, as Judge Posner has pointed out, African Americans have their own word-of-mouth job networks. Those would also be threatened by the EEOC's policies. For example, the Clarence Thomas–Anita Hill hearings revealed a network of African American Yale Law School alumni who refer job candidates to each other, which is how Thomas came to hire Hill. Notwithstanding the antagonistic end to the Thomas-Hill professional relationship, it hardly seems obvious that this sort of networking should be considered illegal discrimination as opposed to a welcome continuation of the African American self-help tradition.

* * *

As a condition of settlement of antidiscrimination lawsuits, the EEOC and private litigants are increasingly demanding that defendant corporations agree to have managers strongly consider supervisors' vigilance in implementing anti-harassment policies when evaluating those employees' performances. Even companies that have not been sued are adopting this policy to attempt to avoid future lawsuits. One common criterion used to judge an employee's zealousness in enforcing anti-harassment policies is whether the employee has expressed his *personal* support for the policies. An employment law expert asserts that managers must "communicate to their employees that they agree with, personally believe in, and will enforce the harassment policy."[38] Yet anti-harassment policies are often controversial within a company, especially when they stifle speech or prohibit dating among coworkers. Employment law expert Walter Olson writes that unless the trend toward requiring absolute fealty to internal anti-harassment policies is reversed, "those who dissent from the official line, harbor doubts or qualms about it, or for any other reason prove unwilling to announce their enthusiasm for it, will sooner or later find themselves excluded from positions of responsibility in the American corporation."[39]

* * *

The Supreme Court has held that the "right of freedom of thought protected by the First Amendment against state action includes both the right to speak freely and the right to refrain from speaking at all."[40] In a stirring opinion overturning a compulsory flag salute statute in the midst of World War II, the Court wrote,

> We set up government by consent of the governed, and the Bill of Rights denies those in power any legal opportunity to coerce that consent. Authority here is to be controlled by public opinion, not public opinion by authority. . . . If there is any fixed star in our constitutional constellation, it is that

no official, high or petty, can prescribe what shall be orthodox in politics, nationalism, religion, or other matters of opinion or force citizens to confess by word or act their faith therein. If there are any circumstances which permit an exception, they do not now occur to us.[41]

We should not let antidiscrimination orthodoxy become the first of what would inevitably turn into many such exceptions.

7. Public Accommodations Laws and the Threat to the Autonomy of Private Organizations

In the late 1960s, John and Ruth Mallery founded a Boys' Club in a poor, blighted neighborhood in Santa Cruz, California. After John died, Ruth, inspired by her childhood memories of boys who got into legal trouble because they had nothing to keep them busy, donated $1.5 million to endow the Club. She stipulated that her gift was to be used only to help boys. Eight-year-old Victoria Isbister, a resident of the neighborhood in which the Boys' Club was located, probably did not understand or even know about Ruth's reasons for marking her donation for boys only. What Victoria did know was that she thought it was unfair that she could not use the only swimming pool in the neighborhood, the one at the Boys' Club. Her parents agreed, and with the help of local American Civil Liberties Union attorneys, Victoria sued the Boys' Club for excluding her from its facilities.[1]

Victoria's lawsuit hinged on a California law banning sex discrimination in all "business establishments." The Club's attorneys argued that the Boys' Club was a charitable recreation facility, not a business establishment, so the law should not apply. The California Supreme Court held that because the Club had a fixed location, it was a business establishment within the meaning of the law. Dissenting Justice Stanley Mosk, a liberal civil libertarian, ridiculed his colleagues: "The majority opinion conjures up visions of young boys, who have been skinny-dipping in their club pool, donning three-piece suits to attend the board meeting of their 'business establishment' where they may discuss such matters as the antitrust implications of a proposed takeover of girl scout cookies. Precocious indeed these teen and preteen youngsters must be."

The Club's attorneys also asserted that it should be exempt from the law for public policy reasons. If enough girls decided to join the

Boys' Club, it might need to drop its open-door policy and limit access to the club at certain hours. The Club's attorneys insisted that it had good reasons to spend its limited resources on boys—namely, that they are far more likely than girls to be arrested and to become the perpetrators or victims of violence. The California Supreme Court majority responded that the Club had presented no hard evidence "that boys need the recreation offered by the Club more than girls, that a sex-segregated 'drop-in' recreational facility is more effective in combating juvenile delinquency than one open to both sexes, or that extension of membership to girls would cause an impractical net increase (or decrease) in membership." In the absence of hard evidence on these issues, the court saw only arbitrary and illegal discrimination.

In contrast, Justice Mosk saw an open and diverse philanthropic arena with room for all kinds of charitable clubs, including sex-specific ones. He observed that allowing philanthropists like Mallery to donate to sex-segregated clubs does not prohibit other donors from sponsoring coed clubs. On the other hand, requiring all children's organizations to be coed, as the California Supreme Court had now done, prevented those with a different vision of how to help children from trying to realize it. Mosk accused his colleagues of quashing "pluralism [and] all the values that connotes—values such as a diversity of views, a variety of ideas, and preservation of traditions." Justice Otto Kaus, who also dissented, cited studies showing that boys and girls benefit from being separated from each other for at least part of their day. He added, "Who are we to say it is unreasonable for the club's management to believe that there is a rational basis for giving boys a few hours a day when they do not have to carry their machismo on their sleeves?"

Chief Justice Rose Bird, concurring with the majority, wrote an opinion scoffing at the dissenters' defense of pluralism, which she reduced to defending the right of "wealthy patrons who prefer to confer largess in a sexually discriminatory fashion." Bird saw Ruth Mallery and people like her not as kindly philanthropists trying to aid society as best they know how, but as a contemptible "select few" who wish to be "insulated from the 20th century." Bird's intemperate opinion attacking an altruistic elderly widow became an issue in a reelection battle that ultimately cost Bird her seat on the state supreme court.

One result of bans on single-sex charitable organizations is that some donors are not able to fully satisfy their preferences. The logical response of these frustrated would-be donors is to either reduce their donations to children's charities or to stop donating at all. Although the California Supreme Court could dictate that Boys' Clubs must admit girls, it could not force donors to continue to fund the clubs. Mallery, upset that the court had thwarted her goal of helping boys, withdrew the unspent portion of her endowment of the Boys' Club. Her view was that if the ACLU and the California Supreme Court wanted Santa Cruz to have a "Boys' and Girls' Club," they could go ahead and pay for it themselves.[2]

* * *

The Boys' Club case exemplifies the vast expansion of public accommodations law at the federal and especially state levels since the passage of the granddaddy of public accommodations laws, Title II of the federal 1964 Civil Rights Act. Title II bans discrimination on the basis of race, color, religion, or national origin in public accommodations.

The law was motivated in part by testimony before Congress that African Americans traveling in the South often had difficulty finding motels and restaurants that would serve them. Title II also reflected a growing belief that any establishment that holds itself out as being open to the public, and that is not otherwise selective about who it admits, should not be permitted to discriminate against members of minority groups.

A few libertarians objected to Title II because it conflicted with property rights and freedom of association. Novelist-philosopher Ayn Rand, for example, wrote that "[j]ust as we have to protect a communist's freedom of speech, even though his doctrines are evil, so we have to protect a racist's right to the use and disposal of his own property."[3] Future Supreme Court nominee Robert Bork, who was more libertarian in those days, famously referred to legally compelled association as a "principle of unsurpassed ugliness." He added that the issue was not "whether prejudice or preference is a good thing but whether individual men ought to be free to deal and associate with whom they please for whatever reasons appeal to them."[4]

Libertarian objections to Title II's regulation of public accommodations were largely overshadowed by southern congressmen's arguments that Title II violated "states' rights" by overturning Jim Crow laws that required segregation in public accommodations. Libertarian concerns regarding *private* accommodations, however, received a serious hearing. At the time, even very liberal members of the legal elite agreed that members of private clubs had a right to choose their associates without government interference. Supreme Court Justice Arthur Goldberg, for example, wrote that there is a constitutional right to close one's home or club "to any person . . . solely on the basis of personal prejudices, including race." Several years later, Justice William O. Douglas proclaimed, "The associational rights which our system honors permit all white, all black, all brown, and all yellow clubs to be formed. They also permit all Catholic, all Jewish, or all agnostic clubs to be established. Government may not tell a man or woman who his or her associates must be. The individual can be as selective as he desires."[5]

Congress ultimately agreed to exempt private clubs from Title II's dictates, but this exemption begged the pivotal question of what makes a club "private." Many restaurants in the South began to call themselves "private" in an attempt to evade Title II, but their alleged privateness was obviously pretextual, as all whites were admitted and all African Americans were excluded.[6] Federal courts eventually developed a test to distinguish private clubs from public accommodations: the factors that weigh in favor of private status include selectivity in membership, limiting use of facilities and services to members and bona fide guests, nonprofit status, and an absence of advertising to the general public.

Consideration of these factors perhaps resulted in a narrower private club exemption than Congress had intended, and led to a broader definition of "public accommodations" than a literal interpretation of the phrase would allow. For example, courts applied Title II to such seemingly private organizations as a swim club, a hunting club, a youth football league, and an African American teachers' association.[7] On the other hand, the Supreme Court rejected—over the dissent of three liberal Justices—an attempt to define all private organizations that receive government licenses and permits as "state actors" subject to the same prohibitions on discrimination as is the government.[8]

Many state and local public accommodations laws prohibit discrimination on bases not covered by Title II, such as sex, sexual orientation, weight, appearance, political affiliation, and even, in Minnesota, membership in a motorcycle gang.[9] Moreover, some laws exempt only "distinctly private" clubs, a narrower category than the "private" clubs exempted by federal law. Some legislatures have even amended their states' laws to ensure that the term "distinctly private" is construed narrowly. New York State, for example, amended its public accommodations law to explicitly state that private clubs with more than 100 members that provide regular meal service are not "distinctly private." This change in the law overturned a judicial decision holding that the Kiwanis Club and other large membership organizations are distinctly private.[10]

In other states, courts, rather than legislatures, have driven the expansion of public accommodations law. For example, in 1969, the New Jersey Supreme Court announced that it would give New Jersey's public accommodations law "a broadly sympathetic construction" to "eradicate the cancer of discrimination."[11] A few years later, the court diverged from federal precedent and held that an organization need not meet in a fixed location to be considered a "place of public accommodation." As a result, the Little League Baseball organization, though certainly not any kind of place at all in normal parlance, was held to be a "place of public accommodation" under New Jersey law and was therefore required to admit girls.[12] A cat fanciers' club is also a "place of public accommodation" in New Jersey and therefore may not discriminate against Jews.[13] Other state courts have held that such membership organizations as a boating club, the United States Jaycees, and the Boy Scouts of America are "places of public accommodation," even though they have no fixed meeting place.[14]

Not content to merely redefine the word "place," state courts have also ignored the ordinary meaning of the word "private" to reject private club defenses to the application of public accommodations laws. Perhaps the most egregious case along these lines involved three of Princeton's 13 historic private eating clubs.[15] Although the clubs have no legal ties to Princeton University, they function as nonresidential fraternities, providing food, entertainment, and social services to most juniors and seniors at the school.

Princeton University junior Sally Frank filed a complaint under New Jersey's public accommodations law against three eating clubs that refused to admit women. New Jersey's law provided an exemption for private clubs, but Frank alleged that the clubs were actually public accommodations because they functioned as "arms of Princeton." After several years of litigation, the New Jersey Supreme Court ruled in Frank's favor. The court acknowledged that the clubs had "assiduously maintained legal separateness" from the university: the clubs operated off-campus, in their own facilities, and they received no university funding. To find that the clubs were nevertheless public because of their purported ties to the university, the court focused instead on the "gestalt" of the clubs' relationship with the school.[16] The state supreme court concluded that "the Clubs and Princeton have an interdependent relationship that deprives the Clubs of private status." *Frank*, as the clubs' attorney, George McCarter, has written, is notable "as an almost defiant exercise of raw judicial power, and for its indifference to traditional legal analysis."[17] One might add a similar note about the New Jersey Supreme Court's refusal to seriously consider the plain English meaning of the statutory language it was charged with interpreting.

Some state courts have interpreted their public accommodations laws much less expansively. Like federal courts, these courts have held that membership organizations with no fixed meeting place, such as the Boys Scouts of America, cannot be considered places of public accommodation.[18] After all, they simply aren't places. Some courts have even held that organizations with fixed meeting places may use discriminatory criteria in selecting members, even when the clubs are not otherwise selective, because membership is not an "accommodation."[19] However, the trend continues to favor an expansive definition of the phrase "places of public accommodation." In 2001, for example, the Supreme Court held that under the Americans with Disabilities Act, the PGA tour is a place of public accommodation and therefore could not "discriminate" against disabled golfer Casey Martin by prohibiting him from using a golf cart.[20] This was obviously a stretch, but the Court didn't stop there. For the ADA to apply to Martin, he had to be a "customer" of the PGA, and so the Court absurdly deemed him to be one—and a very strange customer he is, playing in the PGA tour on his Court-authorized motorized golf cart, sometimes collecting prize money but never seeming to buy anything from the PGA.

* * *

As we have seen, the battle over the scope of public accommodations laws has focused for the most part on the definition of "public accommodation" (or, in California, "business establishment"). Whether Boys' Clubs, eating clubs, or other organizations must comply with antidiscrimination laws depends on whether these organizations fit the statutory definition of places of public accommodation, as construed by the courts.

However, there is more to this story. The expansion of public accommodations laws also has constitutional ramifications. The U.S. Supreme Court has acknowledged that the right to privacy, which arises out of the First and Fourteenth Amendments, protects a sphere of certain intimate relationships from antidiscrimination laws.[21] Therefore, the question arises as to when membership in an organization is such a relationship. In determining whether the right to "intimate association" is implicated, courts must assess "where [a] relationship's objective characteristics locate it on a spectrum from the most intimate to the most attenuated of personal attachments."[22] Protected relationships include, but are not limited to, "creation and sustenance of a family—marriage, childbirth, the raising and education of children, and cohabitation with one's relatives." Between the extremes of a business association and a family lays "a broad range of human relationships that may make greater or lesser claims to constitutional protection."

The Supreme Court has not yet invalidated an antidiscrimination law as a violation of the right to intimate association, and no doubt the parameters of what constitutes a protected relationship will be clearer once it does. The Court, however, has, at least for the time being, put an outer limit on potential intimate association claims by holding that the Rotary Club, a national organization made up of local chapters, some quite small, was not an intimate association, because it lacked selectivity and had a business-oriented agenda.[23] Most recently, the Court declined the Boy Scouts of America's invitation to determine whether its exclusion of gays is constitutionally protected by the right to intimate association, though it found for the Boy Scouts on other grounds (see Chapter 8).[24] Lower courts, meanwhile, have been loathe in the absence of further Supreme Court guidance to find that the right to intimate association trumps antidiscrimination law in particular cases.

Two courts have, however, held that the right of intimate (or "private") association protects specific private clubs from antidiscrimination laws. One case arose in New Orleans, Louisiana—a city that proscribes discrimination by any club that has more than 75 members and provides regular meal service. An African American man filed a complaint with the city's Human Rights Commission against four social clubs, alleging that they had denied him membership because of his race. The Commission initiated an investigation of the clubs' membership policies and practices.

When the clubs sued in federal court seeking to enjoin the Commission from continuing the investigation, the Fifth Circuit Court of Appeals held that the Commission's investigation violated the intimate association rights of the clubs and their members.[25] The court explained that the clubs existed exclusively for private, social purposes, and they prohibited the transaction or discussion of any commercial business on their premises. The clubs had very small memberships and very restrictive admission policies. There were no signs identifying the club's buildings to outsiders, and the clubs did not advertise to the public in any way. Club members shared common social interests and often preexisting family or religious ties, so there was a close nexus between the clubs' purposes and their membership criteria. Finally, the clubs rarely permitted guests. For these reasons, the clubs were held to be sufficiently private to be entitled to constitutional protection.

The court then turned to the issue of whether the Commission was violating the clubs' right of private association by merely investigating charges of discrimination. Association rights, the court noted, "can be abridged even by government actions that do not directly restrict individuals' ability to associate freely." The court concluded that the investigatory techniques at issue did not adequately protect the clubs' private association rights, because the Commission had the authority to force the clubs to turn over their membership lists.[26]

Members of the Pacific Union Club in San Francisco also defeated an antidiscrimination investigation by invoking the right to intimate association.[27] California's Franchise Tax Board had demanded the club's membership list so it could investigate whether members had illegally deducted club dues and expenditures. California tax law forbids members of private clubs that discriminate to deduct their club dues, and the club had admitted that it engaged in age discrimination. But the club argued that its members had a constitutional right to keep its membership list private.

The California Court of Appeal agreed. It found that the club had a purely social purpose; limited its size; did not actively recruit new members; required membership candidates to undergo a rigorous admissions process, including many personal interviews to assess the applicant's congeniality; excluded nonmembers from functions; and kept its membership list strictly private. The court concluded that "the Club is more than sufficiently intimate" to be entitled to claim the right of intimate association. Further, compelled disclosure of the club's membership list to the tax authorities would have a chilling effect on people's willingness to be members of the club, because their membership could lead to an audit. The court held that the goal of investigating potentially illegal tax deductions was not sufficiently compelling to override the privacy rights of the club and its members. The membership list stayed private.

* * *

Public accommodations laws are most effective against outliers who disagree with a broader societal consensus, such as when the rest of the United States imposed nondiscrimination norms on the recalcitrant South in the 1960s. More often, court decisions banning purely social discrimination target discrimination that is already in precipitous decline due to changing social attitudes and that would likely die a natural death if left alone. For example, most of Princeton's eating clubs had already begun admitting women by the time Sally Frank began her litigation in the 1970s. The litigation did not conclude until 1992,[28] by which time changing social mores had led the very clubs Frank was suing to admit women regardless of the outcome of the court battle.[29] Yale and Harvard's fraternal clubs also admitted women voluntarily. The last of Yale's single-sex secret societies, the Order of Skull and Bones, voted to admit women in 1991,[30] and Harvard's last all-male club, the Fly Club, voted to admit women in 1993.[31] The most positive thing one can say about Frank's litigation is that it may have forced sex integration to commence a bit earlier than it would have otherwise. Meanwhile, it established a damaging precedent for freedom of association in New Jersey.

Similarly, although the U.S. Supreme Court held in 1987 that states *may* force service organizations such as the Rotary Club to admit women (see Chapter 8), by 1992, very few states had chosen to enact such rules. Nevertheless, almost all major service organizations— a notable exception being the women-only Junior Leagues—had decided by then to admit both sexes nationwide to avoid the massive membership losses that could result from the perception that they are sexist and anachronistic. As we have seen, the California Supreme Court in 1983 ruled that Boys' Clubs in that state must admit girls. Few states followed California's lead but, by 1987, 80 percent of Boys' Clubs served girls and 60 percent of them admitted girls as members, continuing a trend that had begun before the California ruling for the pragmatic reason that many boys apparently found single-sex organizations to be "uncool." In 1990, the organization officially changed its name to the Boys & Girls Clubs of America. The California court was ahead of the curve, but just barely.

On the other hand, if judicial interpretations of public accommodations laws stray beyond what society supports, the judiciary will generally back down. When she wrote her scathing concurrence in the Boys' Club case attacking single-sex youth organizations, Chief Justice Rose Bird suggested that such organizations were a relic of a less enlightened era and would soon be abolished. She was wrong. The Girls Clubs of America, for example, did not join the Boys' Clubs in turning coed. The GCA leadership continued to believe that many girls, especially girls growing up in poor urban neighborhoods in which teen pregnancy is rampant, benefit from a single-sex social environment. The GCA changed its name to "Girls, Inc." and continues to offer programs tailored to at-risk girls, such as a program that discourages early sexual activity and attempts to reduce adolescent pregnancy rates. Those looking for single-sex youth organizations also still have the option of joining the Boy Scouts or Girl Scouts, among other organizations, while other groups, such as 4-H clubs and most religious youth groups, are coed. The California Supreme Court itself later backed away from the clear implications of its Boys' Club opinion when it held that the Boy Scouts of America is not a business establishment subject to antidiscrimination law. The public seems to support pluralism, and pluralism has triumphed—so far.

College fraternities have also survived the onslaught of antidiscrimination law. Unlike other single-sex social organizations,

"Greek" fraternities have never been forced to go coed. Fraternities are explicitly exempt from the federal prohibition against sex discrimination in education (Title IX),[32] from the Fair Housing Act,[33] and from many states' public accommodations laws. Predictions that the Princeton eating clubs case would lead to the abolition of fraternities in New Jersey have not been vindicated and the California Supreme Court has indicated that, unlike Boys' Clubs and country clubs, fraternities are not business establishments and may engage in sex discrimination.[34]

The different treatment shown to discriminatory country clubs on the one hand and single-sex fraternities on the other is hardly a result of lesser government interest in eliminating discrimination by fraternities. All of the rationales for eliminating discrimination by other clubs apply to fraternities—for example, many important life-long business contacts are made through friendships developed in fraternities. Yet the law has left fraternities alone because single-sex fraternities are still widely accepted as an appropriate form of socialization and because they have a significant political constituency. The public may be ready for the forced integration of golf and tennis clubs, but it is not willing to force frats to go coed, so the courts do not push it.

The inability of public accommodations laws to stray far beyond societal consensus stems from the U.S. system of government. Americans rely on democratically elected representatives to pass laws, and they look to judges, administrators, and juries to enforce them. There is little reason to believe that these government actors hold opinions far different than those of the public regarding whether traditional forms of social discrimination are harmful. Law can accelerate the process of social change somewhat, as voluntary social change is (or at least can be) a more drawn-out process than the enforcement of legislative edicts. The question is whether sacrificing freedom of association—with the attendant risk that the government will unnecessarily stifle pluralism or even ultimately codify regressive social norms, as it so disastrously did in the Jim Crow era—is worthwhile for slightly quicker social change and the suppression of a few outliers who refuse to conform to changing social attitudes.

This question is especially pertinent today, because the social context of discrimination has changed a great deal. At one time, public accommodations laws primarily targeted social organizations dominated by elite Protestant white males. The laws therefore arguably served the cause of pluralism by opening up such organizations to less-established outsiders. Today, by contrast, clubs with policies favoring the traditional elite are increasingly rare, while all-black (e.g., 100 Black Men of America), all-Jewish (e.g., B'nai B'rith), and all-female (e.g., the Junior Leagues), among others, are going strong and creating significant social and economic capital for their members. However, these organizations are at risk of being dissolved by public accommodations laws' nondiscriminatory membership policies because they practice social discrimination. The bottom line is that if the government is permitted to dictate policies to private social organizations, there is a strong chance that American society will be the worse for it.

* * *

Many private organizations that promote political or social messages have been deemed to come within the purview of state public accommodations laws. If these "expressive associations" are forced to obey antidiscrimination mandates, the content of their messages will likely change. For example, B'nai B'rith, an all-Jewish fraternal organization, would likely promote or emphasize a different political agenda if the government required it to admit gentiles. The regulation of expressive associations implicates First Amendment concerns and is the subject of the next chapter.

8. Stifling Expressive Associations

Without a corresponding freedom to associate, the First Amendment rights to freedom of speech, assembly, and to petition government would be trivial because political and social movements advocating changes to the status quo could be easily suppressed by laws dictating the rules under which activists could interact.[1] For example, a pro-vegetarian social movement would not get very far if the government said, "Sure, you can sing the praises of greens and carrots all you like, but you're going to have to let members of a veal-and-pâté-worshipping religion into your group." This point was brought home more seriously and dramatically in the 1950s, when state governments in the South tried to defeat the civil rights movement by curtailing the associative rights of activists. The Supreme Court defeated this stratagem by recognizing the implicit constitutional right to associate for expressive purposes, now known as the right of "expressive association."[2]

In a series of decisions in the 1980s, however, the Supreme Court held that the expressive association right must yield to antidiscrimination laws. Specifically, the Court reasoned that because the government has a compelling interest in eradicating discrimination, public accommodations laws that regulate the membership practices of private organizations trump the First Amendment rights of the organizations and their members. Fortunately, however, the Court seems to have recognized that its rulings created a grave danger to civil liberties and has recently backed away from these decisions.

The first case to reach the Supreme Court involving a clash between a public accommodations law and the First Amendment involved the United States Jaycees, an organization for young business leaders. The Jaycees originally accepted only men, but by the early 1970s it was admitting women as associate members. Associate members could participate in Jaycees activities, but they could not vote, run for office, or receive awards. Some chapters that wished to admit women to full membership, such as the Omaha Jaycees, formed two parallel, separate organizations under the same holding company. One of these organizations admitted women to full membership and conducted the day-to-day activities of the Jaycees. The other entity reserved full member status for men and served as the Jaycees' official link to the national organization. Other Jaycees chapters were free to follow the Omaha model, but two Minnesota chapters instead chose to sue the national organization under Minnesota's public accommodations law, which banned discrimination against women by membership organizations.

The litigation threatened to unalterably change the Jaycees' message. The Jaycees' charter established the organization's central purpose as "promoting the interests of young men." It hardly seems likely that young women admitted as members would use their membership primarily to contribute to this purpose. Moreover, the national, state, and local chapters of the Jaycees (including the Minnesota chapter) took positions on a wide range of political issues. Given the "gender gap" in political views—women on average are more liberal on economic and military issues than are men—forcing the Jaycees to admit women would inevitably affect the Jaycees' political agenda.

For these reasons, a federal appeals court found that by forcing the Jaycees to admit women, Minnesota's public accommodations law violated the Jaycees members' First Amendment right of expressive association.[3] Minnesota appealed to the Supreme Court, which ruled against the Jaycees in a 5–0 opinion written by Justice William Brennan, with Justices Sandra Day O'Connor and William Rehnquist concurring and two other justices recusing themselves.[4]

Justice Brennan acknowledged that the First Amendment protects the right to associate for expressive purposes, but he paid only lip service to that right. He found that the Jaycees had presented no valid evidence that the compelled acceptance of women as members would "change the content or impact of the organization's speech." According to Brennan, the claim that admitting women would inherently change the Jaycees' message relied "solely on unsupported generalizations about the relative interests and perspectives of men and women" that "may or may not have a statistical basis." Therefore, requiring the Jaycees to admit women did not violate anyone's expressive association rights.

Had Justice Brennan's opinion stopped there, it would not have been especially notable. Although critics have attacked Brennan's tendentiousness in ignoring the very real and predictable ways that the Jaycees' message would be changed by admitting women, if his opinion had confined itself to a fact-dependent analysis it would have had limited impact on the law. Instead, Brennan added that the Jaycees would have lost the case even if the Court had found that Minnesota's public accommodations law *had* infringed on the Jaycees' expressive association rights. He reasoned that because the law advanced the compelling interests of eliminating gender discrimination and ensuring "equal access to publicly available goods and services," intrusion into First Amendment rights was permissible.

Reducing sex discrimination is an important goal, but merely stating that fact does not explain why the government's interest in forcing the Jaycees to admit women was sufficiently "compelling" to trump the First Amendment's protection of freedom of expression. Brennan did note that Minnesota claimed a longstanding interest in eradicating discrimination against women, but he failed to explain why a single state's public policy goal creates a federal constitutional interest powerful enough to override the First Amendment. More fundamentally, Brennan did not address the government's lack of a *constitutionally legitimate*—much less *compelling*—interest in eradicating discriminatory attitudes, beliefs, expressions, or associations. The very purpose of the free speech protections of the First Amendment is to prevent the government from squelching the expression or promotion of certain ideas, so it is difficult to see how the government's claimed interest in doing so can trump the First Amendment.

Perhaps the nadir of the Supreme Court's respect for expressive association rights was reached a few years after *Jaycees*. The Court first extended the logic of *Jaycees* to hold that state governments could compel Rotary International to allow the admission of women as members. Then, adding insult to injury, the Court claimed that by approving government interference with RI's membership policies, the Court was serving the Rotarians' own best interests.[5] The Court argued that its ruling would help RI achieve its stated objective of providing humanitarian service and encouraging high ethical standards. The addition of women, the Court added, would also likely promote RI's stated goal of ensuring that Rotary clubs represented a cross-section of their communities. Because the Court believed that admitting women advanced RI's stated goals, the Court reasoned that there was no violation of the right of expressive association. But, as in *Jaycees*, the Court volunteered that it would have ruled against RI even if RI's expressive association rights had been infringed. Public accommodations laws, the Court reiterated, "plainly serv[e] compelling state interests of the highest order."

With the Supreme Court signaling open season on any organization deemed by state law to be a public accommodation, the Boy Scouts of America soon became a leading target of antidiscrimination lawsuits. Activists accused the Scouts of violating state and local public accommodations laws by excluding gays, atheists, and girls. Gays are excluded because the Scouts' leadership believes that homosexual activity violates the Scout Oath, which requires scouts to be "morally straight," a provision Scout leaders have construed to forbid nonmarital sex, including homosexual sex. Atheists and agnostics are excluded because the Scout Oath requires an acknowledgment of a scout's duty to God. Girls are excluded because the Scouts believes that the moral education of boys is best undertaken in a single-sex atmosphere.

Those who objected to the Scouts' policies were (and are) free to found the "Straight and Gay Scouts" or the "Godless Scouts" or the "Boy and Girl Scouts." Dissident scouts also could join one of the many established youth organizations that do not discriminate on the basis of sex, religious belief, or sexual orientation. Some activists nonetheless sued the Scouts with the help of the American Civil Liberties Union, and eventually with help from local government antidiscrimination agencies. Several courts rejected these claims, but only because the Scouts was not a "public accommodation" subject to the relevant antidiscrimination law. Courts, meanwhile, consistently held that the Scouts had no constitutional expressive association right to discriminate to defend its creed.[6] The Connecticut Supreme Court, for example, stated that the Scouts' assertion of a constitutional right to exclude women from serving as scoutmasters had "little merit" in light of *Jaycees* and *Rotary International*.[7]

* * *

A 1995 case, *Hurley v. Irish-American Gay, Lesbian & Bisexual Group of Boston*,[8] suggested that the Supreme Court's deference to antidiscrimination laws at the expense of expressive association rights was waning. The Irish-American Gay, Lesbian & Bisexual Group (GLIB), a gay rights organization, claimed that Massachusetts's public accommodations law obligated the organizers of Boston's St. Patrick's Day Parade to permit GLIB members to march under GLIB's banner. The parade organizers responded that they had a First Amendment right to exclude any group that sought to convey a message (in this case, they claimed, a "sexual message") the organizers did not wish to convey.[9] The trial court ruled in favor of GLIB,[10] relying on *Jaycees* in holding that any "incidental" infringement on expressive association rights was justified by the government's interest in eradicating discrimination against homosexuals. On appeal, the Massachusetts Supreme Court agreed that the organizers had no viable First Amendment defense.[11] So far, it was business as usual, with public accommodations law running roughshod over freedom of association.

The tide turned when the U.S. Supreme Court reversed the GLIB decision in a unanimous opinion written by Justice David Souter. The Court explained that the parade organizers had not excluded gays from the parade. Rather, they had excluded a group that had been formed for the express purpose of marching under its own banner in the parade "in order to celebrate its members' identity as openly gay, lesbian, and bisexual descendants of Irish immigrants." The organizers had a First Amendment right not to promote this theme because "the fundamental rule of protection under the First Amendment, is that a speaker has the autonomy to choose the content of his own message." Justice Souter distinguished *Jaycees* on the grounds that the *Jaycees* court found that enforcing Minnesota's public accommodations law did not affect the Jaycees' message, while enforcing the Massachusetts law would change the parade organizers' message. Souter ignored the compelling interest test, even though it loomed large in *Jaycees* and despite the fact that the trial court and GLIB's brief had relied on it.

Hurley's broader significance became apparent in 2000, when the case of *Boy Scouts of America v. Dale* came before the Supreme Court. James Dale had become a Cub Scout at the age of 8 and had remained in scouting until he turned 18, ultimately achieving the rank of Eagle Scout in 1988.[12] In 1989, Dale applied for adult membership in the Scouts and became an assistant scoutmaster. Meanwhile, Dale "came out" and became active in his university's gay and lesbian advocacy organization. In 1990, a newspaper printed an interview with Dale about his advocacy on behalf of gay youth. Dale subsequently received a letter from the local scouting council revoking his adult membership, because the Scouts "specifically forbid[s] membership to homosexuals."

Dale sued the Scouts for violating New Jersey's public accommodations statute. After protracted litigation, the New Jersey Supreme Court ruled in Dale's favor. The court found that the Scouts' ability to disseminate its message of "moral straightness" was not significantly affected by forced employment of Dale. Moreover, the court added a familiar refrain: even if Dale's employment had infringed on the Scouts' expressive association rights, this infringement would have been justified under *Jaycees* by the government's "compelling interest in eliminating discrimination based on sexual orientation."

The U.S. Supreme Court overruled the New Jersey Supreme Court in a five-to-four opinion in favor of the Scouts, written by Chief Justice William Rehnquist. Rehnquist concluded that to force the Scouts to grant Dale a leadership position would violate the organization's right of expressive association because it "would significantly burden the Scouts' right to oppose or disfavor homosexual conduct." "Dale's presence in the Boy Scouts," Rehnquist wrote, "would, at the very least, force the organization to send a message, both to the youth members and the world, that the Boy Scouts accepts homosexual conduct as a legitimate form of behavior." Just as the coerced presence of GLIB in Boston's St. Patrick's Day parade would have interfered with the parade organizers' choice not to propound a particular point of view, the presence of Dale as an assistant scoutmaster "would surely interfere with the Boy Scouts' choice not to propound a point of view contrary to its beliefs."

Rehnquist stressed that associations "do not have to associate for the 'purpose' of disseminating a certain message" to receive First Amendment protection. They merely have to "engage in expressive activity." If the Scouts wants leaders to teach about sexual morality only by example, this subtle form of expression is protected by the First Amendment. Finally, Rehnquist also made clear that First Amendment protection is not limited to groups that take a strong stand against those they exclude. Rehnquist wrote that "[t]he fact that the organization does not trumpet its views from the housetops, or that it tolerates dissent within its ranks, does not mean that its views receive no First Amendment protection."

Because *Dale* did not explicitly overrule *Jaycees*, one might have expected Rehnquist to meaningfully explore whether New Jersey had a compelling interest in eradicating discrimination against gays, but he did not. Rather, he simply wrote that given the severe intrusion into the Scouts' right to expressive association, the state interests served by New Jersey's public accommodations law were not sufficient to overcome the Scouts' rights. Rehnquist implied that state interests in battling discrimination can overcome expressive association rights only when the infringement on such rights is minor, as the Court found was the case in *Jaycees*.

The four dissenters also did not focus on the compelling interest issue. Instead, they argued that the Scouts case was not sufficiently vociferous in its opposition to homosexual activity to have a First Amendment right to exclude gays. The Scouts' lack of virulence is intentional—the organization seeks to encourage traditional moral values while creating as little offense among its members and supporters as possible. Had they succeeded in limiting expressive-association rights to organizations vociferous in their support of discrimination, the dissenters would have ensured that those rights are available mainly to marginal, extremist organizations. As Northwestern University Law School Professor John McGinnis observes, "the advantage of having a full range of civic associations lies in society's enjoyment of a range and intensity of views on an issue pressed from the different perspectives provided by associations with different civic purposes."[13] The constitutional world contemplated by the dissenters, by contrast, "is one in which shrill advocacy alone supplements the norms encouraged by the government."[14]

Another reason to protect freedom of expressive association from antidiscrimination laws is that government agencies charged with enforcing public accommodations laws tend to target groups with unpopular messages. For example, in 1994, the Nation of Islam, notorious for its racist, sexist, and anti-Semitic views (which are, of course, protected by the First Amendment), requested permission to rent the Cleveland convention center for a men-only meeting. The city of Cleveland sought a court ruling that the men's event would violate Ohio's public accommodations law by excluding women, and that denying the facility to the Nation would not violate the Nation's constitutional rights. The Nation, in turn, asked for a judgment permitting it to restrict its event to men, in accordance with its religious practice.[15]

A federal district court ruled in favor of the Nation on expressive association grounds, a ruling that now seems correct under *Dale*[16] but that was possible at the time only because the court ignored *Jaycees*. The court stated that "[i]f the City is allowed to make the public accommodation law requiring Minister Farrakhan to speak to a mixed audience, the content and character of the speech will necessarily be changed." After the decision was announced, Nancy Lesic, spokesperson for Cleveland mayor Michael White, told reporters that "the city did not deny anyone's rights in this case. It is an unlawful and discriminatory practice to deny a person access to a public facility on account of factors such as gender. In this case, women were being denied access to public accommodations."[17] Yet it is difficult to imagine Cleveland similarly trying to force less controversial religious groups like Catholics, Orthodox Jews, or even Orthodox Muslims to hold coed meetings. Religious groups aside, it is also difficult to imagine Cleveland denying access to its convention center to the Junior League, the Girl Scouts, or other popular single-sex organizations.

* * *

Dale leaves many questions unresolved. For example, can for-profit businesses ever claim the right to expressive association in defiance of antidiscrimination laws, or, as Justice O'Connor suggested in her concurrence in *Jaycees*, can the right only be asserted by "primarily expressive" associations? If the latter, how does one determine whether a nonprofit organization is "primarily commercial," as O'Connor thought the Jaycees to be, or primarily expressive? Under what circumstances must courts apply Jaycees' compelling interest test, and when, if ever, does the government have an interest sufficient to overcome the First Amendment's protection of expressive association? Despite these loose ends, the Court's decision in *Dale* is the greatest victory yet won by civil liberties partisans in the conflict between antidiscrimination laws and civil liberties.

The reaction to *Dale*, however, has largely divided along ideological lines. "Conservatives" generally support *Dale*, because in their eyes it prevents government from taking sides in the culture wars. "Progressives," including many liberals who otherwise have strong civil libertarian instincts, oppose *Dale* because it seems to deal a blow to gay rights. Progressives also fear that organizations that wish to discriminate against other groups will rely on *Dale* for constitutional exemptions from antidiscrimination laws.

As a legal matter, however, *Dale* was not about the conflict between gay rights activists and their opponents, nor was it about a general right to discriminate. Rather, the underlying issue in *Dale* was whether a private, nonprofit expressive association has a First Amendment right to discriminate when needed to prevent dilution of its message. Although the right of expressive association can benefit people on either side of the political spectrum, for the past two decades the right has been primarily raised as a defense to antidiscrimination claims by African Americans, women, and especially homosexuals. As a result, left-leaning organizations have typically sought to limit the scope of the constitutional right, while conservatives have been more supportive of the autonomy of private associations. As discussed below, however, the left may soon find that the constitutional right to expressive association has its uses. It may save one of the left's favorite causes—affirmative action preferences at private universities—from interference by the government.

* * *

Dale's protection of the right of expressive association raises the issue of whether nonprofit expressive associations have a constitutional right to engage in race discrimination when needed to avoid dilution of their message. Even before *Dale*, one court recognized that the Ku Klux Klan had a right to discriminate. Thurmont, Maryland, had denied the KKK a parade permit because the Klan refused to allow African Americans to march in its parade. The Klan sued in federal court, and won.[18] The court found that the Klan had a First Amendment right to exclude African Americans to prevent dilution of the Klan's message of racism and white superiority.

In contrast, the New York City Commission on Human Rights ruled that a black separatist organization had no constitutional right to exclude whites from its otherwise public meetings.[19] The Commission acknowledged that the United African Movement had proved "that there is a nexus between its racially discriminatory membership policies and the group's message that Caucasians and people of African descent should not mix." Therefore, forcing the Movement to admit whites to its meetings would dilute the group's message

105

and consequently infringe upon its right to expressive association.[20] The Commission concluded, however, that New York had a compelling interest in eradicating discrimination on the basis of race, an interest that trumped the Movement's First Amendment rights.[21]

Dale resolves the conflict between the Maryland and New York cases in favor of the expressive association rights of racist organizations. To force racist groups to integrate themselves, or even their audiences, would inhibit the ability of such organizations to preach racism at least as much as forcing the Boy Scouts to employ Dale would have interfered with the Scouts' antihomosexual activity message.

Many people are shocked by the idea that any organization—even a pro-racism advocacy group—has a First Amendment right to indulge in race discrimination when necessary to further its message. Yet, as in many other contexts, protecting the First Amendment rights of unpopular, outrageous, and contemptible organizations will ultimately protect the rights of mainstream and forward-thinking organizations as well. Overtly racist organizations are far from the only expressive groups that have an ideology that leads them to discriminate on the basis of race. Private universities almost universally engage in racial preferences in admission. Although the motivation for these preferences is benign—speeding the social and economic integration of racial minority groups—the preferences nevertheless quite literally involve race discrimination. What critics must realize is that if *Dale* protects the right of the Klan to discriminate against African Americans, it also protects the right of private universities to discriminate in their favor.

Racial and ethnic preferences on behalf of African Americans and Latinos are rampant in American academia. According to a study conducted by a supporter of affirmative action, among the most selective and prestigious law schools, 17.5 times as many African American students were admitted in 1991 as academic qualifications alone would have predicted.[22] At the same time, approximately half of all African American matriculants to law school would not have been admitted to any law school purely on the basis of their grade point average and Law School Admission Test scores.[23] Although grades and test scores don't tell the whole story about an applicant, these statistics show that racial preferences in law school admissions clearly go well beyond choosing the minority candidate when two candidates are equally qualified.

The legality of these preferences is dubious. In the famous *Bakke* case,[24] four Supreme Court justices concluded that racial preferences always violate Title VI of the 1964 Civil Rights Act, which bans racial discrimination by schools that receive federal funds, a category that includes almost all American universities. A fifth justice, Lewis Powell, cast the deciding vote. Powell agreed that admissions quotas were illegal, but he concluded that racial preferences were permissible if they were used as a "plus" factor along the lines of other plus factors universities employ to diversify their student bodies.[25]

Some legal authorities, including one federal appellate court,[26] assert that later Supreme Court decisions on racial preferences have overridden *Bakke*, and *all* racial preference programs by public or private universities now violate federal law. Others argue that Justice Powell's opinion in *Bakke*, as the necessary fifth vote on an issue that has not been directly revisited by the Supreme Court, is a binding statement of law, so that using race as a plus factor is still permitted. As of this writing, two cases that will clarify the law are pending before the U.S. Supreme Court. What the Court will certainly *not* do is endorse the legality of quotas.

It seems clear that any limitation on affirmative action decreed by the Court will be met with tacit and perhaps explicit resistance from many universities. Despite *Bakke*'s ban on quotas, for example, many universities continued to implicitly use them. Some universities discreetly violate the law but others do so overtly. For example, the administration of Rice University, a private school, believes that the law in its home state of Texas forbids it from considering the race or ethnicity of its applicants. Yet Rice's director of admissions boasted to the *New York Times* that the school engages in various subterfuges to defy the law. For example, Rice will not officially give a preference to an African American student for being black, but it will give credit for the student's involvement in a high school African American student club. As a result of such gambits, the percentages of African American and Latino students entering Rice barely changed after racial and ethnic preferences were banned.[27] It would be logical to conclude that Rice not only continues to use race as a factor in admissions but also that it uses an implicit quota system.

Schools like Rice will eventually be targeted with reverse discrimination lawsuits. Private universities could respond to such lawsuits by claiming an expressive association exemption to antidiscrimination laws. The administrators of many universities sincerely believe that their schools should teach students the importance of assisting disadvantaged minorities and ensuring racial diversity in the upper echelons of American society. Not unreasonably, the administrators believe that if the law prohibits them from using racial preferences, they will see their schools' classes become overwhelmingly white (and, increasingly, Asian American) and it will become far more difficult to promote their schools' egalitarian ideals to their students. Just as employing Dale would have diluted the Boy Scouts of America's anti–homosexual activity message, forcing private universities to adopt race-neutral admissions policies would dilute their pro-diversity messages.

Moreover, a university that has a racially homogenous class—or faculty—inherently sends a negative or, at best, indifferent message to its students and the public at large about the importance of racial diversity. Engaging in explicit racial preferences to ensure a diverse student population sends the opposite message. To preserve racial preferences, universities can rely on *Dale*'s dictum that the Boy Scouts of America has a First Amendment right to teach "by example," and argue that they too have a right to promote a moral vision unencumbered by government regulation.[28] Conditioning federal funding of universities on the abolition of affirmative action preferences would place what constitutional scholars call an "unconstitutional condition" on that funding.

Some legal scholars argue that the 1976 Supreme Court case of *Runyon v. McCrary*[29] suggests that, despite *Dale*, private universities cannot claim an expressive association right to discriminate on the basis of race. In *Runyon*, the Supreme Court rejected a freedom-of-association defense to a discrimination lawsuit against a whites-only private school. That opinion, and not *Dale*, is claimed by some to be the controlling precedent when expressive association rights conflict with laws banning race discrimination in education.

This understanding of *Runyon* is mistaken, because the *Runyon* defendants did not advance an expressive association argument. Instead, they made a very short, throwaway argument that compelled integration violated their general right to "freedom of association." No such right appears in the Constitution, and the Supreme Court has never recognized a general right of association independent of any expressive goal. The *Runyon* defendants could have argued (but did not) that forced integration violated their First

Amendment rights by impeding their ability to promote segregation to their students.[30] Even that argument would have been problematic, however, because the schools involved in *Runyon* were organized on a commercial basis, and it is not clear whether commercial entities can claim expressive association rights.[31] In short, the *Runyon* Court did not reach the issue of whether a noncommercial private school could successfully defend discriminatory policies as an exercise of expressive association rights.[32] So, *Runyon* does not prevent universities from relying on *Dale* to protect their affirmative action programs from antidiscrimination suits.

If private universities acknowledged that they engage in racial preferences and successfully asserted an expressive association defense to any subsequent legal challenges, the current racial preferences in admissions would continue, but in a much more open and honest fashion. Because universities refuse to acknowledge that they engage in racial preferences, many otherwise well-informed people, including many of the beneficiaries of racial preferences, are unaware of their existence and scope.[33]

Some schools might not be able to successfully defend their racial preferences in the court of public opinion. On the other hand, if universities were more candid in their acknowledgment and defense of racial preferences in admissions, they might be able to develop a stronger constituency in favor of the preferences. Moreover, a frank acknowledgment by elite universities of the difficulty in finding African American (and to a lesser extent, Latino) applicants meeting the schools' regular standards[34] might lead to some useful national soul-searching regarding the inferior educational opportunities given minority students.

* * *

One commentator, writing before the Court's ruling in *Dale*, suggested that "under the First Amendment, discrimination of any kind in choosing one's fellows in the conscience-forming enterprise must be viewed as protected expression."[35] At least with regard to nonprofit, expressive associations, this is now the law of the land. Political progressives have expressed dismay at the ruling in *Dale* and the potential consequences of the decision. Not only did *Dale* deal a blow to the gay rights movement, they complain; now any nonprofit, primarily expressive group with an ideology that requires discrimination may also have a First Amendment right to discriminate regarding membership, employment, and audience to prevent dilution of its message. The left's reaction is understandable. Many organizations with opprobrious ideas *will* evade antidiscrimination laws, using *Dale* as a defense.

On the other hand, protecting the liberty of those with deplorable views also protects one's own liberty. *Dale* may allow the Boy Scouts of America to discriminate against gays, but it should also provide protection for private universities that discriminate in favor of Latino and African American applicants. In short, *Dale*'s protection of the right of expressive association is about preserving pluralism by allowing organizations with diverse viewpoints to flourish. Given the vagaries of politics, where the majority can easily become a minority and vice versa, *Dale*'s protection of ideological diversity should be supported by Americans from all points on the political spectrum.

9. Regulating Religious Schools

The First Amendment protects the free exercise of religion and prohibits governmental establishment of religion, a concept that includes a prohibition on excessive government entanglement with religion. Accordingly, the Constitution prohibits the government from interfering in the hiring and firing of "ministerial" church employees, including clergy and religion teachers at church-sponsored schools.[1] However, courts have held that antidiscrimination laws can still regulate the employment of teachers of secular subjects in religious schools.

One such teacher, Linda Hoskinson, felt a calling to teach in Christian schools so she "could interpret her lessons with feelings [sic] from the Bible."[2] She found employment as a grade school instructor at Dayton Christian Schools, an affiliate of two of Dayton, Ohio's strict fundamentalist churches.[3] DCS sought to employ only teachers who would "carry with them into their classes the religious fervor and conviction felt necessary to stimulate young minds into accepting Christ as savior." Hoskinson seemed to have found her niche. Eventually, however, church doctrine and Hoskinson's personal life came into conflict. When Hoskinson informed the DCS administration that she and her husband were expecting a baby, she was told that her contract would not be renewed. The school's sponsoring churches believe that mothers of young children should not be employed outside of the home, so continuing to employ Hoskinson would flout church doctrine.[4]

Hoskinson consulted an attorney, who informed DCS that it was violating Hoskinson's rights under federal and state antidiscrimination laws, even though DCS had accepted no government funding. DCS responded by immediately firing Hoskinson for violating the "Biblical Chain of Command,"[5] a belief adhered to by some Christian sects, including DCS's sponsors, that all disputes among members of the church should be resolved within the church. Like all DCS employees, Hoskinson had agreed in her contract to abide by the

Biblical Chain of Command, but had broken that agreement when she took her problems with church policy to an outside lawyer.[6]

Hoskinson filed a sex discrimination complaint with the Ohio Civil Rights Commission.[7] The Commission investigated, and urged DCS to sign a settlement agreement that stipulated, among other things, that contrary to DCS's belief in resolving disputes within the church, DCS "shall make clear in its employment contracts that employees may contact the Commission if they believe they are being discriminated against at any time."

When DCS received the proposed agreement, it filed a suit in federal court asking that the court protect DCS's free exercise of religion by prohibiting the Commission from investigating and prosecuting the school. Joining DCS as plaintiffs were the two sponsoring churches, DCS officials, two parents who alleged that the investigation and potential prosecution of DCS "burdens and endangers the ability of parents to choose a religious education for the children," and a teacher who charged that the investigation "endangers the opportunity of religious teachers and administrators to carry out their religious vocation in the Christian formation and education of young people."[8]

The court rejected DCS's free exercise claim, reasoning that the Commission's enforcement of Ohio's antidiscrimination law placed only "a minimal burden" on the plaintiffs' free exercise rights. No mothers with young children would be forced to work; DCS needed only to refrain from firing Hoskinson. The court did not address the plaintiffs' claim that by forcing DCS to employ a teacher who disobeyed church teachings, the law threatened the plaintiffs' ability to impress upon the students the importance of church doctrine. Although the court downplayed the importance of the case to the plaintiffs, it found that the state had a compelling interest in eliminating "all forms of discrimination," and in preventing young people from being educated "in an atmosphere of discrimination."

An appeals court reversed the lower court decision, finding that the Commission's investigation violated the plaintiffs' free exercise rights, and that those rights were not trumped by the government's interest in eradicating discrimination.[9] The Commission appealed to the Supreme Court. Although religious groups filed briefs uniformly supporting DCS, the case divided liberal civil libertarian organizations. The American Civil Liberties Union sided with the Commission, while Americans United for the Separation of Church and

State supported the school's position. "We are firmly opposed to discrimination," AUSCS executive director Robert Maddox said, "but this principle must not override the right of churches or church schools to hire the pastors or teachers they believe can best teach their faith."[10] The Supreme Court ultimately sidestepped the civil liberties issue by reversing the appeals court on the grounds that the federal courts should not have interfered in ongoing state proceedings.[11]

Finally, after DCS had spent more than $100,000 defending itself, Hoskinson dropped her lawsuit. Hoskinson, who in the meantime had given birth to three children, and who had not returned to teaching, was unapologetic. She said, "If a person who is in a religious institution cannot have the protection of the law, then I think we're in for some serious problems, because if they don't have the protection of the law, there's going to be a vacuum there they're just sucked into."[12] Recall, however, that Hoskinson had not been "sucked into" teaching in a school that taught and enforced conservative Christian values, but had actively sought out such an environment.

* * *

Other Christian schools have run afoul of antidiscrimination laws by trying to enforce religious doctrines that guide personal morality. In a virtual replay of the DCS case, the Michigan Supreme Court held that the government's compelling interest in eradicating discrimination trumped the Providence Christian School's claim of a free exercise right to refuse employment to female teachers with young children.[13] Other cases have involved religious schools firing teachers who became pregnant out of wedlock—such pregnancy being compelling evidence of a violation of the schools' religious conviction against premarital intercourse. In these cases, courts agreed that religious schools' "[r]estrictions on pregnancy are not permitted because they are gender discriminatory by definition."[14] In other words, the schools were discriminating by not firing any unmarried pregnant males! The more plausible legal defense for a school that fired an unmarried pregnant teacher would be to somehow persuade the jury that it would also have fired a male teacher who was discovered to have had sex outside of marriage, as this would be evidence of evenhanded treatment. But only a brave (or perhaps foolish) school administrator would risk his school's fiscal health on its attorneys' ability to prove this sort of counterfactual to a jury's satisfaction. The legal standard enunciated by the courts, then, would likely discourage most schools from enforcing their anti-fornication policies.

The standard itself makes little sense. Courts failed to consider that schools might reasonably choose to distinguish between a visibly pregnant female teacher and a male teacher whose fornication has come to the attention of a school's administration but not to the attention of his students. Christian educators could reasonably believe that sins by teachers that remain private can be overlooked, but employing a sinner whose transgressions have become public sends the wrong signal to students. As one Christian education manual states, teachers are expected to be role models. One such manual advises that students "should see in their teachers the Christian attitude and behavior that is often so conspicuously absent from the secular atmosphere in which they live. Without this witness, living in such an atmosphere, they may begin to regard Christian behavior as an impossible ideal."[15] One court stated that if a school was concerned with the effect a teacher's visible pregnancy might have on impressionable high school students, it should have granted her a paid leave of absence during the term of her pregnancy. To fire her for getting pregnant, the court said, was "inviting a sex discrimination lawsuit."[16] Where the typical financially overextended church school might find the money to finance a teacher's paid leave of absence, the court did not say.

* * *

Like their elementary and secondary school counterparts, religious universities have also been subjected to antidiscrimination claims when they tried to enforce their religious traditions. In the mid-1980s, Georgetown University, a Jesuit school in Washington, D.C., refused to extend "university recognition" to two gay student groups. Without university recognition, the groups could not get university funding and were not entitled to office space or a mailbox on campus. University recognition required the approval of the university's administration and was available only to organizations that were likely to be "successful in aiding the university's educational mission in the tradition established by its founders." Although the university permitted the gay groups to meet on university property and to invite guest speakers, the groups were not eligible for university recognition because they flouted Catholic beliefs about sexual ethics.

The groups sued the university for violating the Washington, D.C., Human Rights Act's ban on discrimination against gays.[17] The D.C. Court of Appeals acknowledged that a religious organization such as Georgetown could not be compelled to endorse a student group that encouraged or accepted homosexuality. However, the court found that D.C. law did not require Georgetown to actually endorse or accept the goals of the gay student groups, but merely to extend the same benefits to them that it offered to other student groups. Although D.C. had a compelling interest in eradicating discrimination against gays, the court said, the Act imposed a relatively minor burden on Georgetown's exercise of religion. The court reasoned that the university already provided limited benefits to the gay groups. The additional tangible benefits that would flow from university recognition were "relatively insignificant." Ironically, the fact that Georgetown was generally tolerant of its gay students apparently meant that it received less constitutional protection than would have been granted to a virulently antigay school—a perverse message from a court delivering a lecture on the importance of not discriminating.

Disturbed by the court's ruling, Congress added an exemption for religious organizations to D.C.'s ban on discrimination against gays.[18] But by this time, Georgetown had been so beaten down by a barrage of negative publicity it had received that it had lost the will to defend its restrictions on gay student groups. The university soon modified its rules, allowing any "nonpolitical" student group, including Georgetown's gay organizations, to receive funding and office space.[19]

* * *

South Carolina's Bob Jones University, which is famously sponsored by a strict fundamentalist Christian sect, screens its students for their religious beliefs to ensure compatibility with the school's mission, and the university requires all students to conform to a stringent code of conduct. Until 1971, the university excluded African American students. In 1971, the school, under pressure from federal civil rights authorities, began admitting married African American students. Following a 1975 court ruling requiring private colleges to admit African Americans, the university began admitting unmarried African American students as well. The university, however, contemporaneously banned interracial dating on penalty of expulsion. The university's founders claimed that the policy stemmed from a belief that the Bible prohibits interracial marriage, but others suspected that such explanations were merely a weak pretext for racial discrimination.[20] And then the tax man got involved.

The Internal Revenue Service revoked Bob Jones' tax-exempt status when it concluded that the university's ban on interracial dating constituted discrimination in violation of public policy. The university sued, alleging that because the university was theologically opposed to interracial marriage, the IRS revocation infringed on the university's free exercise of religion. The case reached the Supreme Court, which acknowledged that IRS denial of tax benefits to universities that discriminated on religious grounds would "inevitably have a substantial impact on the operation of private religious schools."[21] However, the Court held that this IRS policy was constitutionally permissible because the burden on universities was substantially outweighed by the government's "fundamental, overriding interest in eradicating racial discrimination in education."

There are legitimate grounds on which to justify the Court's decision in the Bob Jones case, but claiming that statutory antidiscrimination goals have a higher constitutional status than the First Amendment's protection of free exercise of religion, as the Court did in its opinion, is not one of them. Rather, given the university's historic discrimination against African Americans, the Court could reasonably have questioned the sincerity of the university's religious rationale for banning interracial dating.[22] Indeed, the university abruptly gave up its purportedly "sincere religious belief" in banning interracial dating in 2000, after the university came under withering criticism following a visit by presidential candidate George W. Bush. Facing a loss of credibility, and possibly revenue, the university suddenly discovered that its ban on interracial dating was not theologically required, after all.[23]

* * *

Exactly how autonomous religious organizations should be from antidiscrimination laws has been a controversial question for decades. When it considered the 1964 Civil Rights Act, Congress debated how to deal with the potential conflicts with religious freedom that could arise under the act. Congress ultimately decided to exempt religious organizations from Title VII's prohibition against discrimination in employment, but only under narrow circumstances: when the discrimination is based on religion and the organization is engaging in religious activities.[24] A 1972 amendment to the Civil Rights Act broadened this exemption so that it applied to religious organizations even when they were engaged in nonreligious activities.[25]

The Supreme Court upheld this provision against an Establishment Clause challenge in a case involving an employee of a Mormon church-owned gymnasium who was fired for failing to abide by church doctrine.[26] The employee claimed that his dismissal constituted discrimination on the basis of religion, and that the religious organization exemption was an unconstitutional establishment of religion. The Court disagreed, finding that the exemption was an appropriate accommodation of religion by the government, not an illicit endorsement of religion.

Title VII's religious exemption remains limited in scope. Most courts, for example, have held that engaging in sex discrimination—even for religious reasons as in the DCS case—is not covered by the exemption. Courts consistently reject arguments from church defendants that they fired female employees who violated church doctrine over such issues as childbearing and child-rearing not because the employees were women, but because they had strayed from the church's religious teachings. Meanwhile, some states' employment discrimination laws, which are enforced on top of federal law, grant no religious exemptions at all.[27]

For many years, religious organizations and, to a lesser extent, individuals sought shelter from the mandates of antidiscrimination laws by relying on the free exercise clause of the First Amendment, as interpreted in the 1963 case of *Sherbert v. Verner.*[28] In *Sherbert*, the Supreme Court dealt with the issue of generally applicable laws, such as antidiscrimination laws, that only incidentally interfere with the free exercise of religion. The Court held that free exercise rights trump such laws, unless the law in question serves a "compelling governmental interest." In practice, this seemingly strict test was subsequently enforced so laxly that it provided religious organizations minimal protection from antidiscrimination laws.[29] In 1990, the Supreme Court abandoned the compelling interest test, ruling instead that a generally applicable law that incidentally interferes with the free exercise of religion does not violate free exercise rights.[30] Religious groups now receive no effective federal constitutional free exercise protection from antidiscrimination laws.

Religious organizations can, however, look elsewhere for protection. The Religious Freedom Restoration Act,[31] passed by Congress in 1993, revived the compelling interest test that had been nixed for constitutional purposes in 1990. RFRA provides that laws could substantially burden the exercise of religion only if they constituted the least restrictive means of furthering a compelling governmental interest. Although the Supreme Court held RFRA unconstitutional as to state legislation because it was beyond the power of Congress to force states to define religious freedom so broadly,[32] most courts have held that the RFRA still applies to federal legislation.[33] Many states have passed their own versions of RFRA,[34] and several state supreme courts have interpreted their state constitutions' free exercise clauses as demanding adherence to the compelling interest test. Some of these states have more clearly protected free exercise by adopting a narrow definition of what constitutes a "compelling interest."[35]

An even more important development is that religious organizations seeking a constitutional exemption from antidiscrimination laws can now rely on the right of expressive association. In the 2000 case of *Boy Scouts of America v. Dale* (see Chapter 8), the Supreme Court held that nonprofit, ideological organizations have a First Amendment expressive association right to set employment and membership policies consistent with their beliefs, even if antidiscrimination laws would normally make such policies illegal. *Dale* therefore implies that Christian schools like Dayton Christian Schools have an expressive association right to refuse to employ teachers who behave contrary to church doctrine; that Christian universities like Georgetown have an expressive association right to refuse to fund gay advocacy organizations; and that schools that have a religiously based racist outlook like Bob Jones claimed to have, have the right to discriminate based on race.[36] *Dale*, in short, is likely to protect religious schools from having their free exercise rights violated by courts and agencies acting to enforce antidiscrimination laws.

However, there are still some conflicts between religious freedom and antidiscrimination laws that *Dale* cannot resolve. For example, *Dale* only protects the rights of nonprofit associations, so parties that do not fit into that category, such as the religious landlords described in the next chapter, must either fall back on legislative exemption from antidiscrimination laws or on judicial enforcement of the compelling interest test to protect their freedom to exercise their religion.

10. Religious Landlords: Antidiscrimination Law as a Weapon in the Culture Wars

Paul Desilets and his wife Louise own 23 apartment units in Turners Falls, Massachusetts. The Desiletses are devout Roman Catholics who try to live according to their beliefs. Louise, for example, directs Sunday school at Our Lady of Czestochowa Church and works as a hospice visiting nurse, comforting dying patients. The Desiletses believe that renting an apartment to an unmarried couple would violate Catholic doctrine by facilitating fornication.[1] Paul told the *Seattle Times* that "allowing fornication to occur on property I own places my eternal soul at risk."[2]

The Desiletses' lives changed the day Cynthia Tarail asked Paul about renting an apartment she intended to share with her boyfriend, Mark Lattanzi. According to Tarail, Paul asked if she intended to marry Lattanzi. When she replied that she was unsure, he told her, "Then you'd be living in sin, and we don't go for that. Don't you know it's a criminal act to cohabitate and fornicate?"[3] Paul acknowledges that he rebuffed Tarail but claims he politely informed her of his policy against renting to unmarried couples.

The couple filed a complaint with the Massachusetts Commission Against Discrimination, alleging discrimination on the basis of marital status, and the state attorney general filed suit against the Desiletses. Tarail, a graduate student in social work, described her politics as "very left." "I'm a feminist and a socialist," she told the *Boston Herald*, "and our motivation here is not to stick up for unmarried couples but for tenants' rights. We believe strongly that housing is a right, not a privilege."[4] Lattanzi, a local coordinator for an antihousing discrimination organization, expressed his disgust that "the Desilets seem to think their religious beliefs allow them to discriminate." "Housing is a commodity, like anything else," Lattanzi told the media.[5] Paul Desilets responded, "Must everything today come

121

down to strictly economic terms, the lowest common denominator? Can't we raise our sights and deal with larger issues? We have laws that say I can't smoke in a public building, but people are allowed to fornicate on my property. Don't I have rights, too?"[6]

The trial court held that the Desiletses had violated the Massachusetts fair housing law, but found that the state constitution's protection of religious freedom from government interference precluded enforcing the statute against them. When the case was appealed to the state supreme court, three of the seven justices voted to affirm the lower court's ruling. In dissent, they argued that "[n]either the court nor the Legislature can constitutionally give preference or priority to a so-called 'right' of cohabitation over the . . . guarantees of the free exercise of religion."[7]

A four-justice majority, however, sent the case back to the trial court for further consideration of whether the fair housing statute could properly infringe on religious liberty. The majority opinion acknowledged that the statutory rights of Lattanzi and Tarail were of a "lower order" than the constitutional rights of the Desiletses, and the court strongly hinted that it expected the lower court to once again rule in the Desiletses' favor. The supreme court stated, for example, that it could not conclude that the "simple enactment of the prohibition against discrimination based on marital status" established that the comonwealth had a compelling interest in ending such discrimination.[8] The majority added that to find for the state on remand, the lower court would need to find that Massachusetts had a specific compelling interest not just in combatting discrimination in general, but also "in the elimination of discrimination in housing against an unmarried man and an unmarried women who have a sexual relationship" and wish to rent housing together. The Massachusetts attorney general's office read between the lines and dropped the case, purportedly for lack of resources, but it warned that it reserved the right to prosecute other landlords who refused to rent to unmarried couples for religious reasons.[9]

The Desilets case is one of several in which unmarried heterosexual couples, hardly a beleaguered minority group, have charged religious landlords with discrimination for refusing to rent to them. Columnist George Will calls this "the latest twist in the trivialization of the 'civil rights' movement."[10] In fact, as the Desilets case illustrates, these cases represent an even worse phenomenon—the use of antidiscrimination laws as a weapon in the "culture wars" between the secular left and the religious right.

While their case was being decided by the state supreme court, Lattanzi and Tarail married, but they declined to drop their claim. They told the media, "Some people have said, 'If you're getting married, what's the big deal.' But that's not the issue. We don't want people telling us we have to be married. We want to be married when WE want to be."[11] This suggests that the couple's underlying complaint was not that they were denied needed housing, but that the Desiletses dared to disapprove of their living arrangements and had acted on that disapproval. The goal of Lattanzi, Tarail, and other cohabiting couples who sue religious landlords seems to have less to do with combating invidious discrimination—because unlike, say, African Americans in the 1960s, these couples can almost always find alternative housing quite easily—and more to do with trying to punish religious conservatives for refusing to accommodate liberal secular values. It is not so much a case of "you've prevented me from finding a place to live," as it is a case of "you've acted in a politically incorrect way and now you're going to pay."

* * *

Anchorage, Alaska, landlord Tom Swanner lost his free exercise claim when he faced marital status discrimination charges for refusing to rent to three unmarried couples. After both a hearing examiner and a trial court ruled against Swanner, he appealed to the state supreme court.[12] The court found that the verdict against Swanner could be upheld only if the state could demonstrate a compelling interest sufficient to overcome Swanner's free exercise rights.[13] Swanner insisted that Alaska's interest in prohibiting discrimination against unmarried couples could not possibly be compelling, given that the state itself discriminated in favor of married couples in a variety of other contexts. The court disagreed, ruling that "[b]ecause Swanner's religiously impelled actions trespass on the private right of unmarried couples to not be unfairly discriminated against in housing, he cannot be granted an exemption from the housing antidiscrimination laws." The circularity of this reasoning is evident; the court essentially reasoned that statutory antidiscrimination rights override free exercise rights because . . . they do. The court ordered Swanner to pay $1,000 plus all of the plaintiffs' legal costs.

The U.S. Supreme Court declined to review the case, sparking a vigorous dissent from Justice Clarence Thomas.[14] At the time, the Religious Freedom Restoration Act, later invalidated as to its applicability to the states by the Court on constitutional grounds (see Chapter 9), suggested that Swanner had a federal statutory right to discriminate on the basis of religion unless the government could show it had a compelling interest in quashing the discrimination. Thomas wrote that "if, despite affirmative discrimination by Alaska on the basis of marital status and a complete absence of a national policy against such discrimination, the State's asserted interest in this case is allowed to qualify as a 'compelling' interest—that is, a 'paramount' interest, an interest 'of the highest order'—then I am at a loss to know what asserted governmental interests are not compelling."

* * *

Few laws explicitly protect unmarried couples from housing discrimination.[15] Some jurisdictions do ban discrimination on the basis of marital status, but this bar was intended to aid recently divorced women who sometimes find it difficult to find housing because they have not established their own credit histories. Such bans on discrimination based on marital status arguably do not apply to landlords who willingly rent to single individuals but not to unmarried couples. After all, landlords who refuse to rent only to unmarried couples are not discriminating on the basis of the prospective tenants' marital status—such landlords would be perfectly willing to rent to these same prospective tenants individually—but on the basis of what the landlords perceive as immoral *conduct*.[16]

Several courts have nevertheless held that laws prohibiting marital status discrimination protect unmarried couples. The Minnesota Supreme Court is a rare but welcome exception. Layle French of Marshall, Minnesota, bought a new house for his family. Rather than selling his previous residence right away, he decided to rent it out until the real estate market picked up. He found a couple interested in the house and agreed to rent it to them, but then reneged on the agreement when he discovered that they were not married. French, a Sunday school teacher at a conservative Lutheran church, believed that premarital sex is a sin and that renting his house to an unmarried couple would aid in the commission of that sin or would at least create "the appearance of evil." The rejected couple hired an attorney.

The state filed suit against French after the couple's attorney complained that French had "illegally attempted to enforce his religious prejudices concerning marital status on the marketplace," and was thus "guilty of violating the couple's civil rights." French recognized that he was a combatant in the culture wars. "They're pretty consistent in telling us that we can't push our religion on somebody else," French remarked, "Meanwhile, they are trying to push their beliefs on us."[17] An administrative law judge found that French had violated the Minnesota Human Rights Act and fined him over $1,000. In a four-to-three decision, the state supreme court reversed, holding that the act's prohibition on discrimination based on marital status did not extend to discrimination against unmarried heterosexual couples.[18]

Even if a fair housing law does protect unmarried heterosexual couples from discrimination, landlords may still have a federal or state constitutional right to follow the dictates of their consciences. As discussed previously (see Chapter 9), under federal constitutional precedent a religious believer usually cannot claim a free exercise exemption from general laws that happen to impinge on his religious beliefs. A three-judge panel of the Ninth Circuit Court of Appeals, however, held that fair housing laws that impinge on landlords' religious beliefs are an exception to this rule, because the laws also impinge on associational freedoms and property rights.[19] The Ninth Circuit noted that the Supreme Court has held that when a litigant asserts a "hybrid" constitutional defense that joins a free exercise claim with an assertion of other constitutional rights (such as those protecting property and association), the law in question cannot be enforced unless it serves a compelling governmental interest. The Ninth Circuit panel concluded that there "is simply no support from any quarter for recognizing a compelling government interest in eradicating marital-status discrimination."[20] The court, therefore, held that a landlord has a constitutional right to refuse to rent to unmarried couples for religious reasons. An opportunity to see whether the Supreme Court agreed with the panel's ruling was lost when the full Ninth Circuit reversed the panel's opinion on procedural grounds.[21]

Regardless of federal precedents, many state courts interpret their state constitutions as requiring them to apply the compelling interest test to general laws—including fair housing laws—that impinge on religious freedom. Three members of the majority in the French case, discussed earlier, stated that even if the statute applied to unmarried couples, French's right to exercise his religion under the freedom of conscience provision of Minnesota's constitution outweighed any interest of potential tenants to cohabitate before marriage.

The three dissenters, however, concluded that combating any type of invidious discrimination in housing is an overriding compelling state interest that trumps religious freedom. They justified this view on the grounds that "housing is a basic human need regardless of a person's personal characteristics" and "an individual's marital or familial status ... is irrelevant to ... renting a house, because it bears no relation to the individual's ability to participate in and contribute to society." The dissenters, alluding to America's history of racial segregation, accused the majority of advocating a return to the days of "separate but equal," during which individuals could keep "undesirables" out of their neighborhoods. Demonstrating an incredible lack of perspective, the dissenters argued that discrimination against the unmarried is no less invidious than discrimination against African Americans. The court ignored the fact that being an unmarried couple is a lifestyle choice, not an immutable characteristic like race, and that unmarried couples have not suffered centuries of slavery and persecution. Moreover, since marriage is widely regarded to be beneficial to society and especially to children, discrimination against cohabitating couples, to the extent it encourages them to get married, may actually serve the public interest.

* * *

But what happens when a court decides to focus on how hard it would be for the landlord to avoid discriminating rather than on how compelling the government's interest is in ending the discrimination? The California Supreme Court gave the free exercise issue this interesting twist in a case involving Evelyn Smith, an elderly widow who owned two duplexes in Chico, California, and offered the four apartments for rent.[22] Two tenants gave Smith, a devout Presbyterian, a rental deposit, claiming they were married. When Smith discovered the tenants had lied and were actually single, she returned the deposit. The couple sued and won $454 in compensatory damages and $500 for emotional distress.

126

On appeal, the state supreme court addressed Smith's claim to a religious exemption. Instead of focusing on whether the government's interest was compelling, the court applied a "substantial burden" test, stating that if the law imposed a substantial burden on Smith's free exercise of religion, she would be entitled to an exemption. The court concluded that prohibiting marital status discrimination did not substantially burden Smith's practice of religion because she could voluntarily avoid the conflict without sacrificing her religious beliefs and "without threatening her livelihood, by selling her units and redeploying the capital in other investments." The court, while still purporting to apply the substantial burden test, then disingenuously slipped in other considerations. It found that requiring a landlord to rent to unmarried couples is a relatively insubstantial burden on the landlord's religious freedom because allowing the landlord to rent only to married couples would affect the rights of third parties (that is, the unmarried couples who could not rent). The court did not, and obviously could not, explain how a burden on free exercise somehow diminishes merely because third parties are affected.

* * *

State supreme courts seem to be growing less sympathetic to discrimination claims by cohabiting couples. In 1997, the Illinois Supreme Court summarily reversed a lower court ruling that a religious landlord had no constitutional right to discriminate against an unmarried cohabitating couple.[23] The lower court had found that the government's compelling interest in eradicating discrimination trumped the landlord's free exercise rights.

An even more dramatic reversal occurred in Michigan. Plaintiffs Kristal McCready and Keith Kerr, a cohabiting couple, had sought to rent an apartment from landlord John Hoffius, but he refused them as tenants for reasons of religious conscience. McCready and Kerr soon found another apartment, but they nevertheless filed suit in state court against Hoffius for marital status discrimination. The trial court ruled in Hoffius' favor, finding that the legislature could not possibly have meant to include unmarried couples in the class of people protected under Michigan's fair housing law, because cohabitation remained officially illegal in Michigan. Hoffius not only had the right to refuse to rent to McCready and Kerr, he could have reported them to the police. The state court of appeals affirmed.[24]

The Michigan Supreme Court, however, reversed, noting that the state anti-cohabitation law had not been enforced for decades. The court added that to the extent requiring Hoffius to rent to unmarried couples infringed on his free exercise rights, the infringement was justified under the compelling interest test, the applicable test under the Michigan constitution.[25] Instead of engaging in an independent review of whether combating housing discrimination against unmarried couples is a compelling interest, the court deferred to the state legislature. The court explained that the compelling interest test was satisfied because "[t]he Michigan Legislature has determined that the need for housing is so fundamental as to necessitate the passing of the Civil Rights Act." Meanwhile, Hoffius's "fundamental"—and constitutionally protected—right to exercise his religious beliefs got short shrift. If Hoffius did not want to obey housing discrimination law, the court admonished, he should get out of the real estate business.

The court ordered the case remanded to the trial court for a trial to determine damages. McCready and Kerr, who had suffered no monetary damages and who were comfortably installed in another rental unit, claimed to be suffering from "emotional distress" because Hoffius had refused to rent to them. Hoffius was also potentially liable for the couple's attorneys' fees, which totaled more than $30,000. Before the damages case could be heard in the trial court, however, Hoffius filed a motion for rehearing. In the meantime, an election cycle had passed and new justices had joined the supreme court, including two justices who had decided in favor of Hoffius when they were lower court judges. Hoffius was in luck (or perhaps his prayers were answered). The supreme court granted the motion for rehearing and reversed its earlier ruling without published discussion.[26]

* * *

In the late 1990s, judicial decisions holding that landlords could refuse to rent to unmarried couples on religious grounds destroyed a broad coalition, ranging from religious conservatives to liberal civil liberties groups, that was seeking to enhance legislative protections for religious liberties. The coalition had been lobbying for congressional passage of a successor to the Religious Freedom Restoration Act, the Religious Liberty Protection Act, which would have evaded prior Supreme Court decisions and required courts to apply a compelling interest test when laws infringed on religious liberty. But some liberal groups, most prominently the American Civil Liberties Union, were appalled by the decisions upholding landlords' free exercise rights despite the government's assertion of its "compelling interest" in preventing discrimination.

The ACLU and other prominent civil libertarian groups supported the RLPA in principle. ACLU legislative counsel Christopher Anders testified in Congress that the RLPA would correct erroneous Supreme Court opinions that had construed the Constitution's guarantee of free exercise of religion too narrowly.[27] The ACLU nevertheless felt compelled to oppose the RLPA because its religious exemptions would inevitably extend to antidiscrimination laws. Anders expressed particular concern that recent case law suggested that the RLPA would permit religious landlords to evade laws requiring them to rent to unmarried heterosexual couples. He also worried that laws protecting homosexuals, and perhaps other groups, from discrimination would also be weakened to some degree by the RLPA.[28] But Anders and the ACLU never answered the $64,000 question: Why does an organization purportedly devoted to civil liberties believe that the constitutionally protected right to free exercise of religion should be trumped by antidiscrimination laws?

The ACLU and its allies insisted that the RLPA be amended to exempt antidiscrimination laws from its scope, but conservative groups refused to compromise on this issue. Left-wing groups then abandoned the coalition, effectively killing the legislation. Nathan Diament, director of the Union of Orthodox Jewish Congregations of America's Institute of Public Affairs, decried allegations by some coalition dropouts "that right-wing religious groups were supporting RLPA in order to further their political agenda." Diament accused coalition defectors of being fair-weather friends of religious freedom, stating that "[t]he real test of religious liberty is kind of like the real test of free speech. You defend the right of people even if they're politically incorrect. You really believe in religious liberty if you protect people whose religious views you disagree with.'"[29]

Despite criticism from Diament and others, civil liberties groups are increasingly unwilling to defend religious freedom when the price is a narrowing of antidiscrimination laws. These groups tend to consider all antidiscrimination laws, even trivial laws like those banning discrimination against unmarried heterosexual couples, as more important than the right to free exercise of religion. After several liberal Jewish civil libertarian groups abandoned the pro-RLPA coalition because of concerns about its effect on antidiscrimination law, an unhappy Marc Stern of the American Jewish Congress attacked their implicit idolatry: "The principle of equality is taking on a quasi-religious status," he complained, "Maybe for some people questioning civil rights is like questioning God."[30]

11. The Right to Privacy and the Right to Be Left Alone

Ann Hacklander-Ready rented a four-bedroom house in Madison, Wisconsin, and sublet three of the bedrooms to female housemates. After two housemates moved out, Hacklander-Ready and her remaining housemate, Maureen Rowe, looked for replacements. They initially accepted a rent deposit from a woman named Caryl Sprague, whom they knew to be a lesbian. Upon further reflection, however, Hacklander-Ready and Rowe decided they were not comfortable sharing their living space with a lesbian, and they returned Sprague's deposit.

Sprague responded by filing a discrimination complaint against both Hacklander-Ready and Rowe with the Madison Civil Rights Commission. Sprague's claim relied on Madison's fair housing ordinance, which did not, on its face, indicate whether it applied to roommates. Hacklander-Ready and Rowe argued that it didn't; an administrative law judge decided that it did. The judge awarded Sprague $2,000 for emotional distress, $1,000 for punitive damages, and $300 for the security deposit she lost trying to secure another apartment, along with costs and attorney's fees. Rowe settled, but Hacklander-Ready, convinced that her civil liberties were being violated, appealed.

On appeal, the court agreed that the fair housing ordinance applied to Caryl Sprague's roommate situation. This result was remarkable, because shortly after Sprague filed her discrimination complaint, the Madison City Council had amended the housing ordinance to clarify that "[n]othing in this ordinance shall affect any person's decision to share occupancy of a lodging room, apartment or dwelling unit with another person or persons." The city council was speaking directly to the Sprague case and making clear its support of Hacklander-Ready and Rowe's right to discriminate. The appellate court, however, refused to consider this amendment in resolving the ambiguity in the original law. The court also rejected

Hacklander-Ready's argument that penalizing her for refusing to accept a lesbian housemate violated her constitutional rights to privacy and freedom of intimate association. The court held that these rights apply only in the "home or family" and that Hacklander-Ready gave up these rights when she "rented housing for profit." The court did not explain how living with housemates to defray rental expenses and make ends meet constitutes renting housing "for profit."[1]

The Wisconsin and U.S. Supreme Courts declined to hear further appeals.[2] Meanwhile, the Madison Civil Rights Commission determined that Hacklander-Ready was liable for the more than $23,000 in lawyers' fees Sprague had racked up over the course of the litigation, because the local antidiscrimination ordinance forced losing defendants to pay plaintiffs' expenses.[3] Hacklander-Ready paid dearly for trying to defend her rights.

Nor were Hacklander-Ready's troubles unique. In May 1999, Melissa DeSantis, a young Filipina-American from San Jose, California, placed a sign in her window seeking a roommate to sublet the available bedroom in her two-bedroom apartment.[4] Eric Campbell, an African American man, came to look at the room. Campbell, who was living at the Aconda Hotel at the time, complained that the rent was too high, that the bedroom was too small, and that he couldn't afford to pay the $150 security deposit upfront. He then asked to see the other, larger, room. DeSantis explained that the other room was her room, and was not for rent. For some reason, Campbell was disturbed by DeSantis's honest answer, and he belligerently insisted on seeing the unavailable room, only relenting when DeSantis informed him that her boyfriend was in that room.

Campbell apparently became convinced that DeSantis had refused to show him the larger room because he was black. He contacted Project Sentinel, a nonprofit group that investigates allegations of housing discrimination. The group sent two "testers" to the apartment, a white man and an African American man, to see if they could uncover any discrimination. DeSantis seemed inclined to rent to the white tester, but when the African American tester later inquired about what had become of his application, DeSantis claimed she did not know. DeSantis also offhandedly told the white tester, in regard to another prospective tenant, "Actually, I don't really like black guys. I try to be fair and all, but they scare me."

Armed with this information, Campbell turned the matter into a complaint with the California Fair Housing Commission. The Commission found that his testimony, which made various claims of discriminatory treatment, was internally inconsistent and not credible. The Commission further concluded that he had not been qualified to rent the room, because DeSantis had insisted that her roommate pay in advance the first month's rent and a security deposit, which Campbell could not afford. The Commission therefore found that Campbell was not the victim of illegal discrimination.

The Commission nevertheless awarded Campbell $240 in costs for the pay he lost for attending the hearing and $500 for emotional distress damages; Campbell had testified that when he learned of DeSantis's statement to the tester that she was afraid of black men, he had become upset because he felt he had been judged on the basis of his color. In other words, the Commission ultimately forced DeSantis to pay Campbell for losing work time to pursue a failed claim of housing discrimination and for having his feelings hurt by a comment she made to a "tester" employed specifically to discover such emotionally upsetting information. Strange logic, indeed.

This outcome seems even stranger when one considers that California's fair housing law explicitly exempts persons seeking "boarders" or "roomers" in a single-family house and says nothing about roommates in an apartment, apparently because the drafters did not imagine that the law might ever be applied to such a situation. So that the matter would fall under the law, the Commission treated DeSantis as if she occupied a single-family house, an inaccuracy which nevertheless would normally mean that she was exempt from the fair housing law because she was seeking a "roomer." However, the Commission refused DeSantis this exemption because it only applies to persons who comply with another provision of the law making it "unlawful for a person to make any statement with respect to the rental of a housing accommodation that indicates any preference, limitation, or discrimination based on race." The Commission found that DeSantis had violated this provision with her statement that she didn't like and was scared of black men.

Given constitutional constraints, one hardly expects that a person could be subject to liability for refusing to share an apartment with someone, much less be fined because of an offhand remark made in private conversation. Indeed, the Commission acknowledged in a footnote that "this case raises significant issues of the constitutional protections of freedom of speech and the right to privacy and association." However, according to the Commission, as an administrative agency, it did not have power to declare a statute unenforceable on the basis of its being unconstitutional. This understanding of the Commission's responsibilities, though apparently settled law, is at odds with the accepted notion that all government officials are required to ensure that they act within constitutional strictures. If California law requires the Commission to ignore the federal Constitution, that law is itself unconstitutional. Overall, the Commission's ruling is consistent with the unfortunate tendency of administrative agencies charged with enforcing antidiscrimination laws to expansively interpret the laws and narrowly interpret constitutional rights.

* * *

Although federal, state, and local fair housing laws generally permit discrimination in selecting roommates or housemates, they still prohibit advertisers from mentioning their discriminatory preferences, except for specifying gender.[5] The result is that persons who place classified ads for roommates waste their time, as well as the time of many of those who respond to their ads, by inviting and dealing with inquiries from persons who fail to meet the actual "discriminatory" criteria.

The advertising restriction can be particularly onerous in jurisdictions that ban housing discrimination on the basis of criteria beyond the standard categories of race, sex, religion, and age covered by federal law. For example, Washington, D.C., fair housing law prohibits discrimination on the basis of sexual orientation or political affiliation. In 1998, the Fair Housing Council of Greater Washington sued the *Washington City Paper* for publishing real estate advertisements for roommates and housemates that expressed illegal preferences. Among the examples of illicit advertisements raised in the complaint were the following:

- seeking a gay male to share two-bedroom, one-bath condo
- gay female seeking another gay female to share a house
- housemate needed for a spacious 30ish group house
- housemate needed, no pets, no Republicans
- women-of-color group house seeking a new member
- Jewish cooperative home starting[6]

Some of these ads represent attempts by members of minority groups to find housemates who share the same subculture; others express a desire to live with people of like-minded political views or who are at the same stage in life. In most of these cases, an advertisement that didn't specify the relevant discriminatory preferences would be nearly useless, because the advertisers would be inundated by calls from disfavored heterosexuals, gentiles, 20-year-olds, and so forth. The suit made little sense, but the *City Paper* appears to have capitulated; recent issues do not contain ads stating discriminatory preferences. This puts a great burden on persons with idiosyncratic roommate preferences: District of Columbia residents seeking to establish a group house for gay Jewish Libertarian women of color must either find new housemates by word of mouth or be willing to sift through the random mix of would-be renters that respond to a more generalized ad. Because of the advertisement restrictions, some persons may never be able to find roommates who match their preferences. Such governmental intrusion on the ability to form a relationship as intimate and private as the relationship between people who share living space is unjustifiable.

* * *

Approximately two million American women belong to women-only health clubs.[7] Some women, such as those with religious objections to wearing revealing clothes in front of men, and abuse survivors who find it traumatic to display their bodies in front of unfamiliar men, use these clubs by necessity.[8] Other women join these clubs to avoid unwanted male attention while they exercise. Still others, including overweight women and women who have had mastectomies, feel much less self-conscious exercising in an all-female environment. The owner of one women's health club boasts, "I like to think we're for real women. We don't have everyone looking like a Barbie doll. They're average size and shape. And we don't let men in. We say, 'No men, no mirrors, no kids.'"[9] The owner of a club that holds women-only aerobics classes explains, "It's a privacy issue. The women are sweating, they don't have makeup on, and they feel that the guys are staring at their butts."[10]

Some women find men to be a distraction when they go to coed gyms. Cynthia Parziale, director of research and development at the Naturally Women chain of fitness centers, opines, "If you're really serious about your workout, it's distracting to have people of the opposite sex around. Women will spend time getting dressed or fixing their hair or putting on their lipstick before they come to the gym. The coolest thing about a women's gym is you can be ugly."[11] Joan Pirone, who patronizes a women-only exercise club in Anchorage, Alaska, told CNN that "at coed clubs you feel like you're on TV, like the men are constantly looking at you. Some women enjoy the attention from men, but some of us are intimidated by it. I'm glad I have the choice of going to a women-only gym."[12]

Other users of women's health clubs find that the women-only facilities are cleaner and smell better than coed gyms. Women's clubs also often emphasize the workout equipment that is used more frequently by women, and many even have special equipment built for women. The two women-only clubs in Anchorage, for example, have smaller-than-average Nautilus machines designed for women's bodies, with the weight stacks increasing by 3-pound increments instead of the usual 10. Women-only clubs also emphasize educational programs focusing on women's health concerns, such as preventing osteoporosis and losing weight gained during pregnancy.[13]

Despite their popularity and the privacy interests served by allowing women to work out free from male oglers, women-only clubs have sometimes run afoul of state laws banning sex discrimination in public accommodations. In 1988, the noted feminist attorney Gloria Allred filed a sex discrimination lawsuit on behalf of a Los Angeles man who was denied admission to a women's health club.[14] Allred dismissed the concerns of women who join all-women gyms to avoid male ogling. She contended that the idea that all men ogle is a stereotype and that men who misbehave can be excluded from sex-integrated clubs on a case-by-case basis.[15] Yet common experience suggests that heterosexual men are inclined to "check out" women, particularly women wearing skimpy shorts or tight leotards. Further, Allred did not explain how a club would enforce or prevent an anti-ogling policy on an individual basis. It would be very different to actually prove the subtle act of a man evaluating a woman's body (Mr. Jones, *please* stop undressing Ms. Smith with your eyes), and sensitive women could very well feel ogled whether or not it was actually happening. Despite these arguments, the Los Angeles club ultimately agreed to settle Allred's lawsuit and began admitting men.[16] Successful lawsuits against women-only gyms in Minnesota; Orange County; California; and Wisconsin followed.[17]

Happily, the tide seems to have turned against applying sex discrimination laws to the membership policies of gyms. In 1997, a Massachusetts trial court ruled that a women-only health club, Healthworks Fitness Center, could not exclude men.[18] The decision was met with dismay by the 40,000 female members of that and other such clubs throughout Massachusetts. Despite the National Organization for Women's objections, legislators responded to a flood of protests from angry female exercise enthusiasts by exempting single-sex health clubs from Massachusetts's public accommodations law.[19] Since then, Alaska, Colorado, Hawaii, Illinois, New Jersey, and Tennessee have also passed laws specifically permitting single-sex health clubs, catering to either sex.[20]

The federal Equal Employment Opportunity Commission, meanwhile, has sued women's health clubs for refusing to hire male employees. The most significant case involved the Women's Workout World chain of fitness clubs in the Chicago, Illinois, metropolitan area.[21] After a showing that the chain hired only women, a federal judge granted summary judgment to the EEOC's claim of employment discrimination. In response, Women's Workout World filed a motion for reconsideration supported by a petition signed by more than 10,000 club members.[22] In support of its motion, the chain noted that it specialized in individual attention for its members and that its members did not want men touching them during workouts or seeing them disrobed in the locker room.

The judge concluded that Women's Workout World had articulated a legitimate privacy interest with regard to nudity and withdrew the summary judgment, but he allowed the case to continue. After seven years of crippling litigation expenses, Women's Workout World settled. The company agreed to hire men for certain restructured positions that would (hopefully) maintain members' privacy, and to pay $30,000 to men who had been turned down for jobs. Other all-women clubs have also fought and sometimes lost sex discrimination lawsuits filed by men who were refused employment.[23]

* * *

As workplace use of and reliance on e-mail grows, employers are spending more and more energy monitoring and regulating their employees' e-mails and other computer communications to avoid potential liability under hostile environment law.[24] Even if antidis-crimination law were not a factor, employers would engage in a certain level of monitoring and regulation to ensure that their work-ers were not frittering away the workday instant-messaging their friends and Web surfing. But many employers are going well beyond what is needed to maximize productivity, and are using sophisti-cated surveillance tools to monitor employee e-mail to head off potential discrimination complaints.[25] One-quarter of all large corpo-rations, for example, perform keyword or phrase searches to censor employee e-mails, usually looking for sexual, scatological, or racist language.[26]

Employers are using these techniques in response to a wave of hostile environment lawsuits brought by women and others who either received sexually suggestive e-mails, or who were simply offended to discover that their coworkers had swapped such e-mails among themselves.[27] Almost every hostile environment case contains allegations of offensive workplace e-mails.[28] While it is true that few hostile environment cases succeed solely on the basis of allegations that a corporate defendant tolerated offensive e-mails, such e-mails do hostile environment defendants no favors, so it is most sensible to prohibit them completely. As a leading First Amendment scholar points out, as long as e-mails can be used as part of a hostile environ-ment claim, "the cautious employer must restrict each individual instance of such speech. . . . The employer must say, 'Do not circulate *any* material, even isolated items, that anyone might find racially, religiously, or sexually offensive, since put together such material may lead to liability.'"[29]

When employees are caught using offensive language by software filters or other monitoring devices, they often find that the breach of their privacy is not the worst of their worries. They may also be out of a job. The *New York Times*, for example, fired 20 staffers for sending inappropriate and offensive e-mail. The company "cited a need to protect itself against liability for sexual harassment claims."[30] Jobs are at risk even when no third parties are involved, as two executives at Smith Barney discovered when the company dismissed them for accessing pornography at work and transmitting it between themselves. Although this might seem like excessive punishment, if a company looks the other way, or even lets its workers off with a stern warning, future plaintiffs in sexual harassment suits could use that tolerance as evidence that the company had a lax sexual harassment prevention policy.[31] The looming threat of a hostile environment suit makes terminating an employee who e-mailed the wrong thing the most prudent course.

* * *

Discrimination lawsuits typically proceed with little regard for the privacy interests of the defendant, or even those of third parties not directly involved in the claim. This is an inevitable result of some types of discrimination claims. For example, if a female employee sues a company alleging that she received lower pay than similarly qualified male coworkers, in depositions and at trial the defendant will be forced to directly compare the plaintiff's performance and pay to that of any men with analogous responsibilities. The defendant may also find it useful to compare the performance and pay of other women employees with that of the plaintiff, or with that of other male employees, or with that of each other. To successfully navigate this process, the defendant will need to reveal details about deficiencies in various employees' work, give explanations of whether those deficiencies were related to personal crises, and provide other confidential information likely to embarrass the workers.

In one case, a female attorney sued her firm for sex discrimination after being passed over for partnership. By the time the plaintiff lost her case, everyone in the local legal community knew private details about other lawyers in the firm, including which associate "offended the father-in-law of which senior partner," which associate frequently "disappeared without notice," "whose writing skills were seen as not being up to par," and who was perceived as "more sizzle than steak." Everyone also knew who had said which of these things about whom.[32]

Although such revelations seem an unfortunate but necessary byproduct of some discrimination claims, some of the harm to privacy inflicted by discrimination cases seems gratuitous. For example, recent changes to the rules of evidence allow sexual harassment complaints to turn into massive assaults on privacy. Former president Bill Clinton is the most famous victim of this dynamic. Paula Jones filed a lawsuit against Clinton, claiming that when he was governor of Arkansas he exposed himself to her, made other sexual advances, and implicitly threatened her with retaliation in her job with the state if she refused him. Jones's lawyers, some of whom were at least as interested in embarrassing Clinton as in winning the case, desperately sought an excuse to question Clinton and others about Clinton's rumored affairs with several other women. According to a published report, Jones' husband, Steve, announced that Paula's legal team was going to use subpoena power to reconstruct the secret life of Bill Clinton. Every state trooper used by the governor to solicit women was going to be deposed under oath. "We're going to get names; we're going to get dates; we're going to do the job that the press wouldn't do," Steve Jones said, "We're going to go after Clinton's medical records, the raw documents, not just opinions from doctors, . . . we're going to find out everything."[33]

Eventually, Jones's attorneys stumbled upon Federal Rule of Evidence 415, ironically signed into law by Bill Clinton only a few years earlier. Rule 415 allows plaintiffs in civil cases involving "sexual assault" to present evidence that the defendant engaged in similar acts of sexual assault, in order to show that the defendant had a propensity for abusing women. Sexual assault, as defined by Federal Rule of Evidence 413, includes "contact, without consent, between any part of the defendant's body or an object and the genitals or anus of another person." To take advantage of Rule 415, Jones's attorneys promptly amended their complaint to include a new allegation that Clinton had "put his hand on Plaintiff's leg and started sliding it toward the hem of Plaintiff's culottes, apparently attempting to reach Plaintiff's pelvic area."[34]

Even with this allegation added to the complaint, it seemed like a stretch for Jones's attorneys to inquire about Clinton's past consensual affairs, because such affairs do not meet the rules' criteria for being considered prior sexual assaults. But Jones's lawyers successfully argued that "[t]here is no practical means for this Court, in advance, to limit discovery to non-consensual sexual behavior because only after discovery can the existence of consent be determined."[35] Given the incredibly broad scope courts normally give to discovery requests, the judge had little choice but to accede to the lawyers' request. As a result, Jones's attorneys were able to subpoena the testimony of Monica Lewinsky, and to demand that she turn over her calendars, address books, journals, diaries, notes, letters, and other private information. Lewinsky's attorney filed a motion to quash the subpoena, arguing that complying with it would grossly invade his client's privacy. Before the court could rule on the motion, Kenneth Starr's independent counsel investigation interceded.[36]

Eventually, of course, Clinton's affairs with Lewinsky and other women became public knowledge, Clinton lied about his affairs under oath and to the American people directly, and the world was eventually treated to off-color tales of stained dresses and unusual uses for cigars. Clinton eventually settled the case, which had little if any legal merit, for $850,000—a testament to the blackmail potential of allowing lawyers to delve into the sex lives of their adversaries. One need not be a fan of Bill Clinton's to recognize that permitting sexual harassment complaints to become fishing expeditions for embarrassing information about the intimate lives of defendants is an open invitation to litigants to attempt to satisfy personal grudges, to blackmail defendants, and to otherwise abuse the legal process. All this comes at the expense of the privacy interests that civilized people hold dear. Conservatives did the cause of liberty no favors by helping to open this particular Pandora's box.

* * *

Despite countervailing privacy, academic freedom, and religious freedom considerations, antidiscrimination concerns have made it nearly impossible for colleges and universities to avoid scrutiny and regulation by the federal government, regardless of whether the schools have ever been accused of discrimination. Federal law bans discrimination based on race, sex, and other criteria by schools that receive federal funds, and these laws are accompanied by regulations requiring universities to proactively keep detailed records regarding the race and sex of their applicants, students, and staff.

Several small colleges, including Grove City College, a Christian liberal arts school in Pennsylvania, have tried to preserve their independence from government regulation by refusing all federal funding. Grove City even declined to participate in federal student aid programs that required the college's direct involvement. But these efforts to retain independence were not enough to stave off federal bureaucrats. In 1977, the Office for Civil Rights of the Department of Health, Education, and Welfare demanded that Grove City sign an "assurance of compliance" with federal regulations promulgated under Title IX of the Education Amendments Act of 1972, which bans collegiate sex discrimination. HEW claimed that while Grove City declined direct federal funding, it received indirect funding by accepting tuition payments subsidized by a federal program, even though students applied for this program without any input from or participation by the school. Therefore, according to HEW, Grove City was bound by Title IX.

Grove City's then-president, Charles MacKenzie, refused to sign the assurance of compliance, but he did affirm that the school had "no argument with the spirit or intent of Title IX's support of nondiscrimination."[37] The college had accepted women since its founding in 1876 and had never been accused of sex discrimination, but MacKenzie believed that if Grove City agreed to comply with Title IX, the result would be increased costs to the college, greater expenses for its students, threats to the Christian nature of the college, mandated affirmative action preferences based on race and sex, and a general loss of independence. HEW at least partially validated MacKenzie's suspicions when the department later informed Grove City that colleges subject to Title IX must maintain "detailed records of all student and employee applications, enrollments, academic records, personnel files, suspensions, hirings, firings, promotions, denial of promotions, etc.—all broken down by race, age, sex, and ethnic origin—and submit them upon demand to federal authorities."[38]

The college eventually filed a federal lawsuit against HEW, claiming that it was not a federally funded institution subject to Title IX and that, in any event, it had a First Amendment academic freedom right to refuse to comply with the government's intrusive information demands in the absence of any allegation that the college had discriminated. The college won a victory from a liberal federal trial judge, who admonished the government that it should be spending its resources combating discrimination instead of harassing innocent Grove City College.[39] However, the Supreme Court disagreed and held that Title IX applied to Grove City because its students received financial aid from the federal government.[40] The Court added that even if the college had a First Amendment right to refuse information demands by the government, the right had no bearing on the case because compliance with Title IX regulations was not mandatory: Grove City could avoid Title IX's dictates by refusing federal funds. Of course, the school already had refused federal funds, but to completely free itself of Title IX's reach it would have to stop accepting federally subsidized tuition payments. Only then could it duck the government's demand for information.

The Court tried to limit the damage its holding inflicted on the institutional independence of colleges by ruling that only Grove City's financial aid office was subject to Title IX, because only that part of the university was a recipient of federal aid. The rest of the institution, however, could maintain its autonomy from the federal government. Congress would have none of this. Under the "Civil Rights Restoration Act,"[41] Congress ensured that if a university receives any federal funds at all, including tuition payments from students who receive federal aid, as in Grove City's case, *all* educational programs at that university are subject to Title IX.

Grove City and other institutions of higher learning could either allow the government to regulate all of their programs or turn down all government aid to themselves and their students. Only a few extraordinary institutions could choose the latter option and still survive in the competitive educational marketplace. Grove City turned out to be one of these few institutions, but only because the federal government neglected to enforce Title IX's requirements against it for a decade after passage of the Civil Rights Restoration Act (it took until 1997 for the federal government to promulgate regulations under the Act).[42] By that time, the college had raised enough private money to replace federal aid to its students.[43] Almost every other college and university, however, has agreed to comply with federal Title IX regulations in exchange for federal money— not necessarily because they don't mind Title IX's intrusive meddling, but because they simply cannot survive without the federal funds. And once a school falls under Title IX, the regulations virtually take over. They dictate everything from what sports colleges must offer,[44] to whether a university must favor feminist scholars in tenure disputes,[45] to whether campus speech codes (see Chapter 5) are necessary. The degree to which American universities have lost their autonomy is staggering.

* * *

In the 1960s heyday of the civil rights movement, earnest advocates of antidiscrimination laws would never have imagined that such laws would ultimately forbid advertising for a Republican roommate, prohibit women-only gyms, encourage employers to closely monitor and regulate their employees' interpersonal communications, allow plaintiffs in discrimination lawsuits to go rummaging through defendant's sex lives, and require nearly every university in the United States to "keep detailed records of all student and employee applications, enrollments, academic records, personnel files, suspensions, hirings, firings, promotions, denial of promotions, etc.—all broken down by race, age, sex, and ethnic origin." Yet, antidiscrimination laws have now expanded to the point at which all of these rules exist in some or all jurisdictions in the United States. That this expansion has occurred to general acclaim by—indeed, often at the behest of—antidiscrimination activists highlights the extent to which their movement has changed and demonstrates how little regard they now have for civil liberties.

12. The ACLU and the Abandonment of Civil Liberties

The American Civil Liberties Union has a well-earned public image as a stalwart defender of civil liberties, even when the rights in question conflict with extremely popular and seemingly important legislation. Unfortunately, however, the ACLU, bowing to intellectual trends in left-liberal circles, is increasingly willing to support the enforcement of antidiscrimination laws at the expense of civil liberties. Perhaps the most egregious example of this backsliding is the ACLU's remarkable opposition to the 1999 Religious Liberty Protection Act, described in Chapter 10.

The national ACLU's opposition to the RLPA is just one of many examples of the organization's elevating antidiscrimination principles above free exercise rights. Indeed, the ACLU sided against free exercise in a number of the cases we have already examined. In 1983, for example, the ACLU filed a Supreme Court amicus brief against Bob Jones University, arguing that it was appropriate for the school to be stripped of its tax exemption by the IRS because of the university's (purportedly) religion-based ban on interracial dating (see Chapter 9).[1] A few years later, the ACLU sided with the Ohio Civil Rights Commission and against free exercise of religion in the Dayton Christian Schools case (see Chapter 9).

State ACLU chapters, which act independently of the national ACLU, have also actively supported antidiscrimination cases that are hostile to free exercise rights. The Vermont chapter of the ACLU sued Catholic publisher Regal Arts Press for refusing a project from the abortion rights group Catholics for Free Choice.[2] The Southern California branch of the ACLU filed a brief on behalf of a plaintiff attempting to force the Christian Yellow Pages, a publication created by and for evangelicals, to accept ads from non–born again Christians.[3] In the Hoffius case (see Chapter 10), the ACLU of Michigan filed a brief supporting plaintiffs suing a landlord for refusing to rent to cohabiting unmarried couples for religious reasons.[4]

145

Religious freedom is hardly the only civil libertarian concern the ACLU has downgraded in favor of antidiscrimination concerns. The national ACLU, for example, believes that plaintiffs should be able to win antidiscrimination lawsuits by showing "disparate impact" (demonstrating the discriminatory effects of the defendant's actions, even if there was no discriminatory intent). This places defendants in a very vulnerable position—even if they acted completely innocently, they can be found liable—but the ACLU seems unconcerned. As Cornell University professor Jeremy Rabkin points out, the ACLU is "obsessed with due process, except when it comes to civil rights litigation, where they want no due process for the other side."[5] "There's a certain kind of logic to it," Rabkin adds, "They genuinely think you're in the path of social progress if you object. It's not a personal comment on you; it's that you can't make an omelet without breaking eggs."

To take another example, despite the ACLU's commitment to academic freedom, the organization vigorously supported the Civil Rights Restoration Act of 1987, which was passed in part to force small private colleges like Grove City College (see Chapter 11) to kowtow to heavy-handed government regulation of their admissions and employment policies.[6] Once again, the ACLU was more concerned with paving the road of social progress than with any civil liberties it bulldozed on the way.

The ACLU has also advocated the expansion of state public accommodations laws (see Chapter 7), despite the high costs to freedom of association and to pluralism. For example, the ACLU represented Victoria Isbister in the case that forced the Santa Cruz Boys' Club to admit girls, and it represented Sally Frank in the litigation against the Princeton eating clubs. Even in expressive association cases that directly implicate the First Amendment, the ACLU has tended to take the government's side against private groups asserting their constitutional rights.

The ACLU has been particularly eager to subject the Boy Scouts of America's membership policies to government regulation. Various ACLU chapters have sued the Scouts to force the organization to accept gays and atheists as members and scoutmasters—an effort that was finally rejected by the Supreme Court in 2000 (see Chapter 8). Had the ACLU won its battle against the Scouts, civil liberties would have suffered great damage. For example, the ACLU sued the Scouts on behalf of a gay scoutmaster applicant named Timothy Curran, even though Curran acknowledged that he planned to violate Scouts policy by using his position to promote respect for gays among his youthful charges.[7] By that logic, antidiscrimination laws that ban religious discrimination could require gay organizations to hire fundamentalist Christians who want to use their positions to proselytize against homosexuality. It's hard to imagine the ACLU showing equal enthusiasm for that case.

The ACLU argues—albeit not persuasively—that the Scouts is not truly a private organization, because it benefits from indirect government subsidies, such as the free use of public school facilities.[8] By this logic, organizations ranging from the PTA to voluntary student Bible study groups are also not private. In any event, it is unlikely that the ACLU's position would change if the Scouts cut its ties to the public sector. An ACLU attorney representing a renegade scout differentiated between clearly ideological groups like the Ku Klux Klan, which the ACLU believes have the right to exist autonomously and spread their messages, and the Scouts, which the ACLU views as a nonideological group focused on teaching certain skills. "You're talking about four million kids tying knots," he told the *Washington Post*. "It's not the same thing."[9] Yet many parents enroll their children in the Scouts not because they learn to tie knots, but because the Scouts inculcates traditional moral values. The use of the phrase "he's no Boy Scout" to describe a reprobate is an indication of how much the Scouts' identity is tied to its production of morally upright citizens. One would think that the ACLU would be able to recognize that the Scouts' refusal to recognize avowed homosexuals as morally upright individuals is an ideological decision tied to a particular conception of morality, even though that conception happens to be one the ACLU does not share.

The ACLU's commitment to using government power to thwart discrimination is even threatening the organization's commitment to "pure speech"—expression untied to any act of discrimination against any individual. Several years ago, John Powell, who was then legal director of the ACLU, argued that universities had an obligation to suppress speech that made African American students feel uncomfortable. He stated bluntly that his "concern is less with the strength of the First Amendment than with the wave of racial harassment that has swept the country."[10] Powell also told a reporter that the most important issues for the ACLU were abortion and civil rights.[11]

Pro–free speech forces within the national ACLU, led by its president and strong free speech advocate Nadine Strossen, eventually gained the upper hand, and Powell moved on to a position as a professor at the University of Minnesota School of Law. But even Strossen has been forced to make concessions to the antidiscrimination lobby within the organization, and to left-wing critics who accuse the ACLU of sacrificing important egalitarian goals for abstract civil libertarian principles. Strossen has announced, for example, that the ACLU is committed to "eliminating racial discrimination from society at large."[12] Strossen does not explain how this utopian goal can be actively pursued without resort to coercive means that would violate the restraints on government power that the ACLU has traditionally supported.

Indeed, although the ACLU has generally supported free speech rights over antidiscrimination laws, its record is far from perfect and increasingly reveals schisms within the organization. On the plus side, the Virginia ACLU defended a college fraternity's right to put on an "ugly women" skit;[13] the Kansas City ACLU affiliate waged a long fight for the KKK's right to use a public access television channel,[14] and the Illinois ACLU filed a brief on behalf of Matthew Hale, a law school graduate who was denied admission to the Illinois bar because of his racist beliefs.[15] The ACLU also filed successful lawsuits against state university speech codes in Wisconsin and Michigan (see Chapter 5), and was active in defending neighborhood activists from the federal Department of Housing and Urban Development's charges that their political activities constituted illegal housing discrimination[16] (see Chapter 4). The New York branch of the ACLU supported the right of the Ancient Order of Hibernians to exclude a contingent from the Irish Lesbian and Gay Organization in its New York St. Patrick's Day Parade.[17] The District of Columbia branch of the ACLU, meanwhile, filed a friend of the court brief asking that Georgetown University not be forced to recognize and fund gay student groups[18] (see Chapter 9).

On the minus side, the national ACLU took the opposite side of the Georgetown case. The national ACLU also declined to defend the right of organizers of a Boston St. Patrick's Day parade to exclude a gay rights group, even though, as in the New York parade, gay marchers were welcome as individuals but not as members of an organized group seeking to use the parade as a forum for gay rights advocacy (see Chapter 8).[19] The Virginia ACLU filed a complaint with the Virginia Fair Housing Office against neighborhood activists opposing a home for AIDS sufferers, in part because the activists "had made public statements designed to foster opposition to the . . . home . . . based on irrational prejudice, fear and animus toward those who will reside there."[20] After an investigation, the Fair Housing Office determined that the activists' actions were protected by the First Amendment.[21] In that case, government bureaucrats were more supportive of the First Amendment than was the Virginia ACLU!

Meanwhile, all three California ACLU affiliates have endorsed government-imposed university speech codes. And while the national ACLU has generally opposed using otherwise protected speech as evidence of discrimination in harassment cases, and the Florida ACLU opposed the broad injunction against "sexually suggestive" speech in the Robinson case (see Chapter 2),[22] the national organization supported the Northern California ACLU's brief advocating a broad injunction against offensive speech at an Avis Rent A Car outlet at the San Francisco International Airport[23] (see Chapter 2).

* * *

The ACLU's growing preference for social equality over individual freedom, although antithetical to its stated purpose, is not new. The ACLU's support of civil liberties has been threatened by the temptation of egalitarian political goals since the organization's earliest years. Roger Baldwin, who founded the ACLU in 1920 and led the organization for decades, came out of the radical, pacifist, prolabor, socialist left of the World War I years. Baldwin flirted with Stalinist communism throughout the late 1920s and most of the 1930s,[24] and in 1934 wrote that he favored civil liberties only to ultimately aid workers in gaining power. "If I aid the reactionaries to get free speech now and then," he wrote, "if I go outside of the class struggle to fight against censorship, it is only because those liberties help to create a more hospitable atmosphere for working class liberties."[25] Early ACLU policies reflected Baldwin's socialist agenda. For example, despite its purported commitment to free speech, the organization supported the National Labor Relations Board when it penalized the Ford Motor Company for handing out anti-union literature. The ACLU's paradoxical position was that Ford could say what it wanted to in newspapers or in the chamber of commerce, but the government could restrict Ford's speech in its own factories.[26]

Soviet communism lost its luster among many American leftists, including Baldwin, when Stalin formed a pact with Hitler in 1939. The following year, the ACLU board of directors voted to expunge all communist influence from the organization. The board declared that it was "inappropriate for any person to serve on the governing committees of the Union or its staff, who is a member of any political organization which supports totalitarian dictatorship in any country, or who by his public declarations indicates his support of such a principle."[27] For the next 30 years or so, before its drift toward becoming an adjunct of the civil rights movement, the ACLU was a staunch and consistent defender of the First Amendment.

The growth of an aggressive antidiscrimination agenda at the ACLU at the expense of traditional civil liberties concerns has been a long, gradual process. According to Ira Glasser, longtime executive director of the ACLU, as late as the mid-1960s the "received wisdom" at the ACLU was "that there was a distinction between civil liberties and civil rights, and that while we supported each other, the division of labor was that we handled civil liberties cases, and the NAACP handled civil rights."[28] When civil rights and civil liberties objectives clashed, the ACLU sided with civil liberties. For example, the NAACP opposed jury trials for violators of court decrees in civil rights cases out of fear that Southern juries would not convict such violators, while the ACLU supported jury trials as a matter of principle.[29]

Cracks in the ACLU's defense of civil liberties began to appear in the late 1960s, when the ACLU—which was founded in large part to defend the rights of labor unions—supported African American community activists asserting "local control" of Brooklyn public schools against claims by the teachers' union that its members were being denied due process.[30] In 1972, the ACLU endorsed "anti-blockbusting statutes which prohibit false or deceptive statements concerning changes in the racial, religious, or national character of a neighborhood, and/or the effect of those changes, made with the intent for commercial gain, to promote the sale of property."[31] This policy was sufficiently vague that it arguably did not conflict with

First Amendment norms. But three years later, the board of directors voted down an amendment opposing fair housing laws to the extent the laws violated "the constitutional guarantee of free speech."[32]

Also in 1972, the ACLU reversed its long-standing opposition to government-mandated racial quotas in employment and university admissions. Many ACLU board members seemed more concerned with how the ACLU would be perceived among liberals than with whether racial quotas, particularly when mandated by the government, were actually consistent with civil liberties. One board member, for example, argued that liberals think that "to be against quotas is to be against the aspirations of blacks and other minorities to achieve equality in employment," and the ACLU could not afford to be perceived by liberals as being hostile to minorities.[33]

Over time, the ACLU's commitment to civil liberties has progressively weakened. In the early 1970s, the ACLU's membership rose from around 70,000 to almost 300,000. Many new members were attracted by the organization's opposition to the Vietnam War and its high-profile battles with President Nixon, but such members were not committed to the ACLU's broader civil libertarian agenda. However, the organization's defense of the KKK's right to march in Skokie, Illinois, in the late 1970s weeded out some of these fair-weather supporters and attracted some new free speech devotees. But George H. W. Bush's criticisms of the ACLU during the 1988 presidential campaign again attracted many liberal members not especially devoted to civil liberties.

To maintain its large membership base, the ACLU recruits new members by directing mass mailings to mailing lists rented from a broad range of liberal groups.[34] The result of the shift of the ACLU to a mass membership organization is that it is gradually transforming itself from a civil libertarian organization into a liberal organization with an interest in civil liberties. This problem has been exacerbated by the growth within the ACLU of autonomous, liberal, special interest cliques known as "projects." These projects have included an AIDS Project, a Capital Punishment Project, a Children's Rights Project, an Immigrants' Rights Project, a Lesbian and Gay Project, a National Prison Project, a Women's Rights Project, a Civil Liberties in the Workplace Project, a Privacy and Technology Project, and an Arts Censorship Project. These projects tend to distract the ACLU from its traditional civil libertarian agenda—freedom of expression, free exercise of religion, freedom of assembly and association, and freedom from discriminatory *government* policies. This loss of focus has led Harvard Law School professor Alan Dershowitz to waggishly suggest that "perhaps the Civil Liberties Union needs a civil liberties project."[35]

Dershowitz explains that for a time the ACLU chose board members for affirmative action reasons (because they were African American, female, or gay) in preference to white males with stronger demonstrated commitments to civil liberties. These affirmative action appointees naturally felt that their primary function was to represent within the ACLU the interests of their groups, rather than to preserve civil liberties generally.[36] According to one study, in 1948 the ACLU's traditional civil liberties agenda constituted 94 percent of the ACLU's cases; by 1987 this was down to 45 percent.[37] Mark Lambert, former legislative director of the Iowa ACLU, explains that "the changes started when the ACLU got involved in the civil rights movement. That opened the door for all of these other issues that have nothing to do with the First Amendment."[38]

* * *

Perhaps the ACLU's current drift away from defending civil liberties in favor of antidiscrimination and other concerns could be arrested if the ACLU adhered to a formal constitution—an immutable statement of civil libertarian principles to which the organization could refer any time its mandate became cloudy. Instead, the ACLU makes its policy democratically, by majority vote of the 83 members of the board of directors, which includes all chairs of state affiliates. Immediate political considerations inevitably weigh against timeless principles, and, as Dershowitz notes, political expediency wins out far too often.[39]

Current ACLU president Nadine Strossen is by all accounts a strong, consistent civil libertarian—she even wrote a book defending the legality of pornography from its feminist critics. But Strossen cannot single-handedly reinvent the organization as one devoted solely to civil liberties, given the strong foothold other constituencies have achieved within the ACLU. Strossen concedes that when antidiscrimination laws and civil liberties conflict, the ACLU uses an ad hoc balancing test, choosing "between them in the context of particular facts, weighing the potency and applicability in each instance of the general values of liberty and equality."[40] As the left has generally turned its back on civil liberties in favor of antidiscrimination concerns, the ACLU has become increasingly reluctant to defend civil liberties at the expense of antidiscrimination laws. The ACLU has even given an honorary position to Georgetown University law professor Mari Matsuda, who is perhaps the nation's leading academic advocate of government censorship of "hate speech."[41]

To some extent, the slack left by the ACLU has been taken up by right-of-center groups, including the Individual Rights Foundation and the Center for Individual Rights, and by the Foundation for Individual Rights in Education, an ideologically ecumenical organization that focuses on protecting civil liberties on university campuses. Each of these organizations has been responsible for several civil libertarian triumphs over antidiscrimination laws described in this book. However, none of these organizations currently has the ACLU's resources, prestige, or long-standing civil liberties credentials. Nor, perhaps more crucially, do these organizations have the ACLU's credibility with left-liberals, although FIRE, the newest of these groups, seems to be gradually earning the civil libertarian left's respect.

The ACLU is desperately needed as a left-liberal voice willing to defend civil liberties even when they conflict with antidiscrimination laws. In his history of the ACLU, Samuel Walker has argued that the ACLU is distinguished from other liberal organizations by its "skepticism of government power and a willingness to challenge extensions of that power justified in the name of social betterment."[42] In the antidiscrimination context, however, the organization has increasingly become the voice of statism, not civil liberties. The ACLU is at a crossroads: Will it live up to its reputation as a skeptic of government power and return to a defense of the First Amendment and other rights against the state, or will it continue to evolve into just another liberal organization that supports the evisceration of constitutional liberties in the name of "eliminating discrimination"?

Conclusion

As argued throughout this book, antidiscrimination laws should not be exempt from the First Amendment's and other constitutional provisions' limits on government power. The contrary position, increasingly promoted in law reviews, the popular media, and legislatures throughout the United States, is that antidiscrimination considerations should almost always override any competing concerns, including First Amendment rights. The primary rationale for antidiscrimination law is no longer bringing previously marginalized groups into the economic mainstream. Rather, antidiscrimination laws are justified on the ground that the offense taken by people who face discrimination is an especially serious moral harm—so serious, in fact, that even antidiscrimination laws with no direct economic impact should be exempted from the Constitution's protection of civil liberties. For example, many distinguished academics argue that because of the offense taken by the listener, even the core First Amendment protection of freedom of speech must yield to "hate speech" laws targeting malicious (and sometimes merely inadvertently offensive) speech.[1]

Punishing expression because it creates offense has absurd and totalitarian implications. This has been amply demonstrated on university campuses that have prohibited their faculties and students from offending each other in politically incorrect ways. Sarah Lawrence College, for example, a small liberal arts school in Bronxville, New York, punished a student for "inappropriate laughter" after snorting when his roommate called another student a "fag." Other colleges have banned inconsiderate jokes, speech that threatens a student's self-esteem, inappropriate eye contact (or lack thereof), and licking one's lips in a provocative manner.[2]

More generally, campus intolerance of any speech deemed offensive to designated victim groups has led to serious miscarriages of justice, as campus activists groups use speech codes to suppress dissent from politically correct orthodoxy.[3] One egregious example

155

of the precarious state of freedom of expression on campus is the blind eye that is turned to the theft and destruction of campus newspapers containing stories or advertisements deemed offensive—a modern campus analogy to book burnings (worse, in a way, because book burners at least often own the books they incinerate). This widespread practice is generally tolerated by university administrations even though it evinces a decidedly authoritarian intolerance for open debate. Private universities have the right to enact and enforce foolish policies. Campus authoritarianism, however, may very well provide a glimpse at the sort of antidiscrimination policies that will be pursued at all levels of American government if civil liberties protections are not maintained.

One of the easiest ways to understand the frightening implications of eroding civil liberties with antidiscrimination policies is to take a look at English-speaking democracies in which the sensitivity police have made more gains than they have in the United States. In 1990, for example, the Canadian Supreme Court upheld hate speech laws against a freedom of speech defense. James Keegstra, a public high school teacher, had consistently propagated Holocaust denial and anti-Semitic views to his public high school students, despite repeated warnings from his superiors to stop. Even in the United States, someone in Keegstra's position could be disciplined, even fired, for ignoring his obligations to stick to his assigned curriculum, and for using his classroom as a forum for promoting hatred (see Chapter 5). Instead of merely firing Keegstra, the Canadian government arrested him. Keegstra was convicted of the crime of "willfully promoting hatred against an identifiable group," which carries a penalty of up to two years in jail. On appeal, the Canadian Supreme Court upheld the conviction, despite the Canadian Constitution's protection of freedom of expression. Criminalizing hate speech, the Court stated, was a "reasonable" restriction on expression, and it therefore passed constitutional muster.[4]

Two years later, the Canadian Supreme Court held that obscenity laws are unconstitutional to the extent they criminalize material purely on the basis of its sexual content. However, any "degrading or dehumanizing" depiction of sexual activity—including material that the First Amendment would clearly protect in the United States—was deprived of constitutional protection to protect women and other "victimized" groups from discrimination.[5] The opinion drew heavily on language from a brief coauthored by the feminist censorship advocate Catharine MacKinnon.

The inevitable result of these decisions has been the gradual but significant growth of censorship and suppression of civil liberties across Canada. The Canadian Supreme Court, meanwhile, turned down an appeal by a Christian minister convicted of inciting hatred against Muslims. An Ontario appellate court had found that the minister did not intentionally incite hatred, but was properly convicted for being willfully blind to the effects of his actions. Robert Martin, a professor of constitutional law at the University of Western Ontario, commented that he increasingly thinks that "Canada now is a totalitarian theocracy. I see this as a country ruled today by what I would describe as a secular state religion [of political correctness]. Anything that is regarded as heresy or blasphemy is not tolerated."[6]

Indeed, it has apparently become illegal in Canada to advocate traditional Christian opposition to homosexual sex. For example, the Saskatchewan Human Rights Commission ordered the *Saskatoon Star Phoenix* newspaper and Hugh Owens to each pay $1,500 (approximately $1,000 U.S.) to each of three gay activists as damages for publication of an advertisement placed by Owens conveying the message that the Bible condemns homosexual acts.[7] The ad conveyed this message by citing passages from the Bible, with an equal sign placed between the verse references and a drawing of two males holding hands overlaid with the universal nullification symbol—a red circle with a diagonal bar. In another incident, after Toronto print shop owner Scott Brockie refused on religious grounds to print letterhead for a gay activist group, the local human rights commission ordered him to pay the group $5,000 (approximately $3,400 U.S.), print the requested material, and apologize to the group's leaders. Brockie, who always accepted print jobs from individual gay customers, and even did pro bono work for a local AIDS group, is fighting the decision on religious freedom grounds.[8] An appellate court has upheld the fine, though it did add that it would have ruled the other way had the material in question impinged more directly on Brockie's "core beliefs," such as a publication advocating homosexual behavior.[9] As of this writing, another appeal is pending, with Brockie already having spent $100,000 (approximately $68,000 U.S.) in legal fees.[10]

Any gains the gay rights movement has received from the crackdown on speech in Canada have been Pyrrhic, because as part of the

Canadian government's suppression of obscene material, Canadian customs frequently target books with homosexual content. Customs seizures have included *Pornography*, a book by MacKinnon collaborator and prominent feminist Andrea Dworkin, and several serious novels. A gay organization had to spend $14,000 (approximately $9,600 U.S.) in legal fees to force customs agents to allow *The Joy of Gay Sex* into the country. Police raids searching for obscene materials have disproportionately targeted gay organizations and bookstores. Two gay activists at the University of Toronto were fined for selling *Bad Attitude*, a lesbian magazine with sadomasochistic content.[11] According to the ACLU, "more than half of all feminist bookstores in Canada have had materials confiscated or the sales of some materials suspended by the government."[12] The Canadians are, therefore, living proof of the way progressive censorship rules can come back to bite the constituencies that endorsed them.

One Canadian incident, at least, had a satisfactory ending. The Canadian teachers' accreditation authority attempted to refuse accreditation to graduates of Trinity Western University, a private Christian institution in British Columbia, claiming that they are too bigoted to become teachers because they agree as students to abide by traditional Christian teachings about sex by refraining from "premarital sex, adultery, and homosexual behavior."[13] The Canadian Supreme Court ordered that TWU alumni be deemed eligible for accreditation. Nevertheless, civil liberties in Canada remain in jeopardy, and a great deal more censorship in Canada seems inevitable. British Columbia, for example, has an extremely broad hate speech law that prohibits the publication of any statement that "indicates" discrimination or that is "likely" to expose a person or group or class of persons to hatred or contempt.[14] It seems highly probable the worst is yet to come from the Canadian thought police.

Things look equally bleak in Australia. In 1998, *The Australian Financial Review* published a short opinion column on the Middle East by journalist Tom Switzer. In his piece, Switzer wrote that "the Palestinians cannot be trusted in the peace process." Switzer also noted that since 1993 the Palestinians had engaged in more than 300 terrorist attacks against innocent Israeli civilians, and so "it would appear that the Palestinians remain vicious thugs." When the local Palestinian Authority representative filed a complaint with the New South Wales Anti-Discrimination Board, a tribunal found the publisher guilty of inciting hatred against Palestinians in violation of the racial vilification provisions of the Anti-Discrimination Act. This ruling was later overturned on appeal, but in a narrow decision that gave little comfort to free speech advocates. Similarly, an Australian radio talk-show host was fined $6,000 (approximately $3,600 U.S.) for making disparaging comments about Aborigines while criticizing a recent fair housing decision.[15] Meanwhile, outspoken left-wing Australian columnist Phillip Adams was investigated for "racial vilification" of Americans after he wrote an anti-American column in the wake of the terrorist attacks of September 11, 2001.[16] This led an American wag to write to *The Sydney Morning Herald*, "The next time [Adams] bitches the US out, even if she deserves it, he ought to consider the fact that, here at least, he would be left alone. Sorry, Phil. Them's the breaks, I guess."[17] Beyond their poor showing with regard to protecting speech deemed offensive to protected classes, Australian courts have also banned Jewish and age-specific dating services as discriminatory.[18]

The ban on Jewish dating services was eventually overruled, following public ridicule. But the authoritarian logic of the antidiscrimination movement is inexorable, and supports the original anti–dating service ruling. If, as antidiscrimination activists argue, all discrimination against members of identifiable groups should be punished, then group-specific dating services, which inherently exclude other groups, should be banned. Never mind individual preferences in choosing compatible life partners—antidiscrimination goals are more important. An article in the *Harvard Law Review* even argued that race-specific personal ads should be banned (no more SWF or SBM), though the author conceded that enabling legislation is unlikely, for now.[19]

In fact, when one honestly applies the logic of the antidiscrimination movement, it is difficult to fault the law review article's conclusion that personal ads should be forcibly shorn of discriminatory preferences. Modern antidiscrimination ideology suggests that those who refuse to date (and, therefore, to ultimately marry) members of certain groups should be punished. After all, discriminatory dating not only offends those excluded, but, given the difference in median wealth among groups, it is also a leading cause of societal inequality. Taken to their logical ends, antidiscrimination principles suggest that singles in the dating market should be prohibited from preferentially choosing African Americans or whites, the able-bod-ied or the disabled, Catholics or Protestants, or even same-sex or opposite-sex partners, lest offense and inequality result.

Once the folly of this reductio ad absurdum is conceded, it becomes clear that some limits must be placed on the scope of antidiscrimination law. The only question is where to draw the line, and the First Amendment is the obvious place to start. Mainstream liberal civil libertarians, as represented by the ACLU, agree that the pursuit of antidiscrimination objectives must be limited by constitu-tional restraints on government power. However, they often believe that the First Amendment should only prohibit laws that regulate pure speech, such as hate speech laws and hostile environment regulations. By contrast, they believe that laws banning discrimina-tory acts—such as public accommodations laws that prohibit private organizations from banning gays from membership or employment discrimination laws that prevent church schools from firing teachers who get pregnant out of wedlock—should be beyond the reach of First Amendment. Defenders of such laws draw analogies to tres-pass, copyright and trademark infringements, and other acts that often have expressive aspects, but that can nevertheless be banned without violating the First Amendment.

Adopting this reasoning would have dangerous consequences because in contrast to trespass and other torts that may also have expressive aspects, antidiscrimination law has no clear definitional boundaries. The concept of antidiscrimination is almost infinitely malleable. Almost any economic behavior, and much other behavior, can be defined as discrimination. Is a school admitting students based on SAT scores? The U.S. Department of Education has pro-posed that using such tests in college admissions be considered discrimination against groups that get below-average scores.[20] Is a credit card company denying applications to the non-creditworthy? That's discrimination based on financial status. (Sound absurd? Tell it to the New Zealand Human Rights Commission, a body modeled after American civil rights enforcement agencies, which has deter-mined that refusing service on credit to a customer who is unem-ployed, has no credit card, earns less than $10,000 [approximately $5,500 U.S.] a year, and does not own a home is illegal discrimination on the grounds of employment status.)[21] Is an employer hiring only the best qualified candidates? Well, that might be discrimination against everyone else!

160

The obvious retort from exasperated antidiscrimination activists is that only laws prohibiting "real" discrimination should receive constitutional exemption. Legislatures and courts should not allow the definition of discrimination to expand beyond what is reasonable. The problem is, of course, that there is no consensus about what constitutes "real" discrimination, nor does there appear to be any principled definition that legislatures have followed. What counts as discrimination will always depend on which interest groups have the power to influence legislatures to define their particular goals as antidiscrimination goals, and not on any objective definition of discrimination.

Already, definitions of discrimination have proven extremely tractable. Some define discrimination as treating the alike unequally on the basis of invidious preferences, but, even outside of the controversial area of affirmative action preferences, antidiscrimination law does not always follow this definition. The Americans with Disabilities Act defines discrimination not only as the unwillingness to treat the disabled and nondisabled alike but also as the unwillingness to make "reasonable accommodations" for the disabled. In the first enforcement action under the ADA, the government ordered a company to pay for a full-time sign translator for a hearing-impaired student in its review class for the CPA exam, even though the interpreter cost far more than the student's tuition.[22] Undertaking this measure was obviously not treating the hearing-impaired student just like everybody else.

Similarly, Title VII of the 1964 Civil Rights Act's ban on discrimination based on religion actually mandates preferential treatment for religious employees. The statute requires that employers accommodate the religious beliefs and observances of their employees, unless doing so would cause the employer "undue hardship." Some hardship to the employer, which in economic terms constitutes a subsidy to the religious employee, is mandated where necessary.[23] If failure to give members of a group a subsidy constitutes discrimination, then just about any law can be defined as an antidiscrimination statute that is potentially exempt from constitutional limitations. In short, exempting antidiscrimination laws from the civil liberties protections manifested in the Constitution might destroy those protections.

* * *

Although much legal writing focuses on court decisions and the resulting legal precedent, responsibility for preserving civil liberties rests first and foremost with the legislative branch of government. Courts can only correct the constitutional mistakes of legislatures. Legislatures can avoid these mistakes in the first instance, and, when appropriate, provide protections for civil liberties that go beyond minimum constitutional requirements. Moreover, courts are influenced by the political winds, and are more likely to protect civil liberties when they see concern for such liberties emanating from legislatures.

Conscientious legislators should halt the expansion of antidiscrimination law, and, wherever possible, reduce its scope. There should be a presumption of freedom of association, both because such a presumption protects freedom in and of itself—what is freedom if it does not include some protection of the right to choose one's associates?—and because the growth of antidiscrimination law creates inevitable conflicts with civil liberties and diminishes the autonomy of the institutions of civil society that serve as buffers between the individual and the state.

A good start for legislatures concerned with civil liberties would be to roll back public accommodations laws (see Chapter 7) so that they apply only to truly public commercial entities such as restaurants, theaters, hotels, and stores—not to private clubs and associations. Other legislative tasks beckon. Sexual harassment law should be modified to explicitly prohibit constitutionally protected speech from being used to support a hostile environment claim (see Chapter 2). In addition, state universities should be more closely monitored to ensure that they are protecting student and faculty freedom of expression (see Chapter 5).

Given the precarious state of constitutional free exercise rights in the federal courts (see Chapter 9), legislatures have become the primary guardians of religious freedom from the excesses of antidiscrimination laws. A few states lack religious exemptions to their antidiscrimination laws, an oversight that should be remedied. Many states are protecting free exercise through state laws that create a presumption that religious activity should not be impinged upon by legislation. These laws should not be altered to include special exemptions for antidiscrimination laws, as the ACLU and many other liberal groups have advocated.

The religious exemptions that do currently exist should be broadened to explicitly include such things as allowing small-scale religious landlords to refuse to rent to unmarried couples. Such landlords have little effect on the housing market, but forcing them to rent to cohabitating unmarried couples interferes with their perceived religious duties (see Chapter 10). Church schools, meanwhile, should be free to fire teachers who disobey church doctrine, such as by getting pregnant out of wedlock (see Chapter 9). Even if the legislature believes that this is morally repugnant discrimination, "its direct effects are purely internal to the religious group; only those who chose to become part of the religious community . . . are governed by its rules."[24] It is unfair and illogical to allow a teacher to claim the benefits of teaching at a religious school while retaining the right to sue the school for upholding the rules of its religion.

Legislatures must also monitor courts and administrative agencies to ensure that they are not interpreting antidiscrimination laws more broadly than is warranted either by the language of the statutes or by legislative intent. Some legislatures have been notably quiescent in this regard, allowing antidiscrimination laws to be applied wildly beyond their intended scope. The New Jersey legislature, for example, has allowed the New Jersey Supreme Court to make a mockery of its public accommodations law. As described previously (see Chapter 7), that court has held that the state's public accommodations law applies to everything from Little League baseball to small private eating clubs to cat fanciers' clubs to the Boy Scouts of America. Several states have allowed their administrative agencies and courts to interpret fair housing laws banning discrimination on the basis of marital status to include protections for unmarried heterosexual couples, despite rampant discrimination by the states themselves against such couples in other contexts (see Chapter 10). By contrast, the Madison, Wisconsin, City Council properly stepped in when local courts and agencies decided that the city's fair housing law applied to the residents' choice of roommates, albeit too late to save Ann Hacklander-Ready from a financially ruinous lawsuit (see Chapter 11).

The task for courts, meanwhile, is simple—do not give antidiscrimination laws special status, either in statutory interpretation or in constitutional analysis. On the statutory interpretation front, courts have been prone to expansively interpret antidiscrimination laws, to the point at which the language of the statutes in question cannot bear the weight of the interpretations. Courts justify this bias on the grounds that they are acting consistent with the "purpose" of the laws, such as when the Supreme Court asserted that "eradicating discrimination" was a "central statutory purpose" of Title VII of the 1964 Civil Rights Act.[25] Yet an examination of the statute reveals that its provisions are consistent with the purpose of *reducing* discrimination, not eradicating it. For example, Title VII applies only to employers with more than 15 employees, contains special damage caps and limitations, requires Equal Opportunity Employment Commission approval before private plaintiffs may file suit, and contains a religious exemption.[26] If Congress's goal had been to completely eliminate all discrimination, these caveats would not have been included.

With regard to constitutional analysis, from the mid-1970s through the early 1990s, the Supreme Court consistently favored antidiscrimination laws over constitutionally protected civil liberties. The Court often did so by tendentiously construing the facts of cases to allow it to evade conflicts between antidiscrimination laws and the First Amendment. Beyond that, the Court suggested that when such conflicts do arise, preventing discrimination is such a "compelling interest" that, for reasons never clearly explicated, antidiscrimination statutes trump constitutional rights. Fortunately, the Court has recently backed away from such slipshod reasoning. The results of *Boy Scouts of America v. Dale* (see Chapter 8) suggest that all nine justices have all but abandoned the "compelling interest" reasoning, and that five of the justices are now willing to directly confront conflicts between antidiscrimination laws and civil liberties. Thankfully, the Court seems on the verge of treating antidiscrimination laws as normal statutes, subject to standard rules of constitutional and statutory interpretation.

Ultimately, defending civil liberties from antidiscrimination laws is not only a job for courts and legislatures. Citizens, too, have a responsibility to organize and defend these civil liberties against the encroachment of laws promoting social equality. In some states, the ACLU is still dominated by traditional civil libertarians and these state chapters could become the nucleus for a movement to restore protection of civil liberties to the top of the national ACLU's agenda. A revitalized, consistently civil libertarian ACLU would lose some of its more authoritarian members, but it could lure back principled civil libertarians, such as author Nat Hentoff, who have quit in protest of the organization's neglect of, and sometimes outright opposition to, civil liberties. Such an ACLU would also attract libertarian-leaning conservatives who currently distrust the organization's creeping statism, giving the organization a broader and therefore more influential base.

Citizen support can also help other organizations fill at least part of the vacuum currently left by the ACLU's neglect of civil liberties. In particular, the Foundation for Individual Rights in Education, founded by attorney Harvey Silverglate and Professor Alan Kors of the University of Pennsylvania to protect civil liberties on college and university campuses, has the potential to become a broad-based, ecumenical, civil libertarian organization. The Center for Individual Rights has also done yeoman's work in defending civil liberties from antidiscrimination laws, and deserves support for its efforts.

Finally, if civil liberties are to be preserved, Americans will need to develop thicker skin. One price of living in a free society is having to tolerate those who intentionally or unintentionally offend you. The current trend, however, is to give offended parties a legal remedy, so long as the offense can be construed as "discrimination." Yet the more the American legal system offers people remedies for offense, the more they are likely to feel offended. This is true for two reasons. First, as economists point out, when you subsidize something, you get more of it. Therefore, if the legal remedies of antidiscrimination law, particularly monetary remedies, subsidize feelings of outrage and insult, we will get more feelings of outrage and insult, a net social loss. Second, economists have also noted the psychological endowment effect, which, in effect, means that people tend to consider something they own to be more valuable than it would be if they did not own it. Similarly, once people are endowed with a right, they tend to overvalue it and react passionately when it is interfered with.

Unfortunately, Americans increasingly coddle and even reward the hypersensitive, perversely encouraging ever more hypersensitivity. In one notorious incident, a Washington, D.C., city official was forced to resign for using the word "niggardly" at a meeting because the word sounded like a racial epithet, even though it is actually a word of Scandinavian origin meaning "miserly."[27] It should hardly be surprising, then, that people are suing for and winning damages when they are offended by colleagues at work, when they are excluded by private clubs or turned down as roommates, or when they are fired from church-run schools after reneging on promises to obey church doctrine. Nor should it be surprising that legislatures are increasingly succumbing to the temptation to expand the laws to protect from discrimination every group with a grievance, including the vertically challenged (short people, protected in San Francisco and Michigan), the body-pierced (among those protected in various jurisdictions, including Washington, D.C., that ban discrimination on the basis of personal appearance), recovering drug addicts (protected by the federal Americans with Disabilities Act and local equivalents), and the Hell's Angels (protected, along with other motorcycle gang members, in Minnesota).

Preserving the liberalism that defines the United States, and the civil liberties that go with it, requires Americans to show a certain level of virtue, including a phlegmatic tolerance of those who intentionally or unintentionally offend and sometimes—when civil liberties are implicated—even of those who blatantly discriminate. A society that undercuts civil liberties in pursuit of the "equality" offered by a statutory right to be free from all slights, protected by draconian antidiscrimination laws, will ultimately end up empty-handed with neither equality nor civil liberties to show for its efforts. The violation of civil liberties required to achieve this kind of equality will diminish constitutional restraints on the government, while the additional power garnered by the government, introduced for noble purposes, will end up in the hands of people who use it to promote their own interests.[28] In these days of the Oprahization of public discourse, when even presidential candidates swear that they feel the public's pain, asking Americans to display a measure of fortitude in the face of offense and discrimination is asking for a lot. But in the end, it is a small price to pay for preserving civil liberties.

Notes

Introduction

1. Susan Ferriss, "Free Speech Advocates Find a Fight in Berkeley," *San Francisco Examiner*, July 22, 1994, p. A6.

2. Michelle Tauber, "Dancer's Image: Charging Body-size Bias, Krissy Keefer Fights to Have Her 9-year-old Daughter Admitted to Ballet School," *People*, March 5, 2001, p. 79.

3. Al Knight, "Webb Deaf to Free Speech," *Denver Post*, October 1, 2000.

4. *Ganzy v. Allen Christian School*, 995 F. Supp. 340, 348 (E.D.N.Y. 1998).

5. Carl S. Kaplan, "In Library Filtering Case, an Unusual Ally," *New York Times*, October 2, 1998.

6. Kirsten Lagatree, "Fighting Words: Efforts to Avoid Housing Discrimination Have Changed the Way Realty Ads Are Written," *Los Angeles Times*, February 12, 1995, p. 1.

7. The federal government has specified that using these phrases, along with other words and phrases that do not facially express a discriminatory preference, is permissible under federal law, but not all state and local agencies follow federal guidelines when enforcing their fair housing laws. See generally U.S. Department of Housing and Urban Development, Advertisements Under 804(c) of the Fair Housing Act, January 9, 1995, available at www.fairhousing.com/hud_resources/hudguid2.htm.

8. *Stanley v. Lawson*, 993 F. Supp. 1084 (N.D. Ohio 1997); Tom Puleo, "Former Dairy Mart Manager in Ohio May Sue for Return of Her Job," *Hartford Courant*, January 13, 1992, p. A1.

9. Interview with Benjamin Bull, attorney for Ms. Stanley, January 11, 2002.

10. Senator Hubert H. Humphrey explained his support for the employment discrimination provisions of the federal 1964 Civil Rights Act this way: "The Negro American is the principal victim of a vastly complex system of self-perpetuating practices, traditions, and processes that has denied him true parity in the national job market. He has consistently and effectively been kept from participating fully in the job opportunities developed by the American free enterprise system." *Congressional Digest*, March 1964, p. 76.

11. C. C. Burlingham, et al., Letter to the Editor, "Faults Found in Ives Bill," *New York Times*, February 13, 1945. Not all civil libertarians shared this caution. Also in 1945, the ACLU called for federal and state fair employment practices laws, and restrictions on housing discrimination. Samuel Walker, *In Defense of American Liberties: A History of the ACLU* (New York: Oxford University Press, 1990), p. 168.

12. Hannah Arendt, "Reflection on Little Rock," *Dissent*, No. 1, 1959, p. 45.

13. Elizabeth Jacoway and David R. Colburn, eds., *Southern Businessmen and Deseg-regation* (Baton Rouge: Louisiana State University Press, 1981); Robert Weems, *Desegre-gating the Dollar: African-American Consumerism in the Twentieth Century* (New York: New York University Press, 1998).

14. At common law, innkeepers and others who made a profession of public employment were prohibited from refusing, without good reason, to serve a customer. See *Lane v. Cotton,* 88 Eng. Rep. 1458, 1464–1465 (K.B. 1701) (Holt, C. J.).

15. At the time, hate speech laws were known as "group libel" laws. See Samuel Walker, *Hate Speech: The History of an American Controversy* (Lincoln, Neb.: University of Nebraska Press, 1994), pp. 85, 100.

16. See David E. Bernstein, *Only One Place of Redress* (Durham, N.C.: Duke University Press, 2001), p. 107.

17. Veto message of President George H. W. Bush, October 22, 1990.

18. See, for example, Terry Eastland, *Ending Affirmative Action* (New York: Basic Books, 1996), pp. 189–90.

19. Along with other, more minor incidents, for a period of several months during my childhood my family and I were subjected to anti-Semitic vandalism, taunts, and threats, a situation eventually resolved through police intervention. I mention this as a preemptive response to what I suspect is the inevitable ad hominem argument that my views result from insensitivity to the victims of discrimination, having never personally experienced it myself.

Chapter 1

1. George Kateb, "The Value of Association," in Amy Gutmann, ed., *Freedom of Association* (Princeton, N.J.: Princeton University Press, 1998), p. 59.

2. *Swanner v. Anchorage Equal Rights Comm'n,* 874 P.2d 274 (Alaska 1994).

3. See, for example, *Roberts v. United States Jaycees,* 468 U.S. 609 (1984); *Robinson v. Jacksonville Shipyards, Inc.,* 760 F. Supp. 1486, 1542 (M.D. Fla. 1991).

4. See, for example, Akhil Reed Amar, "The Case of The Missing Amendments: *R.A.V. v. City of St. Paul,*" *Harvard Law Review* 106 (1992): 124. Amar's argument is persuasively rebutted in Alex Kozinski and Eugene Volokh, "A Penumbra Too Far," *Harvard Law Review* 106 (1993): 1639.

5. See, for example, Mari J. Matsuda, "Public Response to Racist Speech: Consider-ing the Victim's Story," in Mari J. Matsuda et al., *Words That Wound: Critical Race Theory, Assaultive Speech, and the First Amendment* (Colorado: Westview Press, 1993); Charles R. Lawrence III, "If He Hollers Let Him Go: Regulating Racist Speech on Campus," in Mari J. Matsuda et al., *Words That Wound,* pp. 53, 61; Catharine MacKin-non, *Only Words* (Cambridge, Mass.: Harvard University Press, 1993), p. 71; Richard Delgado, "Campus Antiracism Rules: Constitutional Narratives in Collision," *North-western University Law Review* 85 (1991): 343, 346; Mary Ellen Gale, "Reimagining the First Amendment: Racist Speech and Equal Liberty," *St. John's Law Review* 65 (1991): 119, 162; Brian Owsley, "Racist Speech and 'Reasonable People': A Proposal for a Tort Remedy," *Columbia Human Rights Law Review* 24 (1993): 323, 324. This argument has also infiltrated the civil libertarian community, and commands a great deal of support within the ACLU. See Dennis Cauchon, "Civil Dispute within the ACLU," *USA Today,* March 31, 1993.

6. See Eugene Volokh, "Freedom of Speech and the Constitutional Tension Method," *University Chicago Roundtable* 3 (1996): 223.

7. *R.A.V. v. City of St. Paul*, 505 U.S. 377 (1992).

8. *Hurley v. Irish-American Gay, Lesbian & Bisexual Group of Boston*, 515 U.S. 557 (1995).

9. *Boy Scouts of America. v. Dale*, 120 S. Ct. 2446 (2000).

10. Catharine MacKinnon, *Only Words* (Cambridge, Mass.: Harvard University Press, 1993), p. 107.

11. Mari J. Matsuda, "Public Response to Racist Speech: Considering the Victim's Story," *Michigan Law Review* 87 (1989): 2320, 2359.

12. See, for example, Owen M. Fiss, *Liberalism Divided: Freedom of Speech and the Many Uses of State Power* (Boulder, Colo.: Westview Press, 1996), p. 115; Cass R. Sunstein, *Democracy and the Problem of Free Speech* (New York: The Free Press, 1993), pp. 186–95; Frank Michelman, "Universities, Racist Speech and Democracy in America: An Essay for the ACLU," *Harvard Civil Rights–Civil Liberties Law Review* 27 (1992): 339, 351–52.

13. Thomas W. Hazlett, "Looking for Results," Interview with Ronald Coase, *Reason*, January 1997, pp. 40, 45; see also R. H. Coase, "The Economics of the First Amendment: The Market for Goods and the Market for Ideas," *American Economic Review* 64 (1974): 384; Aaron Director, "The Parity of the Economic Market Place," *Journal of Law and Economics* 7 (1964): 1; Richard A. Epstein, "Property, Speech, and the Politics of Distrust," *University of Chicago Law Review* 59 (1992): 41.

14. Fiss, see note 12; Morton Horwitz, "The Constitution of Change: Legal Fundamentality without Fundamentalism," *Harvard Law Review* 107 (1993): 30; Frederick Schauer, "Uncoupling Free Speech," *Columbia Law Review* 92 (1992): 1321; Sunstein, see note 12, p. 16; Cass Sunstein, "Free Speech Now," *University of Chicago Law Review* 59 (1992): 255; see also Edwin Baker, "Of Course, More Than Words," *University of Chicago Law Review* 61 (1994): 1181, 1187; Paul H. Brietzke, "How and Why the Marketplace of Ideas Fails," *Valparaiso University Law Review* 31 (1997): 951.

15. Richard A. Epstein, *Forbidden Grounds: The Case against Employment Discrimination Laws* (Cambridge, Mass.: Harvard University Press, 1992).

16. See David F. McGowan and Ragesh K. Tangri, "A Libertarian Critique of University Restrictions of Offensive Speech," *California Law Review* 79 (1991): 825; Michael S. Greve, "Remote Control Tuning for Speech," *Washington Times*, November 9, 1996, p. D3.

17. *American Booksellers Association v. Hudnut*, 771 F.2d 323, 330 (7th Cir. 1985), *aff'd mem.*, 475 U.S. 1001 (1986).

18. Frederick Schauer, *Free Speech: A Philosophical Inquiry* (Cambridge, U.K.: Cambridge University Press, 1982), p. 86.

19. *American Booksellers Association*, 771 F.2d p. 330.

20. John O. McGinnis, "Reviving Tocqueville's America: The Supreme Court's New Jurisprudence of Social Discovery," *California Law Review* 90 (2002): 485.

21. Ibid.

22. Stanley Fish, *There's No Such Thing as Free Speech—And It's a Good Thing, Too* (New York: Oxford University Press, 1994), p. 125.

23. McGinnis, see note 20.

24. Andrew Koppleman, *Antidiscrimination Law and Social Equality* (New Haven, Conn.: Yale University Press, 1996), p. 230.

25. See George Will, "Reason One of the Few Things Not Included in Spending Bill," *Seattle Post-Intelligencer*, October 26, 1998, p. A9.

26. See Cal. Educ. Code § 943671(a) (West Supp. 1999); Cal. Educ. Code § 48950 (West 1993); Nat Hentoff, "Magna Carta for Students," *Washington Post*, January 30, 1993, p. A21.

27. See Henry J. Hyde and George M. Fishman, "The Collegiate Speech Protection Act of 1991: A Response to the New Intolerance in the Academy," *Wayne Law Review* 37 (1991): 1469. The bill stipulated that no university "shall make or enforce any rule subjecting any student to disciplinary sanctions solely on the basis of conduct that is speech or other communication protected from governmental restriction by the first article of amendment to the Constitution of the United States."

28. Transcript of discussion in Gary LaMarche, ed., *Speech and Equality: Do We Really Have to Choose?* (New York: New York University, 1996) p. 75; see also Michael S. Greve, "The Libertarian Case for Speech Codes," *Reason*, July 1995, available at www.reason.com/9507/GREVEcol.jul.shtml.

29. *Boy Scouts of America v. Dale*, 120 S. Ct. 2446 (2000); see generally Henry Louis Gates Jr., "Let Them Talk," *New Republic*, September 20 and 27, 1993, pp. 37, 42–43; Mari Matsuda, "Public Response to Racist Speech: Considering the Victim's Story," *Michigan Law Review* 87 (1989): 2320, 2371.

30. Fish, see note 22.

31. Jack Bass, *Unlikely Heroes* (Tuscaloosa, Ala.: University of Alabama Press, 1986); David E. Bernstein, "Lochner, Parity, and the Chinese Laundry Cases," *William and Mary Law Review* 41 (1999): 211.

32. James Weinstein, *Hate Speech, Pornography, and the Radical Attack on Free Speech Doctrine* (Boulder, Colo.: Westview Press, 1999), p. 5.

33. Fish, see note 22, p. 102.

34. Ibid., p. 109.

35. Weinstein, see note 32.

36. William Graham Sumner, "Democracy and Plutocracy," in Robert Bannister, ed., *On Liberty, Society, and Politics: The Essential Essays of William Graham Sumner* (Indianapolis, Ind.: Liberty Press, 1985), p. 134.

Chapter 2

1. *Mackenzie v. Miller Brewing Co.*, 623 N.W.2d 739 (Wis. 2001).

2. Bernard J. Wolfson, "Office Clinton Jokes Could Lead to Lawsuits," *Orange County Register*, October 5, 1998, p. A1.

3. Kathleen M. Moore, "Workers' Talk Dwells on Case, But Discreetly Sensitive Issue at Water Cooler," *Bergen Record*, February 2, 1998, p. A6.

4. Yochi Dreazen, "Talking Dirty: In Our Brazen Era of Monica and Viagra, What Subjects Should Be Off-limits at Work?" *Florida Times Union*, August 16, 1998, p. F1.

5. The classic text is Catharine MacKinnon, *Sexual Harassment of Working Women* (New Haven, Conn.: Yale University Press, 1979).

6. *Harris v. Forklift Systems, Inc.*, 510 US 17, 21 (1993), quoting *Meritor Savings Bank, FSB v. Vinson*, 477 U.S. 57, 65, 67 (1986).

7. See generally Jonathan Rauch, "Offices and Gentlemen," *New Republic*, June 23, 1997, p. 22; Eugene Volokh, "What Speech Does Hostile Work Environment Harassment Law Restrict?" *Georgia Law Review* 85 (1997): 627, 637; Jeffrey Rosen, "In Defense of Gender-Blindness," *New Republic*, June 29, 1998, p. 25; Kingsley R. Browne, "Title VII as Censorship: Hostile-Environment Harassment and the First Amendment," *Ohio State Law Journal* 52 (1991): 481, 539.

8. *Oncale v. Sundowner Offshore Services, Inc.*, 523 U.S. 75 (1998).

9. See *Davis v. Monroe County Bd. of Educ.*, 526 U.S. 629, 665, 682 (1999) (Kennedy, J., dissenting).

10. See, for example, *Cardin v. Via Tropical Fruits, Inc.*, 1993 U.S. Dist. LEXIS 16302, *24–25 and n. 4 (S.D Fla.).

11. See, for example, *Baskerville v. Culligan Int'l Co.*, 50 F.3d 428, 430 (7th Cir. 1995) (reversing jury award of $25,000); *Black v. Zaring Homes, Inc.*, 104 F.3d 822, 823 (6th Cir. 1997) (reversing jury award of $250,000).

12. U.S. Department of Labor, "Sexual Harassment: Know Your Rights" (1994), discussed in Eugene Volokh, "What Speech Does Hostile Work Environment Harassment Law Restrict?" *Georgia Law Review* 85 (1997): 627, 633.

13. *Olivant v. Department of Environmental Protection*, 1999 WL 430770 (N.J. Admin. April 12).

14. *Brown Transportation Corp. v. Commonwealth*, 578 A.2d 555, 562 (Pa. Commw. 1990).

15. *Pakizegi v. First National Bank*, 831 F. Supp. 901, 908–909 (D. Mass. 1993).

16. Eugene Volokh, "Thinking Ahead about Freedom of Speech and Hostile Work Environment Harassment," *Berkeley Journal Employment and Labor Law* 17 (1996): 305.

17. Ibid., pp. 307–08 (discussing *EEOC v. Hyster*, No. 88-930-DA [D. Or. filed August 15, 1988]).

18. For details, see *Reid v. O'Leary*, 1996 U.S. Dist. LEXIS 10627 (D.D.C. July 15, 1996).

19. Ibid.

20. Interview with Gary Simpson, attorney for the plaintiff, July 19, 2001.

21. Steve Miletich, "Gay Man Withdraws His Complaint against Company," *Seattle Post-Intelligencer*, July 7, 1994, p. B2; Steve Miletich, "Gay Man Claims Hostility at Work," *Seattle Post-Intelligencer*, June 21, 1994, p. B4; John Carlson, "When Political Correctness Becomes Political Coercion," *Seattle Times*, June 21, 1994, p. B4.

22. *Robinson v. Jacksonville Shipyards, Inc.*, 760 F. Supp. 1486 (M.D. Fla. 1991).

23. Ibid., pp. 1492, 1502.

24. Ibid., p. 1535.

25. *NLRB v. Local Union No. 3*, 828 F.2d 936 (2d Cir. 1987); *Hospital & Serv. Employees Union, Local 399 v. NLRB*, 743 F.2d 1417, 1428 n.8 (9th Cir. 1984).

26. *NLRB v. Gissel Packing Co.*, 395 U.S. 575, 617, 618 (1969); *NLRB v. Douglas Div.*, 570 F.2d 742, 747 (8th Cir. 1978); *Sheet Metal Workers Int'l Ass'n v. Burlington N.R.R. Co.*, 736 F.2d 1250, 1253 (8th Cir. 1984); *Dow Chem. Co. v. NLRB*, 660 F.2d 637, 644–45 (5th Cir. Unit A November 1981).

27. See, for example, *Pacific Gas & Elec. Co. v. Public Util. Comm'n*, 475 U.S. 1, 20 (1986); *Consolidated Edison Co. v. Public Serv. Comm'n*, 447 U.S. 530, 536 (1980).

28. *Madsen v. Women's Health Center, Inc.*, 512 U.S. 753 (1994) (discussing the right to protest outside an abortion clinic).

29. *Cohen v. California*, 403 U.S. 15, 21 (1971).

30. See, for example, *Jenson v. Eveleth Taconite Company*, 824 F. Supp. 847 (D. Minn. 1993); *Berman v. Washington Times Corp.*, 1994 WL 750274, *5 n.4 (D.D.C.); *Baty v. Willamette Industries, Inc.*, 985 F. Supp. 987 (D. Kan. 1997).

31. *Bowman v. Heller*, 1993 WL 761159, *1 (Mass. Super. Ct.) (unpublished disposition).

32. Hustler *Magazine v. Falwell*, 485 U.S. 46 (1988).

33. *Aguilar v. Avis Rent A Car System, Inc.*, 87 Cal. Rptr. 2d 132 (1999).

34. *Avis Rent A Car System v. Aguilar*, 120 S. Ct. 2029 (2000) (Thomas, J., dissenting from denial of cert.).

35. *Davis v. Montrose County Bd. of Educ.*, 119 S. Ct. 1661, 1682, 1690 (1999) (Kennedy, J., dissenting).

36. See, for example, *DeAngelis v. El Paso Municipal Police Officers Ass'n*, 51 F.3d 591, 596–97 (5th Cir. 1995).

37. *Johnson v. County of Los Angeles Fire Dept.*, 865 F. Supp. 1430, 1438, 1442 (C.D. Cal. 1994); *Mauro v. Arpaio*, 147 F.3d 1137, 1141 (9th Cir. 1998).

38. "Anchorage Tells Fire Halls to Eliminate Risqué Magazines," *Juneau Empire Online*, February 18, 2002, available at www.juneauempire.com/stories/021802/sta_stbriefs.shtml.

39. See Eugene Volokh, "Squeamish Librarians," www.reason.com/hod/ev060401.html.

Chapter 3

1. This chapter's discussion of Keefer's lawsuit relies on Joan Acocella, "A Ballerina Body," *The New Yorker*, March 5, 2001, p. 38; Paul Ben-Itzak, "Keefer's Crazy Crusade: A Wounded Ballet Mom Strikes Out Blindly," available at www.danceinsider.com/f1213_1.html; Janice Berman, "The Rejection Seat: Fredrika Near Keefer's Rejection from the San Francisco Ballet Company," *Dance Magazine*, March 1, 2001, p. 14; Edward Epstein, "Girl Fights for a Chance to Dance: Complaint Filed over School's Body-type Rules," *San Francisco Chronicle*, December 7, 2000; Welton Jones, "It's Unnatural Selection, but That's Ballet," *San Diego Union-Tribune*, January 28, 2001, p. F4; Joan Ryan, "I Asked My Mother What Will I Be . . . ," *San Diego Union-Tribune*, December 24, 2000, p. G4; Michelle Tauber, "Dancer's Image: Charging Body-size Bias, Krissy Keefer Fights to Have Her 9-year-old Daughter Admitted to Ballet School," *People*, March 5, 2001, p. 79; Joanna Weiss, "Fight for Future of Dance Ideal Is Taking Shape: S. F. Ballet Battle Furthers Clash between Politics, Art," *Boston Globe*, January 16, 2001, p. E1; *Good Morning America*, Transcript, December 21, 2000.

2. Beth Gardiner, "Stretching Title IX: N.Y. Group Seeks to Use Anti-bias Law to Get More Women's Artwork in Museums," *Associated Press*, www.s-t.com/daily/03-98/03-08-98/e04li202.htm; Beth Piskora, "Artists Paint Bleak Picture of Museums," *New York Post*, January 27, 1998, p. 23; Tunku Varadarajan, "Art World in Brush with US Women over Bias," *Times of London*, January 28, 1998.

3. Beth Gardiner, "Women Artists Seeking the Benefits of Title IX; Group Argues Museums Should Put Them On Par with Female Athletes," *Chicago Tribune*, March 26, 1998, p. C8.

4. Wis. Stat. §§ 111.32 (13).

5. Montana Human Rights Commission, "Model Equal Employment Opportunity Policy: A Guide for Employers" (no date).

6. Nat Hentoff, "Sexual Harassment by Francisco Goya," *Washington Post*, December 27, 1991, p. A21.

7. See Eugene Volokh, "Thinking Ahead about Freedom of Speech and Hostile Work Environment Harassment," *Berkeley Journal Employment and Labor Law* 17 (1996): 305.

8. Ibid.

9. Jonathan Rauch, "Offices and Gentlemen," *New Republic*, June 23, 1997, p. 22.

10. *Henderson v. City of Murfreesboro*, Tennessee, 960 F. Supp. 1292 (M.D. Tenn. 1997).

11. See Dave Kopel, "Naked Justice," *National Review Online*, February 25, 2002.

12. Francis X. Gilpin, "Unsettling Settlement," *Tampa Bay Weekly Planet*, July 26, 2001, available at http://www.weeklyplanet.com/2001-07-26/notebook.html; Kevin Graham, "Art or Porn: USF Opts Not to Fight," *St. Petersburg Times*, July 4, 2001, p.

A1; Joe Humphrey, "Students Outraged by Removal of TA Who Showed Sex Photo to Student," *USF Oracle*, November 5, 1999, available at www.studentadvantage. lycos.com/lycos/article/0,4683,c4-i7-t41-a17728,00.html; www.oracle.usf.edu/archive/ 199911/19991108/.

13. *Stanley v. Georgia*, 394 U.S. 557, 566 (1969).

14. *Robinson v. Jacksonville Shipyards, Inc.*, 760 F. Supp. 1486, 1542 (M.D. Fla. 1991).

15. 2000 WL 272263, pp. *1, *3, *5-*7 (6th Cir. March 14).

16. David Patch, "Panel Backs Deaf Patron's Claim against Club," *Toledo Blade*, March 6, 2001.

17. Federal law states that "it shall not be an unlawful employment practice for an employer to hire and employ employees . . . , on the basis of his religion, sex, or national origin . . . where religion, sex, or national origin is a bona fide occupational qualification reasonably necessary to the normal operation of that particular business." 42 U.S.C. § 2000e-2(e)(1).

18. Ruth Shalit, "Melrose Case," *New Republic*, January 26, 1998.

19. *EEOC v. Mike Fink Corp.*, M.D. Tenn., No. 3-96-0790, consent decree approved 9/12/00; Stacey Hartmann, "Male-Server Policy Loses Out in Court," *The Tennessean*, March 16, 2000.

20. Joe D. Jones, "Have 'Equal' Employment Laws Gone Too Far?" *Mississippi Business Journal*, April 3, 2000, available at www.msbusiness.com/archives/22v14n/ Editorial/9904.php.

21. *Sambo's Restaurants, Inc. v. City of Ann Arbor*, 663 F.2d 686 (6th Cir. 1981); but see *Urban League v. Sambo's of Rhode Island* (Rhode Island Commission for Human Rights, 1981), holding that prohibiting the use of the name "Sambo's" did not violate the First Amendment.

22. "Hooters Agrees to Hire Men in Support Roles, but It Will Still Hire Scantily Clad Women," *Baltimore Sun*, October 1, 1997, p. 3C.

23. "Hooters Moms Sue over Policy," *Baton Rouge Sunday Advocate*, December 17, 2000, p. I7.

24. Ralph Reiland, "Selecting Targets," *The Free Market*, January 1998.

25. See 29 Code of Federal Regulations § 1604.2(2) (1997) (allowing sex to be considered in the hiring of actors).

26. *Wilson v. Southwest Airlines Co.*, 517 F. Supp. 292 (D.C. Tex. 1981).

27. Reiland, see note 24.

28. Ibid.

Chapter 4

1. See Heather MacDonald, "Free Housing Yes, Free Speech No," *Wall Street Journal*, August 8, 1994, p. A12.

2. Debra Caldon, "On Equity and Affordable Housing," *Flatland News*, February 1993, p. 2.

3. Fair Housing Issues: Hearings before the Subcommittees on Civil and Constitutional Rights of the House Comm. on the Judiciary, 103d Cong., 1st Sess. (1994).

4. *White v. Lee*, 227 F.3d 1214 (9th Cir. 2000).

5. Ibid.

6. See, for example, Sigfredo A. Cabrera, "HUD Continues Its Assault on Free Speech," *Wall Street Journal*, June 7, 1995, p. A15; Lou Chapman, "Free Speech an Issue in Suit against Ridgmar Group," *Fort Worth Star-Telegram*, November 19, 1994,

p. 27; Editorial, "Intimidating Political Protest," *Washington Post*, August 22, 1994, p. A16; Edmund Mahony, "Judge Dismisses Suit against Neighborhood," *Hartford Courant*, February 12, 1995, p. B1; Joyce Price, "Federal Government Sues Five for Fighting Group Home: Act of Getting a Restraining Order Called Discriminatory," *Washington Times*, May 31, 1995, p. A3; Joyce Price, "HUD Sues Texans in Home-Sale Battle—Citizens Fought to Stop Deal in 1991," *Washington Times*, November 19, 1994, p. A4; Brian J. Taylor, "No Retreat in Feds' War on Free Speech," *Sacramento Bee*, November 19, 1994, p. F1.

7. Mahony, see note 6, p. B1.

8. See, for example, Editorial, "Free the Berkeley Three: HUD vs. Free Speech," *Virginian-Pilot*, August 18, 1994, p. A20; Editorial, "No More Speech Police," *Boston Herald*, September 3, 1994, p. 12; Editorial, "Intimidating Political Protest," see note 6; MacDonald, see note 1; Justin Raimondo, "The Hidden Agenda of Radical Egalitarians," *San Francisco Examiner*, August 17, 1994, p. A17.

9. Memorandum from Roberta Achtenberg, Assistant Secretary for Fair Housing & Equal Opportunity, U.S. Department of Housing & Urban Development (September 2, 1994) (on file with author).

10. See Roberta Achtenberg, "Sometimes on a Tightrope at HUD," *Washington Post*, August 22, 1994, p. A17.

11. See Editorial, "Government by Intimidation," *Washington Post*, February 26, 1996, p. A18.

12. Achtenberg, see note 10, p. A17.

13. Deval L. Patrick, Letter to the Editor, *Washington Post*, February 19, 1996, p. A24.

14. *United States v. Wagner*, Civ. No. 3:94-CV-2540-H, 1995 WL 841924, p. *5 (N.D. Tex. December 11, 1995).

15. *White v. Julian*, 227 F.3d 1214 (9th Cir. 2000).

16. *Salisbury House, Inc. v. McDermott*, No. CIV.A.96-CV-6486, 1998 WL 195693, p. *10 (E.D. Pa. Mar. 24, 1998); *Michigan Prot. & Advocacy Serv., Inc. v. Babin*, 799 F. Supp. 695 (E.D. Mich. 1994).

17. Quoted in Jeremy Rabkin, "Developers Nail Free Speech," *American Spectator*, December 2000, p. 46.

18. Robyn E. Blumner, "Political Correctness Threatens to Swallow Free Speech," *St. Petersburg Times*, September 19, 1999; Eugene Volokh, "Is Criticizing Affirmative Action Illegal in Chicago?" *Free Speech & Election Law News*, Summer 1999, p. 10.

19. Volokh, see note 18.

20. For Deming's account, see David Deming, "Free-Speech Hypocrisy at the University of Oklahoma," *Front Page Magazine*, January 25, 2001.

21. Lucia Perri, Letter to the Editor, *The Oklahoma Gazette*, available at Oklahoma Women Organizing for Change Web site, www.members.aol.com/okamwoc/deminged.html.

22. "Bats in the Belltower: Sexual Harassment by Analogy," *Clarion*, Vol. 4, March/April 2000, available at the Pope Center for Higher Education Web site, www.popecenter.org/clarion/2000/mar-apr/bats.html.

23. Ed Godfrey, "Professor's Letter Draws Ire," February 26, 2000, available at Oklahoma Women Organizing for Change Web site, http://members.aol.com/okamwoc/ddeming.html.

24. Ibid.

25. "Bats in the Belltower," see note 22.

26. Deming, see note 20.

27. See *Brown v. Board of Trustees of Boston University*, 891 F2d 337, 350–51 (1st Cir. 1989); J. Edward Pawlick, *Freedom Will Conquer Racism and Sexism* (Wellesley, Mass.: Mustard Seeds Incorporated, 1998), pp. 221–23.

28. Ibid., p. 227.

29. *Wirtz v. Basic, Inc.*, 786, 787 (D. Nev. 1966).

30. *Sweeney v. Keene State College*, 569 F.2d 169, 179 (1st Cir. 1978).

31. Walter Olson, *The Excuse Factory* (New York: Free Press, 1997), p. 256.

32. See, for example, Federal Rules of Evidence 403.

33. The cartoon can be viewed at www.detnews.com/AAEC/summer99/kirk/kirk.html.

34. "St. Paul Human Rights Director Files Complaint over *Pioneer Press* Cartoon," *Pioneer Press*, June 10, 1999.

35. V. Cullum Rogers, "Kirk Anderson Cartoon Stirs Tempest in St. Paul," www.detnews.com/AAEC/summer99/kirk/kirk.html.

Chapter 5

1. For details, see *Doe v. University of Michigan*, 721 F. Supp. 852, 867 (E.D. Mich. 1989).

2. Ibid.

3. *UWM Post, Inc. v. Board of Regents of the University of Wisconsin System*, 774 F. Supp. 1163, 1181 (E.D. Wis. 1991) (striking down the university's rule against directing discriminatory epithets at individuals as unduly vague and overbroad); *Doe v. University of Michigan*, 721 F. Supp. 852, 867 (E.D. Mich. 1989) (striking down speech limitation as overbroad).

4. *Dambrot v. Central Michigan University*, 55 F.3d 1177 (6th Cir. 1995).

5. *R.A.V. v. City of St. Paul*, 505 U.S. 377 (1992).

6. Ibid., pp. 383–84.

7. Some legal scholars argue that the Supreme Court's decision the following year in *Wisconsin v. Mitchell*, upholding a law providing sentence enhancements for hate crimes, essentially overruled *R.A.V.* by allowing extra punishment on the basis of the ideological motivation of the perpetrator. David E. Rovella, "Critics See Threat to Free Speech as States Stiffen Penalties on Bias-motivated Crime," *National Law Journal*, August 29, 1994, p. A1. The cases are clearly distinguishable, however, because *R.A.V.* was charged under a law banning speech, while the defendant in Mitchell was charged with criminal conduct. That the Court itself recognized this distinction is evidenced by the fact that all of the justices who joined the majority opinion in *R.A.V.* also joined the unanimous opinion in Mitchell.

8. See *Dambrot v. Central Michigan University*, 55 F.3d 1177 (6th Cir. 1995).

9. For an account of the incident, see Eugene Volokh, "Freedom of Speech in Cyberspace from the Listener's Perspective: Private Speech Restrictions, Libel, State Action, Harassment, and Sex," *University of Chicago Legal Forum* (1996): 377, 419, and n. 148.

10. The University of Maryland College Park's sexual harassment rules are described in www.inform.umd.edu/EdRes/Topic/WomensStudies/GenderIssues/SexualHarassment/UMDManual/handout1.

11. Conciliation Agreement between the U.S. Department of Labor, Office of Federal Contract Compliance Programs, and The Ohio State University, September 14, 1992.

12. See Nat Hentoff, "Sombrero Scrap," *Washington Post*, January 1, 1994, p. A23.

13. The brochure's contents may be found at www.nas.org/affiliates/westvirginia/wvu98codes.htm.

14. See www.nas.org/affiliates/westvirginia/wvu98.html.

15. Ibid.

16. Richard Bernstein, *Dictatorship of Virtue: Multiculturalism and the Battle for America's Future* (New York: Alfred A. Knopf, 1994), p. 209; Alan Charles Kors and Harvey A. Silverglate, *The Shadow University: The Betrayal of Liberty on America's Campuses* (New York: The Free Press, 1998), pp. 180–81.

17. Doug Grow, "College Republicans Can Thank 'U' Official for Their Sudden Fame," *Minneapolis Star Tribune*, September 19, 1993, p. 3B.

18. Maura Lerner, " 'U' Backs off Ban on Literature Making Fun of Clinton," *Minneapolis Star Tribune*, September 22, 1993, p. 1B.

19. Maura Lerner, "Did You Hear the One About . . . The Republican Student and the 'U' President?" *Minneapolis Star Tribune*, April 27, 1994, p. 1A.

20. "Free Speech or Sexual Harassment? Student Suspended for Material in Dorm Newsletter," *Student Press Law Center Report*, Fall 1997, p. 28; www.aclu-sc.org/news/openforum/of712.pdf.

21. "Kvederis Lawsuit against CMC Settled on Confidential Terms," www.cmcstudent.com/kvederis.html.

22. Mary Becker, "The Legitimacy of Judicial Review in Speech Cases," in Laura Lederer and Richard Delgado, eds., *The Price We Pay: The Case against Racist Speech, Hate Propaganda, and Pornography* (New York: Hill and Wang, 1995), pp. 208, 211.

23. See, for example, *Hardy v. Jefferson Community College*, 260 F.3d 671 (6th Cir. 2001).

24. See, for example, *Dambrot v. Central Michigan University*, 55 F.3d 1177 (6th Cir. 1995) ("An instructor's choice of teaching methods does not rise to the level of protected expression"). The Supreme Court has explicitly held that in public schools below college level, regulation of curriculum-related speech does not raise First Amendment concerns if it is "reasonably related to legitimate pedagogical concerns." *Hazelwood School Dist. v. Kuhlmeier*, 484 U.S. 260, 268–69 (1988).

25. See, for example, *Martin v. Parrish*, 805 F.2d 583, 586 (5th Cir. 1986).

26. See, for example, *Cohen v. San Bernardino Valley College*, 92 F.3d 968 (9th Cir. 1996) (holding that a college's sexual harassment policy was too vague to be used against a professor who used explicit language and provocative examples in class); *Dambrot v. Central Michigan University*, 55 F.3d 1177 (6th Cir. 1995) (finding that a policy that vests authority in university administration to determine ex post what speech constitutes harassment is unconstitutional).

27. *Silva v. University of New Hampshire*, 888 F. Supp. 293 (D.N.H. 1994).

28. Ibid.

29. Center for Individual Rights, Docket Report, First Quarter, 1995. For a case in which a court held that a public university had the authority to sanction a professor for using obscene language after warning him that it was against university policy, see *Bonnell v. Lorenzo*, 241 F.3d 800 (6th Cir. 2001).

30. Kors and Silverglate, pp. 120–21.

31. Linda Chavez, "Boston College Fires Feminist Prof for Excluding Men," *Austin Review*, September 15, 1999.

32. Kors and Silverglate, see note 16, p. 121.

33. Vicki Schultz, "Reconceptualizing Sexual Harassment," *Yale Law Journal* 107 (1998): 1683, 1793.

34. Michael Krauss, "When You Face the PC Inquisition," *Washington Times*, January 27, 1995, p. A27.

35. The text of the remarks can be found at www.print.indymedia.org/front.php3?article_id'923.

36. "Police Get Hate-crimes Complaint against Thobani," *National Post*, October 10, 2001, p. A4.

37. Albert J. Nock, "The Criminal State," *American Mercury*, March 1939.

Chapter 6

1. *West Virginia v. Barnette*, 319 U.S. 624 (1943).

2. Title VI Enforcement Agreement between the United States Department of Housing and Urban Development and Bonnie L. Jouhari/Pilar D. Horton and Roy E. Frankhouser, No. 03-98-0797-8 (August 28, 1998), available at www.splcenter.org/cgi-bin/oframe.pl?dirname'/egalaction&pagename'la1.html&anchorname'centerhud.

3. The text of the settlement may be found at www.splcenter.org/cgi-bin/frame.pl?dirname'/enterinfo&pagename'lci-15.html.

4. Michael Kelly, "Cuomo's Thought Police," *Washington Post*, May 17, 2000.

5. Ibid.

6. Dennis Roddy, "Deal Making Nazi a Martyr," *Pittsburgh Post-Gazette*, May 20, 2000.

7. See Editorial, "Intimidating Political Protest," *Washington Post*, August 22, 1994, p. A16.

8. *Torres v. Union Market*, Mass. Comm'n against Disc., no. 94-SEM-0066 (December 7, 1998), reported in *The Quincy Patriot Ledger*, December 11, 1998, p. 6.

9. "Other Ideas," *Las Vegas Review Journal*, April 1, 2000.

10. Jeff Jacoby, "Banned in Boston," *Boston Globe*, April 6, 2000.

11. Eugene Volokh, "Freedom of Speech, Cyberspace, Harassment Law, and the Clinton Administration," *Law & Contemporary Problems* 63 (2000): 299.

12. 24 C.F.R. 109.30a.

13. See, for example, *Ragin v. New York Times Co.*, 923 F.2d 995, 1000 (2d Cir. 1991).

14. *Ragin v. Harry Macklowe Real Estate Co.*, 801 F. Supp. 1213 (S.D.N.Y. 1992), *aff'd* in part *and rev'd* in part, 6 F.3d 898 (2d Cir. 1993).

15. Such damages were awarded in *Spann v. Colonial Village, Inc.*, 899 F.2d 24 (D.C. Cir. 1990); *Fenwick-Schafer v. Winchester Homes*, No. 90066002/CL110092 (Cir. Ct. Baltimore).

16. *Ragin*, 923 F. 2d, p. 100.

17. L. Pendlebury, "Civil Rights Fight on Ads Leaves Bitter Aftertaste," *Legal Times*, July 20, 1987, p. 13.

18. *Ragin v. Steiner, Clateman and Assocs.*, 714 F. Supp. 709 (S.D.N.Y. 1989).

19. Michael E. Rosman, "Ambiguity and the First Amendment: Some Thoughts on All-White Advertising," *Tennessee Law Review* 61 (1993): 289.

20. *Housing Opportunities Made Equal, Inc. v. Cincinnati Enquirer, Inc.*, 943 F.2d 644 1353 (6th Cir. 1991) (Keith, J., dissenting).

21. 24 C.F.R. 108.

22. www.hud.gov/fhe/109.html.

23. *Spann v. Colonial Village, Inc.*, 662 F. Supp., 541, 545 (D.D.C. 1987).

24. *Housing Opportunities Made Equal, Inc. v. Cincinnati Enquirer, Inc.*, 943 F.2d 644 1353 (6th Cir. 1991).

25. *EEOC v. Consolidated Service Systems*, 989 F.2d 233, 235 (7th Cir. 1993).

26. *EEOC v. Consolidated Service Systems*, 777 F. Supp. 599, 609 (N.D. Ill. 1991), *aff'd*, 989 F.2d 233 (7th Cir. 1993).

27. James Bovard, "The Latest EEOC Quota Madness," *Wall Street Journal*, April 27, 1995, p. A14. See also James Bovard, *Lost Rights* (New York: St. Martin's Press, 1994), pp. 172–73.

28. 989 F.2d, pp. 237–38.

29. Michael A. Fletcher, "Childhood Lessons Still Inspire New Leader of EEOC," *Washington Post*, November 30, 1998, p. A23.

30. *Equal Employment Opportunity Commission v. O & G Spring and Wire Forms Specialty Company*, 705 F. Supp. 400, 402 (N.D. Ill. 1988), *aff'd*, 38 F.3d 872 (7th Cir. 1994).

31. Bovard, see note 26.

32. *Equal Employment Opportunity Commission v. O & G Spring and Wire Forms Specialty Company*, 38 F.3d 872, 890 (7th Cir. 1994).

33. 38 F.3d 890, and "Appellate Summaries, Civil Rights—Racial Discrimination," *Chicago Daily Law Bulletin* 1 (December 1, 1994).

34. 38 F.3d 893.

35. Ibid., p. 885.

36. See generally Seth Kupferberg, "Civil Rights Law and Breaking Down Patterns of Segregation: The Case of Nepotism," *Hofstra Labor and Employment Law Journal* 16 (1999): 355.

37. Richard A. Epstein, *Forbidden Grounds: The Case against Employment Discrimination Laws* (Cambridge, Mass.: Harvard University Press, 1992), pp. 67–68.

38. Abraham McLaughlin, "When Others Harass, Now Managers Lose Pay," *Christian Science Monitor*, September 10, 1999.

39. Ibid.

40. *Wooley v. Maynard*, 430 U.S. 705, 714 (1977).

41. *West Virginia State Bd. of Educ. v. Barnette*, 319 U.S. 624 (1943).

Chapter 7

1. *Isbiter v. Boys' Club of Santa Cruz, Inc.*, 707 P.2d 212, 214 (Cal. 1985).

2. "The State," *Los Angeles Times*, November 6, 1985.

3. Ayn Rand, *The Virtue of Selfishness: A New Concept of Egoism* (New York: New American Library, 1964), p. 134.

4. Robert Bork, "Civil Rights—A Challenge," *New Republic*, August 31, 1963, p. 21.

5. *Moose Lodge No. 107 v. Orvis*, 407 U.S. 163, 179–80 (1972).

6. See, for example, *Katzenbach v. Jack Sabin's Private Club*, 265 F. Supp. 90, 91–92 (E.D. La. 1967).

7. *United States v. Lansdowne Swim Club*, 713 F. Supp. 785, 790 (E.D. Pa. 1989), *aff'd*, 894 F.2d 83 (3d. Cir. 1990); *Durham v. Red Lake Fishing & Hunting Club, Inc.*, 666 F. Supp. 954 (W.D. Tex. 1987); *United States v. Slidell Youth Football Ass'n*, 387 F. Supp. 474 (E.D. La. 1974); *Auerbach v. African Am. Teachers Ass'n*, 356 F. Supp. 1046, 1047 (E.D.N.Y. 1973).

8. *Moose Lodge No. 107*, 407 U.S. 163.

9. Minn. Stat. § 604.12, subd 2(a) (1998) ("A place of public accommodation may not restrict access, admission, or usage to a person solely because the person operates

a motorcycle or is wearing clothing that displays the name of an organization or association.")

10. N.Y. Exec. Law § 292(9) (McKinney 1993); *Kiwanis Club of Great Neck, Inc. v. Board of Trustees of Kiwanis Int'l*, 363 N.E.2d 1378 (N.Y. 1977).

11. *Jackson v. Concord*, 253 A.2d 793, 799 (N.J. 1969).

12. *National Org. for Women v. Little League Baseball, Inc.*, 127 N.J. Super. 522, 318 A.2d 33 (App. Div.), *aff'd*, 338 A.2d 198 (N.J. 1974).

13. *Brounstein v. American Cat Fanciers Assoc.*, 839 F. Supp. 1100 (D.N.J. 1993).

14. See, for example, *Quinnipac Council, Boy Scouts of America, Inc. v. Commission on Human Rights and Opportunities*, 528 A.2d 352, 354 (Conn. 1987); *United States Power Squadrons v. State Human Rights Appeal Bd.*, 452 N.E.2d 1199, 1204 (N.Y. 1983); *United States Jaycees v. McClure*, 305 N.W.2d 764, 772 (Minn. 1981).

15. *Frank v. Ivy Club*, 576 A.2d 241 (N.J. 1990).

16. Ibid., p. 257.

17. See George W. C. McCarter, "Look Before You Leap: New Jersey's Experience with (Covert) Strict Gender Scrutiny," *Seton Hall Constitutional Law Journal* 6 (1996): 991–92.

18. See, for example, *Seabourn v. Coronado Area Council*, 891 P.2d 385 (Kan.1995); *Schwenk v. Boy Scouts of America*, 551 P.2d 465, 469 (Ore. 1976).

19. See, for example, *Benevolent and Protective Order of Elks v. Reynolds*, 863 F. Supp. 529 (W.D. Mich. 1994); *Maine Human Rights Comm'n v. Le Club Calumet*, 609 A.2d 285, 287 (Me. 1992).

20. *PGA Tour, Inc. v. Martin*, 121 S. Ct. 1879 (2001).

21. *Roberts v. United States Jaycees*, 468 U.S. 609 (1984).

22. Ibid.

23. *Board of Dirs. of Rotary Int'l v. Rotary Club of Duarte*, 481 U.S. 537, 546 (1987).

24. *Boy Scouts of America v. Dale*, 120 S. Ct. 2446 (2000).

25. Louisiana Debating and Literary Association, 42 F.3d 1483, 1493 (1995).

26. Ibid., p. 1498 (citing *Lyng v. International Union, United Auto. Aerospace & Agric. Implement Workers of Am.*, 485 U.S. 360, 367 [1988]).

27. *Pacific-Union Club v. Superior Court*, 283 Cal. Rptr. 287 (Ct. App. 1991).

28. After the New Jersey Supreme Court ruled in Frank's favor, the eating clubs challenged that ruling on constitutional grounds in federal court.

29. Meg Nugent, " 'Eating Clubs' Settle Discrimination Suit," *Newark Star-Ledger*, June 4, 1992.

30. "Last Yale Secret Society Votes to Allow Women," *Orlando Sentinel Tribune*, December 20, 1991, p. A16.

31. "Nation in Brief," *St. Petersburg Times*, October 31, 1993, p. 7A.

32. 20 U.S.C. § 1681(a)(6) (1994).

33. 20 U.S.C. § 1144 (1994); 42 U.S.C. § 1975a(b)(1994).

34. See *Warfield v. Peninsula Golf & Country Club*, 896 P.2d 776, 790 (Cal. 1995).

Chapter 8

1. *Roberts v. United States Jaycees*, 468 U.S. 609, 622 (1984).

2. See, for example, *NAACP v. Alabama ex rel. Patterson*, 357 U.S. 449, 453 (1958); *NAACP v. Button*, 371 U.S. 415, 419 (1963).

3. *United States Jaycees v. McClure*, 709 F.2d 1560 (8th Cir. 1983), *rev'd sub nom. Roberts v. United States Jaycees*, 468 U.S. 609 (1984).

4. *Roberts v. United States Jaycees*, 468 U.S. 609 (1984).

5. *Board of Dirs. of Rotary Int'l v. Rotary Club of Duarte*, 481 U.S. 537, 546 (1987).

6. See, for example, *Randall v. Orange County Council, Boy Scouts of America*, 28 Cal. Rptr. 2d 53 (Ct. App. 1994); *Anderson v. Boy Scouts of America, Inc.*, 589 N.E.2d 892 (Ill. Ct. App. 1992); Quinnipiac Council, *Boy Scouts of America, Inc. v. Comm'n on Human Rights & Opportunities*, 528 A.2d 352, 356 n.5 (Conn. 1987). But see *Welsh v. Boy Scouts of America*, 993 F.2d 1267, (7th Cir. 1993) (Cummings, J., dissenting) (stating that if the issue arose, he would probably conclude that the Scouts has a First Amendment right to exclude atheists).

7. *Anderson v. Boy Scouts of America, Inc.*, 589 N.E.2d 892 (Ill. Ct. App. 1992).

8. 515 U.S. 557 (1995).

9. See *Irish-American Gay, Lesbian & Bisexual Group of Boston v. City of Boston*, No. 9-21518, 1993 WL 818674, p. *2 n.5 (Mass. Super. Ct. Dec. 15, 1993), *aff'd*, 636 N.E.2d 1293 (Mass. 1994), *rev'd* sub nom., *Hurley v. Irish-American Gay, Lesbian & Bisexual Group of Boston*, 515 U.S. 557 (1995).

10. Ibid., p. *14.

11. See *Irish-American Gay, Lesbian & Bisexual Group of Boston v. City of Boston*, 636 N.E.2d 1293, 1300 (Mass. 1994), *rev'd* sub nom., *Hurley v. Irish-Am. Gay, Lesbian & Bisexual Group of Boston*, 515 U.S. 557 (1995).

12. The background facts are found in *Boy Scouts of America v. Dale*, 120 S. Ct. 2446 (2000).

13. John O. McGinnis, "Reviving Tocqueville's America: The Supreme Court's New Jurisprudence of Social Discovery," *California Law Review* 90 (2002): 485.

14. Ibid.

15. *City of Cleveland v. Nation of Islam*, 922 F. Supp. 56 (N.D. Ohio 1995).

16. As the Massachusetts Supreme Court has held in a similar case. *Donaldson v. Farrakhan*, 436 Mass. 94 (2002).

17. Richard Carelli, "Court Denies Cleveland Bid to Avoid Legal Fees," *Cleveland Plain Dealer*, January 21, 1998, p. 2B.

18. *Invisible Empire of the Knights of the Ku Klux Klan v. Mayor of Thurmont*, 700 F. Supp. 281 (D. Md. 1988).

19. *Southgate v. United African Movement*, No. MPA 95-0851, PA 95-0031, 1997 WL 1051933 (N.Y.C. Com. Hum. Rts. June 30, 1997).

20. Ibid.

21. Ibid.

22. Linda F. Wightman, "The Threat to Diversity in Legal Education: An Empirical Analysis of the Consequences of Abandoning Race as a Factor in Law School Admission Decisions," *New York University Law Review* 72, (1997): 1, 30, tbl. 6.

23. Ibid., p. 22, tbl. 5.

24. *Regents of the Univ. of Cal. v. Bakke*, 438 U.S. 265 (1978).

25. Ibid., pp. 314, 317–18 (Powell, J., concurring).

26. *Hopwood v. Texas*, 78 F.3d 932 (5th Cir. 1996).

27. John Roberts, "It's Academic: Universities Discriminate Despite Court Orders," *Washington Times*, January 21, 2003, p. A17.

28. *Boy Scouts of America v. Dale*, 530 U.S. 640 (2000).

29. 27 U.S. 160 (1976).

30. Petitioner's Brief, *Runyan v. McCrary*, 427 U.S. 160 (1976) (No. 75-62).

31. Justice O'Connor, a member of the five-vote majority in *Dale*, has suggested that they cannot. *Roberts v. United States Jaycees*, 468 U.S. 609 (1984) (O'Connor, J., concurring).

32. *Runyon v. McCrary*, 427 U.S. 160, 175–76 (1976). See David E. Bernstein, "The Right of Expressive Association and Private Universities' Racial Preferences and Speech Codes," *William and Mary Bill of Rights Law Journal* 9 (2001): 619.

33. Some minority students believe that many schools discriminate against them in admissions. As of early 2001 the official Web site of the Law School Admissions Council stated: "We often hear . . . in the Office of Minority Affairs at Law School Admission Council: 'Is it okay to say I'm a minority student when I apply to law schools? I've heard it's better not to tell.' www.lsac.org/LSAC.asp?url/lsac/minorities-in-legal-education-selected-articles.asp. Needless to say, the Web site encouraged students to reveal their minority status.

34. See John E. Morris, "Boalt Hall's Affirmative Action Dilemma," *American Lawyer*, November 1997, p. 4. For example, in 1996–97 only 103 African Americans and 224 Hispanics had a college GPA of 3.25 or above and LSAT scores at or above the 83.5 percentile, and only 16 African Americans and 45 Hispanics achieved the 92.3 (164 LSAT) percentile with a 3.50 or higher GPA. The latter credentials are lower than the averages at the elite "Top 15" law schools, which matriculate several thousand students each year.

35. Andrew R. Varcoe, "The Boy Scouts and the First Amendment: Constitutional Limits on the Reach of Anti-Discrimination Law," *Law and Sex.* 9 (1999–2000): 163, 276.

Chapter 9

1. See, for example, *E.E.O.C. v. Roman Catholic Diocese of Raleigh, N.C.*, 213 F.3d 795 (4th Cir. 2000); *Starkman v. Evans*, 198 F.3d 173 (5th Cir.1999); *E.E.O.C. v. Catholic Univ. of Am.*, 83 F.3d 455, 461-63 (D.C. Cir.1996).

2. UPI, "Religious Schools Await Supreme Court Ruling," *Bergen Record*, March 3, 1986, p. 10.

3. Ibid. The quotation here is from the news story, not from Mrs. Hoskinson.

4. *Dayton Christian Schools v. Ohio Civil Rights Comm'n*, 578 F. Supp. 1004, 1018–19, 1012 (D. Ohio 1984).

5. William Choyke, "Supreme Court Will Rule on Church-School Dispute," *Dallas Morning News*, March 30, 1986, p. 4A.

6. 578 F. Supp. 1012–113.

7. 578 F. Supp. 1014.

8. Ibid.

9. *Dayton Christian Schools v. Ohio Civil Rights Comm'n*, 766 F. 2d. 932 (6th Cir. 1985).

10. UPI, "Religious Schools Await Supreme Court Ruling," *Bergen Record*, March 23, 1986, p. O12.

11. *Ohio Civil Rights Comm'n v. Dayton Christian Schools, Inc.* 477 U.S. 619 (1986).

12. "Church Worker Seeks Ruling on Job Bias," *Houston Chronicle*, March 27, 1986, p. 15.

13. *McLeod v. Providence Christian School*, 408 N.W.2d 146, 152 (Mich. 1987).

14. *Ganzy v. Allen Christian School*, 995 F. Supp. 340, 348 (E.D.N.Y. 1998); see also *Dolter v. Wahlert High School*, 483 F. Supp. 266 (N.D. Iowa 1980).

15. Sacred Congregation for Catholic Education, "Lay Catholics in Schools: Witnesses to Faith," paragraph 32 (October, 15, 1982).

16. *Dolter*, 483 F. Supp. 270.

17. *Gay Rights Coalition of Georgetown University Law Center v. Georgetown University*, 536 A.2d 1 (D.C. 1987).

18. District of Columbia Appropriations Act, 1990, Pub. L. No. 101–168, 103 Stat. 1267, 1284 (1989).

19. Rebecca Sinderbrand, "Taking Pride in Promoting Tolerance," *The Georgetown Hoya*, October 20, 1998, available at www.thehoya.com/features/102098/features3.htm.

20. See *Bob Jones Univ. v. United States*, 461 U.S. 574 (1983).

21. Ibid., p. 599.

22. See Mayer G. Freed and Daniel Polsby, "Race, Religion and Public Policy: *Bob Jones University v. United States,*" *Supreme Court Review* 1(1984).

23. Brian Blomquist and Kenneth Lovett, "Jones Reaches '18th Century' on New Dating Policy: McCain," *New York Post*, March 5, 2000, p. 18.

24. 42 USC § 2000e-1(a) (1970).

25. 42 USC § 2000e-1(a) (1994).

26. *Corporation of the Presiding Bishop of the Church of Jesus Christ of Latter Day Saints v. Amos*, 483 U.S. 327 (1987).

27. See, for example, Ohio Rev. Code Ann. § 4112.01(B) (providing no religious exemption).

28. 374 U.S. 398, 403–10 (1963).

29. As noted, Dayton Christian Schools claimed a rare victory in a federal appellate court under the *Sherbert* test.

30. *Employment Division v. Smith*, 494 U.S. 872 (1990).

31. 42 USC §§ 2000bb-2000bb-4 (1994).

32. *Flores v. City of Boerne*, 521 U.S. 507 (1997).

33. See, for example, *Adams v. Comm'r of Internal Revenue*, 170 F.3d 173 (3d Cir. 1999); In re *Young*, 82 F.3d 1407, 1416-17 (8th Cir. 1996).

34. See, for example, Conn. Gen. Stat. Ann. §§ 52-571b (West Supp. 1999); Fla. Stat. Ann. § 761 (West Supp. 1999); R.I. Gen. Laws §§ 42-80.1.3 (1997).

35. As of February 1999, among states interpreting their constitutions, approximately 15 apply a strong compelling interest test, 6 give less protection to religion, and the rest have not clearly spoken to the issue. Steve France, "Not under My Roof You Don't," *American Bar Association Journal* 85 (April 1999): 26, 28.

36. See David E. Bernstein, "Antidiscrimination Laws and the First Amendment," *Missouri Law Review* 66 (2001): 83; David E. Bernstein, "The Right of Expressive Association and Private Universities' Racial Preferences and Speech Codes," *William and Mary Bill of Rights Law Journal* 9 (2001): 619.

Chapter 10

1. *Attorney General v. Desilets*, 636 N.E.2d 233, 234 (Mass. 1994).

2. Michael Matza, "Rent and a Religious Landlord," *Seattle Times*, April 21, 1994, p. A3.

3. Ibid.

4. *The Boston Herald*, February 10, 1994, p. 20.

5. Professor Marie Failinger responds to this type of argument by noting that to "discount such landlords' interests as merely economic is to send the wrong message about the kind of local communities we may hope to have. That is, it may signal that we do not want landlords who are interested in their tenants' needs or their tenants' misbehavior, that we want landlords who are indifferent to who their tenants are as persons, whose choices will be based solely on economics. To discount [a

landlord] as merely a commercial enterprise is to move farther along to the day when the engaged landlord disappears, and our only landlords will be large corporations with absentee managers who govern through rules rather than relationships, who ignore disruptive tenants and habitability issues until it hurts their bottom line. The blessing of anonymity is also its curse: the landlord who may murmur disapproval at an indigent woman's poor choice in relationships is also the landlord who may fix the heat faster because she knows the woman's children." Marie A. Failinger, "Remembering Mrs. Murphy: A Remedies Approach to the Conflict between Gay/Lesbian Renters and Religious Landlords," *Capital University Law Review* 29 (2001): 383.

6. "So Saith the Landlord," *Boston Globe*, February 13, 1994, p. 74.

7. *Attorney General v. Desilets*, 636 N.E.2d 233, 234 (Mass. 1994).

8. *Desilets*, 636 N.E.2d 240.

9. John Auerbach, "Some Hail AG's Inaction on Tenant Case," *Boston Globe*, January 31, 1995.

10. George F. Will, "Mass. Anti-Bias Law Clashes with Religious Rights," *Chicago Sun-Times*, March 13, 1994, p. 48.

11. Matza, see note 2.

12. *Swanner v. Anchorage Equal Rights Comm'n*, 874 P.2d 274 (Alaska 1994).

13. Ibid., p. 283–84.

14. *Swanner v. Anchorage Equal Rights Comm'n*, 513 U.S. 979, 982 (1994) (Thomas, J., dissenting from denial of cert.)

15. See Maureen E. Markey, "The Landlord/Tenant Free Exercise Conflict in a Post-RFRA World," *Rutgers Law Journal* 29 (1998): 487 (21 states ban marital status discrimination in housing; none explicitly bans discrimination against unmarried heterosexual couples).

16. *County of Dane v. Norman*, 497 N.W.2d 714 (Wis. 1993) (making this argument in a related context).

17. Quoted in George Grant, "Trial and Error: The American Civil Liberties Union and Its Impact on Your Family" (undated), available at www.freebooks.commentary.net/freebooks/docs/a_pdfs/ggte.pdf.

18. 460 N.W.2d 2 (Minn. 1990).

19. Employment Division v. Smith, 494 U.S. 872 (1990).

20. Ibid., p. 717.

21. 220 F.3d 1134, 1137 (9th Cir. 2000).

22. *Smith v. Fair Employment and Housing Comm'n*, 913 P.2d 909 (Cal. 1996).

23. *Jasniowski v. Rushing*, 678 N.E.2d 743 (Ill. App.), judgment vacated, 685 N.E.2d 622 (Ill. 1997).

24. George C. Leef, "Housing Discrimination Laws and the Continuing Erosion of Property Rights," *Freedom Daily*, May 1999, available at www.fff.org/freedom/0599e.asp.

25. *McCready v. Hoffius*, 586 N.W.2d 723 (Mich. 1998).

26. *Cready v. Hoffius*, 1999 WL 226862 (Mich.).

27. American Civil Liberties Union Statement on H.R. 1691 Religious Liberty Protection Act of 1999 before the Subcommittee on the Constitution of the House Committee on the Judiciary Presented by Christopher E. Anders, Legislative Counsel May 12, 1999.

28. Ibid.; see also Christopher E. Anders and Rose E. Saxe, "Effect of a Statutory Religious Freedom Strict Scrutiny Standard on the Enforcement of State and Local Civil Rights Law," *Cardozo Law Review* 21 (1999): 663.

29. Eric Fingerhut, "Jewish Groups Back Away from Religious Protection Act," *Washington Jewish Week*, October 7, 1999, p. 5.

30. Ibid.

Chapter 11

1. State ex rel. *Sprague v. City of Madison*, 555 N.W.2d 409 (Wis. Ct. App. 1996).

2. *Sprague v. City of Madison*, 207 Wis.2d 284 (1997); *Hacklander-Ready v. Wisconsin* ex rel. Sprague, 520 U.S. 1212 (1997).

3. *Sprague v. Hacklander-Ready*, Equal Opportunities Commission Case No. 1462 (February 9, 1995), available at www.ci.madison.wi.us/eoc/Cases/01462.htm.

4. *Department of Fair Employment and Housing v. DeSantis*, FEHC Dec. No. 02-12, 2002 WL 1313078 (Cal. F.E.H.C. 2002).

5. See, for example, 24 C.F.R. §§ 109.20(b)(5) (withdrawn). This regulation has been withdrawn, directive no. FR-4029-F-01, effective May 1, 1996, but it probably still reflects HUD's interpretation of the Fair Housing Act. This section was withdrawn because of concern that its restrictions on specific wording of advertising swept too broadly. See Memo from HUD Assistant Secretary Roberta Achtenberg, Guidance Regarding Advertisements under 804(c) of the Fair Housing Act, available at www.fscn.com/members/text/hudadmem.htm. But experts believe that the general policy of prohibiting discriminatory advertising is still in place. See www.fairhousing.com/legal_research/regs/fhr_109-20.htm; www.fscn.com/members/text/c2fhous.htm.

6. Complaint, In re *Fair Housing Council of Greater Washington v. Washington City Paper*, www.fairhousing.org/Casenotes/docs/CityPaper/dcComplaint.rtf.

7. Ellen Goodman, "Desire for Women-only Health Clubs Is No Show of Strength," *Fresno Bee*, February 13, 1998, p. B7.

8. Ibid.

9. Doug Thomas, "Female-friendly Fitness Curves for Women Centers Are Designed to Make the Average Woman Comfortable with Getting Fit without Distractions," *Omaha World-Herald*, December 18, 2000.

10. Michael R. Zahn, "Bias Case against Fitness Club Dropped," *Milwaukee Journal*, December 20, 1993, p. B1.

11. Hanna Miller, "Exercising Their Fitness Options," *Arizona Daily Star*, March 8, 2001, p. F8.

12. Suzanne Schlosberg, "Women-Only Health Clubs Gain Popularity, Draw Controversy," *CNN*, May 31, 2000, available at www.cnn.com/2000/HEALTH/diet.fitness/05/31/women.only.wmd/.

13. Miriam A. Cherry, "Exercising the Right to Public Accommodations: The Debate over Single-Sex Health Clubs," *Maine Law Review* 52 (2000): 97, 104–07.

14. Laura-Lynne Powell, "Anaheim activist Roots Out Bias against Men," *Orange County Register*, April 17, 1992, p. 1.

15. Ibid.

16. "Health Club to Admit Men," *Los Angeles Times*, August 3, 1988, p. Metro 2.

17. "St. Paul Man Files Sex Discrimination Suit against Women-Only Health Club," *Minneapolis Star Tribune*, March 20, 1990, p. 7B; Powell, see note 14; Zahn, see note 10.

18. "Women Only," *Providence Journal Bulletin*, November 3, 1997, p. C1.

19. J. M. Lawrence, "Law Lets Women Sweat Where the Boys Aren't," *Boston Herald*, February 7, 1998, p. 7.

20. "The International Health, Racquet & Sportsclub Association, Single Sex Health Clubs," available at www.ihrsa.org/publicpolicy/industryissues/womenonly.html.

21. *EEOC v. Sedita*, 755 F. Supp. 808 (N.D. Ill. 1991).

22. Ibid.

23. Cherry, see note 13, p. 126.

24. For citations on this point, see Eugene Volokh, "Freedom of Speech, Cyberspace, Harassment Law, and the Clinton Administration," *Law and Contemporary Problems* 63 (2000): 299.

25. Paul McNamara, "Keeping an Eye on E-mail," *Network World*, October 5, 1998, p. 80.

26. Dana Hawkins, "Lawsuits Spur Rise in Employee Monitoring," *U.S. News & World Report*, August 13, 2001.

27. Volokh, www.law.ucla.edu/faculty/volokh/harass/cyberspa.htm.

28. Hawkins, see note 26.

29. Volokh, www.law.ucla.edu/faculty/volokh/harass/cyberspa.htm.

30. Ibid.

31. Ibid.

32. "Victory in Sex Bias Suit Would Only Do So Much," *New York Times*, August 21, 1992. *See Ezold v. Wolf, Block, Schorr and Solis-Cohen*, 983 F.2d 509 (3d Cir. 1992).

33. Ambrose Evans-Pritchard, *The Secret Life of Bill Clinton* (Washington: Regnery Publishing, 1997), p. 363.

34. See Jeffrey Rosen, "I Pry," *New Republic*, March 16, 1998.

35. Quoted in Jeffrey Rosen, "Privacy in Public Places," *Cardozo Studies of Law and Literature* 12 (2000): 167, 183.

36. Ibid.

37. Becky Rees, *Grove City College v. T.H. Bell, Secretary, U.S. Dept. Of Education*, available at Grove City College Web site, www.gcc.edu/pr/Rees.asp.

38. Ibid.

39. *Grove City College v. Harris*, 500 F. Supp. 253 (D.C. Pa. 1980).

40. *Grove City College v. Bell*. 465 U.S. 444 (1984).

41. 20 U.S.C. §§ 1687, 29 U.S.C. §§ 794, 42 U.S.C. §§ 2000d-4a, and 42 U.S.C. §§ 6101.

42. John Leo, "Gender Police: 'Pull Over,'" *U.S. News & World Report*, March 23, 1998, p. 11.

43. John Ritter, "School Puts Its Principles First," *USA Today*, December 9, 1996.

44. See Jessica Gavora, *Tilting the Playing Field: Schools, Sex, Sports and Title IX* (San Francisco: Encounter Books, 2002).

45. *Lynn v. Regents of the University of California*, 656 F.2d 1337 (9th Cir. 1981).

Chapter 12

1. The ACLU's position was that because Bob Jones was still free to express its opposition to interracial dating and marriage, the university's constitutional rights were secure. Brief of the American Civil Liberties Union and the American Jewish Committee, Amici Curiae in support of Affirmance at 37-38, *Bob Jones Univ. v. United States*, 461 U.S. 574 (1983).

2. William A. Donohue, *The Politics of the American Civil Liberties Union* (New Brunswick, N.J.: Transaction Books, 1985), p. 131.

3. *Pines v. W. R. Tomson*, 206 Cal. Rptr. 866 (Cal. App. 1984).

4. *McCready v. Hoffius*, 586 N.W.2d 723 (Mich. 1998).

5. Quoted in Daniel J. Popeo, *Not Our America* (Washington: Washington Legal Foundation, 1989), p. 71.

6. Nadine Strossen, "Regulating Racist Speech on Campus: A Modest Proposal," *Duke Law Journal* (1990): 484, n. 343.

7. *Curran v. Mount Diablo Council of the Boy Scouts of America*, 17 Cal. 4th 670, 674, 952 P.2d 218 (1998).

8. See, for example, Linda Hills, "Court Decision Tarnishes Justice and Boy Scouts," *San Diego Union-Tribune*, March 27, 1998. (The executive director of the San Diego ACLU writes that the Boy Scouts of America should be regulated because it receives "significant support from government.")

9. Julie Makinen Bowles, "D.C. Panel to Examine Boy Scouts' Ban on Gays," *Washington Post*, January 20, 1998, p. B1.

10. Jonathan D. Karl, "Stifled Speech on Campus," *Christian Science Monitor*, August 23, 1990, p. 19.

11. Charles Oliver, "The First Shall Be Last?" *Reason*, October 1990, pp. 20, 25.

12. Strossen, see note 6.

13. See *Iota Xi Chapter of Sigma Chi v. George Mason Univ.*, 773 F. Supp. 792 (E.D. Va. 1991).

14. Samuel Walker, *In Defense of American Liberties: A History of the ACLU* (New York: Oxford University Press, 1990), p. 373.

15. Evan Osnos and James Janega, "ACLU Sides with Supremacist on Right to Obtain Law License," *Chicago Tribune*, August 8, 1999.

16. See Guy Gugliotta, "ACLU Alleges Free Speech Violations in HUD Probes," *Washington Post*, August 17, 1994, p. A20.

17. Rita Delfiner, "St. Pat's Parade Heads to Court," *New York Post*, January 25, 1992, p. 7.

18. "ACLU v. ACLU," *Legal Times*, November 7, 1987, p. 3.

19. The ACLU's brief before the Supreme Court supported neither party. The brief acknowledged that private parades are inherently expressive and are entitled to full First Amendment protection, but concluded that the case should be sent back to the trial court for a determination regarding whether the parade in question was truly private. That issue had already been raised in the courts below, rejected, and was not appealed, but apparently the ACLU simply could not bring itself to oppose enforcement of the antidiscrimination law in question.

20. Nat Hentoff, "Government's Place," *Sacramento Bee*, September 24, 1994, p. B6.

21. Alan Cooper, "Organization Fighting AIDS Homes Wins Round," *Richmond Times-Dispatch*, October 13, 1994, p. B5.

22. Nat Hentoff, "The Onliest Robyn Blumner," *Village Voice*, November 4, 1997, p. 20.

23. John Leo, "Watch What You Say," *U.S. News & World Report*, March 20, 2000.

24. Upon returning from a trip to the Stalinist Soviet Union in 1928, he criticized the "bourgeois mind" concerned with "individual liberties" instead of the economic freedom purportedly enjoyed by Soviet peasants, "a freedom vastly more real to the average worker than shadowy intellectual liberties." Roger N. Baldwin, *Liberty under the Soviets* (New York: Vanguard Press, 1928), p. 24. In 1934, when millions of Soviet citizens were dying in government-engineered famines, Baldwin defended the Soviet dictatorship on the grounds that "the Soviet Union has already created liberties far greater than exist elsewhere in the world." Quoted in Cletus E. Daniel, *The ACLU and the Wagner Act* (Ithaca, NY: Cornell ILR Press, 1980).

25. Daniel, see note 24.

26. Peggy Lamson, *Roger Baldwin: Founder of the American Civil Liberties Union* (Boston: Houghton Mifflin Co., 1976), p. 217.

27. See Robert C. Cottrell, *Roger Nash Baldwin and the American Civil Liberties Union* (New York: Columbia Univeristy Press, 2001), pp. 216–17.

28. Tamar Lewin, "A.C.L.U. Boasts Wide Portfolio of Cases, but Conservatives See Partisanship," *New York Times*, October 2, 1988, § 1, p. 24.

29. See Sanford Levinson, "Investigatory Bodies and the Due Processes of Law," in Robert I. Rotberg and Dennis Thompson, eds., *Truth v. Justice: The Moral Efficacy ofTruth Commissions: South Africa and Beyond* (Princeton University Press, forthcoming); Loren Miller, "A Color-Blind Commonwealth," in Alan Reitman, ed., *The Price of Liberty* (New York: W. W. Norton and Co., 1968), pp. 187, 200.

30. Walker, see note 14, pp. 275–76.

31. Donohue, see note 2, p. 71.

32. Ibid.

33. Jessica Gavora, "The Quota Czars," *Policy Review*, May 15, 1997, p. 22.

34. Oliver, see note 11, p. 24.

35. John T. Leeds, "The A.C.L.U.: Impeccable Judgments or Tainted Policies?" *New York Times Magazine*, September 10, 1989, p. 72.

36. Interview with Alan Dershowitz, February 26, 2002. Former ACLU of Florida president Robyn Blumner makes the same point. Robyn Blumner, "Glasser Will Leave a Lasting Imprint on the ACLU," *Jewish World Review*, September 6, 2000.

37. Mark S. Campisano, "Card Games: The ACLU's Wrong Course," *The New Republic*, October 31, 1988, p. 10.

38. Oliver, see note 11, p. 23.

39. See Dennis Cauchon, "Civil Dispute within the ACLU," *USA Today*, March 31, 1993.

40. Mary Ellen Gale and Nadine Strossen, "The Real ACLU," *Yale Journal of Law and Feminism* 2 (1989): 161, 172.

41. Blumner, see note 36.

42. Walker, see note 14, p. 5.

Conclusion

1. See, for example, the influential article by Mari J. Matsuda, "Public Response to Racist Speech: Considering the Victim's Story," *Michigan Law Review* 87 (1989): 230.

2. All of these restrictions are noted in John Leo, "A Tangled Web of Incorrect Thoughts," *ex Femina*, June 2001, available at www.iwf.org/pubs/exfemina/June2001h.shtml.

3. Many of these incidents are documented in Alan Charles Kors and Harvey A. Silverglate, *The Shadow University: The Betrayal of Liberty on America's Campuses* (New York: The Free Press, 1998).

4. *R. v. Keegstra*, 3 S.C.R. 687 (1990).

5. *R. v. Butler*, 1 S.C.R. 452 (1992).

6. Mirko Petricevic, "Preaching . . . or Spewing Hate? A Thin Line Separates the Right of Canadians to Free Expression and the Crime of Promoting Hatred," *The Record* (Kitchener-Waterloo, Ontario), February 1, 2003, p. J8.

7. Ian Hunter, "Worshiping the God Equality," *Globe and Mail*, July 5, 2001, p. A15.

8. Susan Martinuk, "Religious Freedom Goes Public, Sort Of," *National Post*, May 21, 2001, p. 14.

9. *Brillinger v. Brockie*, No. 179/00 (Ont. Super. Ct. June 17, 2002).

10. Royal Hamel, "Can Christians Let the Gospels Be Muzzled?" *Guelph Mercury*, October 4, 2002, available at 2002 WL 26223201.

11. Zacharias Margulis, "Canada's Thought Police," *Wired*, March 1995.

12. "Why the ACLU Opposes Censorship of 'Pornography,'" available at www.eff. org/Censorship/aclu_opposes_porno_censorship.article.

13. Denise O'Leary, "A Velvet Oppression," *Christianity Today*, April 2, 2001.

14. British Columbia Human Rights Act, Ch. 22, Pt. 1, § 2(1).

15. Both cases are described in Richard Ackland, "Defending the Right to Be Obnoxious," *Sydney Morning Herald*, August 4, 2000, available at www.smh.com.au/news/0008/04/text/features2.html.

16. Quoted in Tim Blair, "May I Speak Freely Here?" *The Australian*, December 11, 2001.

17. Letter to the Editor, "Phillip Adams and the Case for a Bill of Rights," *Sidney Morning Herald*, December 8, 2001.

18. JDC Enterprises Pty Ltd., Tribunal Reference No. 28/98, April 2, 1998.

19. Note, "Racial Steering in the Romantic Marketplace," *Harvard Law Review* 107 (1994): 877.

20. John Leo, "The Feds Strike Back," *U.S. News & World Report*, May 31, 1999, p. 16.

21. *N. v. E.*, Complaints Division W31/99 (N.Z. Human Rights Comm'n October 26, 1999), available at www.hrc.co.nz/org/legal/teritojuly00.htm.

22. Walter Olson, *The Excuse Factory: How Employment Law Is Paralyzing the American Workplace* (New York: The Free Press, 1997).

23. Equal Employment Opportunity Act of 1972, Pub. L. No. 92-261, §§ 2(7), 86 Stat. 103 (codified as amended at 42 U.S.C §§ 2000e(j) (1994)); Americans with Disabilities Act, 42 U.S.C. §§ 12112(b)(5)(A) (1994); 34 C.F.R. §§ 104.12(b)(2) (1999); 42 U.S.C. §§ 12111(10)(B) (1994) (definition of "undue harship").

24. Michael W. McConnell, "Free Exercise Revisionism and the *Smith* Decision," *University of Chicago Law Review* 57 (1990): 1109.

25. *Albemarle Paper Co. v. Moody*, 422 U.S. 405, 421 (1975).

26. See 42 U.S.C. §§ 2000e(b) (1994); 42 U.S.C. §§ 1981a(b)(3) (1994); 42 U.S.C. §§ 2000e-5 (1994); 42 U.S.C. §§ 2000e-1(a) (1994).

27. Yolanda Woodlee, "Top D.C. Aide Resigns over Racial Rumor," *Washington Post*, January 27, 1999, p. B1.

28. This is a paraphrase of Milton and Rose Friedman, *Free to Choose* (New York: Harcourt Brace Jovanovich, 1980), p. 159.

Index

Religious Liberty Protection Act,
129–30, 145
religious schools' regulation
anti-fornication policies, 113–14
Bob Jones University, 115–16
Civil Rights Act (1964) exemptions,
117–18
gay student groups, 114–15
Hoskinson case, 111–13
protections for, 163
rent-seeking, 17
Resources for Community
Development (Berkeley, Calif.),
47–51
Rice University, 107
Robinson, Lois, 30, 149
Roca, Octavio, 36–37
Roddy, Dennis, 74
roommate discrimination
Campbell case, 132–34
real estate advertisement case,
134–35
Sprague case, 131–32
Rotary Club, 91, 94
Rotary International, 99–100
Rowe, Maureen, 131
Runyon v. McCrary (1976), 108–9

Sambo's (restaurant), 44
San Francisco, Pacific Union Club
antidiscrimination investigation, 92
San Francisco Ballet, 2, 35–37
San Francisco Chronicle, 36, 37
San Francisco Human Rights
Commission, 36
Santa Rosa Community College, 60
Sarah Lawrence College, 155
Saskatchewan Human Rights
Commission, 157
Saskatoon Star Phoenix, 157
Seattle, Wash., HUD compelled speech
case in, 75
Seattle Times, 121
severe and pervasive liability standard,
25
sex discrimination, 99–100, 112, 141–43
sexual assault, Federal Rule of
Evidence 415 and, 140
sexual harassment
artistic freedom constraints under,
38–39
costs of complaints, 25–26
definitions of, 26
development of laws on, 24

employers' settlement of claims of,
25, 82
Miller Brewing Company case, 23–24
modifications to laws on, 162
University of Maryland policy, 61
Sherbert v. Verner (1963), 117–18
Silber, John, 54–55
Silva, Donald, 68–69
Silvergate, Harvey, 165
single-sex charitable organizations,
85–87
Smith Barney, 138
Smith College, 55–56
Smith, Evelyn, 126–27
Snow, John T., 54
Souter, David, 101
South Park, 34
Southern California ACLU, 145
Southwest Airlines, 45
speech codes
ACLU defense of, 148, 149
inappropriate laughter and, 155
politically correct orthodoxy and,
155–56
of private educational institutions,
64–65
of public educational institutions,
59–61
Sprague, Caryl, 131
St. Patrick's Day parades, 13, 100–101,
148–49
St. Paul, Minn., *Pioneer Press,* 56–57
Stalin, Joseph, 150
Stanley, Dolores, 3
Starr, Kenneth, 141
state ACLU affiliates, 145, 148–49,
164–65
state courts
compelling interest of
antidiscrimination laws under,
11–12
on compelling interest to general
laws that impinge on religious
freedom, 125–26
legislative monitoring of, 163
on marital status discrimination,
127–28
state governments
antidiscrimination laws of, 26
on employment discrimination by
religious groups, 117
hostile environment laws of, 33–34
public accommodations laws of,
89–90

About the Author

David E. Bernstein is an associate professor at the George Mason University School of Law. He is a graduate of Yale Law School, where he was senior editor of the *Yale Law Journal* and a John M. Olin Fellow in Law, Economics, and Public Policy. After clerking for Judge David Nelson of the Sixth Circuit Court of Appeals and working as a litigator at Crowell & Moring, he served as a Mellon Foundation Research Fellow at Columbia University School of Law. Professor Bernstein is the author of more than 60 scholarly articles, book chapters, and think tank studies. He is author of *Only One Place of Redress: African-Americans, Labor Regulations, and the Courts from Reconstruction to the New Deal* (Duke University Press, 2001), coeditor of *Phantom Risk: Scientific Inference and the Law* (MIT Press, 1993), and coauthor of *The New Wigmore: Volume on Expert and Demonstrative Evidence* (forthcoming). He has been named one of the most cited professors among those who have entered law teaching since 1992.

Cato Institute

Founded in 1977, the Cato Institute is a public policy research foundation dedicated to broadening the parameters of policy debate to allow consideration of more options that are consistent with the traditional American principles of limited government, individual liberty, and peace. To that end, the Institute strives to achieve greater involvement of the intelligent, concerned lay public in questions of policy and the proper role of government.

The Institute is named for *Cato's Letters*, libertarian pamphlets that were widely read in the American Colonies in the early 18th century and played a major role in laying the philosophical foundation for the American Revolution.

Despite the achievement of the nation's Founders, today virtually no aspect of life is free from government encroachment. A pervasive intolerance for individual rights is shown by government's arbitrary intrusions into private economic transactions and its disregard for civil liberties.

To counter that trend, the Cato Institute undertakes an extensive publications program that addresses the complete spectrum of policy issues. Books, monographs, and shorter studies are commissioned to examine federal budget, Social Security, regulation, military spending, international trade, and myriad other issues. Major policy conferences are held throughout the year, from which papers are published thrice yearly in the *Cato Journal*. The Institute also publishes the quarterly magazine *Regulation*.

In order to maintain its independence, the Cato Institute accepts no government funding. Contributions are received from foundations, corporations, and individuals, and other revenue is generated from the sale of publications. The Institute is a nonprofit, tax-exempt, educational foundation under Section 501(c)3 of the Internal Revenue Code.

CATO INSTITUTE
1000 Massachusetts Ave., N.W.
Washington, D.C. 20001
www.cato.org